Dostoevsky

Dostoevsky

A Theological Engagement

P. H. Brazier

Foreword by Murray Rae

PICKWICK *Publications* · Eugene, Oregon

DOSTOEVSKY
A Theological Engagement

Pickwick Publications
An Imprint of Wipf and Stock Publishers
199 W. 8th Ave., Suite 3
Eugene, OR 97401

www.wipfandstock.com

ISBN 13: 978-1-4982-1837-5
HARDBACK ISBN: 978-1-4982-1839-9

Cataloging-in-Publication data:

Brazier, Paul.

Dostoevsky : a theological engagement / P. H. Brazier.

xviii + 200 p. ; 23 cm. Includes bibliographical references and index.

ISBN 13: 978-1-4982-1837-5
HARDBACK ISBN: 978-1-4982-1839-9

1. Dostoevsky, Fyodor, 1821–1881—Religion. 2. Dostoevsky, Fyodor, 1821–
1881—Philosophy. 3. Religion in literature. 4. Religion and literature—Russia.
I. Title.

PG3328.Z7 B734 2016

Manufactured in the U.S.A.

Typeset by P. H. Brazier, Ash Design
Minion Pro 10.75pt on 14pt

For Hilary

Contents

List of Ilustrations

Acknowledgements

This work grew out of my PhD thesis from eleven years ago. This was on the influence of the Russian prophet, novelist, and philosopher Fyodor Mikhailovich Dostoevsky on the Swiss theologian Karl Barth, which was published seven years ago by Paternoster in the UK and by Wipf and Stock in the USA. Approximately 18,000 words were written on a theological reading of Dostoevsky, which was to have formed the first chapter in my PhD thesis, however, by the time the research and writing were finished there was no room—so this first chapter was dropped. Stephen R. Holmes, my tutor, suggested I might consider working the un-used material up into a book. Ten years on—after numerous other projects—the working-up is complete. So my thanks and acknowledgement go to Steve.

The quotations from Dostoevsky's novels in this work are essentially from the Constance Garnett translations from the late nineteenth and early twentieth centuries. Though written in somewhat prosaic Victorian/Edwardian English they are, I believe, superior to the pedestrian English of later-twentieth-century translations. In addition, I have gone back to Dostoevsky's Russian to actually work up my own translations of some passages in many instances, also consulting the excellent German translations from the early twentieth century. Quotations from Eduard Thurneysen's *Dostojewski*, are also my own translation.

My thanks also go to Brendan N. Wolfe for invaluable proof reading and linguistic advice. Also, finally, to Robin Parry, editor at Wipf and Stock, for countless hours of reading and advice.

Foreword

One might suggest that the whole of Dostoevsky's authorship is dedicated to the Psalmist's question, "what is man?"—or, as we would prefer to put it today, "what are human beings?" Dostoevsky believes, of course, that the question cannot be asked except in relation to God. In this study of Dostoevsky's theological anthropology, Paul Brazier takes us into the heart of Dostoevsky's wrestling with the questions posed by human suffering and by human fallenness and he shows us that what matters most for Dostoevsky is whether, in the end, human beings consent to the forgiveness, and thus the fullness of life, that is offered by God.

Among European intellectuals in the West, and to a degree in popular Western culture, the nineteenth century in which Dostoevsky lived was a century of optimism about humanity. Still riding the wave of Enlightenment confidence in the power of human reason to lead us to truth and to virtue, and buoyed by the technological advancements of the age, many in Europe appear to have agreed with Herbert Spencer's confident assertion that "progress is not an accident but a necessity. Surely must evil and immorality disappear; surely must man become perfect."[1] Drawing variously upon Kant and upon Hegel, Christian theologians too developed a vision of the ideal human society established on the basis of human reason and accomplishment. Meanwhile, the critique of religion set forth by Ludwig Feuerbach offered encouragement for the view held by some that progress would be accelerated all the more as the constraints of religious belief were cast off.

There were not many who dissented from this optimistic analysis of humanity's prospects, but among those who did, Dostoevsky, an onlooker from the East, must rank alongside Kierkegaard in the West as one of the most profound. Like Kierkegaard, Dostoevsky was a deeply insightful

1   Spencer, *Social Statics*, 32.

analyst of the human condition. He recognized the contradictions in humanity, its capacity for evil, its ready capitulation to demonic power, its propensity to self-delusion, and, above all, its defiance of God. Forged on the anvil of his own brutal imprisonment and Siberian exile, and shaped further by the battering he received from his epilepsy, Dostoevsky offers a grim portrait of human existence. When he defined man as "the creature that can get accustomed to anything," he spoke from his own experience of human depravity and of human resilience. He recognized, as well, that the brutal elements of human existence, while often a consequence of our defiance of God, can serve sometimes as a powerful justification for the protest atheism that we find in characters like Ivan Karamazov.

The presentation in Dostoevsky's writing of the grim reality of human suffering and evil challenges the optimistic outlook of the nineteenth century, and leaves in tatters the presumptions and the platitudes of superficial, bourgeois religion. More pertinently still, it challenges the presumption that humanity can get along without God. As Paul Brazier explains, without God, there is no limit to the depravity and the evil that humanity can sink to, and humanity is nothing. With God, humanity still fails, but with God, humanity might be of value. Despite the bleakness of Dostoevsky's portrayal of humanity, despite the almost relentless attention given to suffering and crime and struggle, one finds nevertheless in reading his work, the promise of forgiveness and a mercy without limit. The reality of humanity's creation in the image of God is not finally obscured; nor is the sufficiency of divine grace. As Father Zossima testifies in *The Brothers Karamzov*, "Man cannot commit a sin so great as to exhaust the infinite love of God." (Bk II, ch.3). Or, as Eduard Thurneysen writes, "over the dark abysses of the humanity which [Dostoevsky] depicts there glows from the beyond the light of a great forgiveness."[2]

Helmut Rex once observed that, "in Dostoevsky, life and literary work are intimately related."[3] That is also true of Paul Brazier's work. His account in this book of Dostoevsky's theological anthropology is informed by his own close acquaintance with suffering and by his astute attentiveness to the reality of human fallenness. It is shaped as well by a vision shared with Dostoevsky of divine mercy and grace. It is thus on account of his own

2 Thurneysen, *Dostojewski*, 39.

3 Rex, "Dostoevsky: God-Man or Man-God," 200.

wrestling with the questions posed by human existence that Paul is able to provide insight into the truth that Dostoevsky tells. I am confident that Paul's book will encourage readers to return with renewed appreciation to the work of Dostoevsky himself, and perhaps also to Dostoevsky's recognition that despite everything there is reason for hope.

Murray Rae
University of Otago

P. H. Brazier, "Dostoevsky ~ Light and Peception"
(Oil on Linen Board, 15.7 x 11.8 in.)

Introduction

The nineteenth-century Russian writer and prophet Fyodor Mikhailovich Dostoevsky had no theological or philosophical training as such, and yet his novels exude a profound understanding of the gospel. Is he therefore to be considered a theologian? For many the answer is yes. There is no apparent systematic or structured theology in his works, yet his writings reflect and cohere with a traditional theology.

1. AIMS AND OBJECTIVES

So, can we write a theological reading of Dostoevsky's works? That is the aim of this volume. Essentially what follows is an encounter with his beliefs expresed through his writings. The objective is to critically analyze the theology implicit in Dostoevsky's works—taking into consideration the influence of his life, upbringing, and background on his beliefs—and how his theology evolved.

Initially, in Part One, we will look at Dostoevsky's life, which spanned a tumultuous period in Russian, and European, history. This will involve examining Dostoevsky's career and the factors and events that influenced his faith and beliefs. It will also include the influence that the New Testament exerted over him, that is, the foundation of the biblical world of his novels, which he based explicitly on the Russian New Testament. Importantly this will cause us to consider the role Dostoevsky's epilepsy had in the formulation of his beliefs, in informing and shaping—perhaps subliminally—how different his beliefs were in subtle ways from those of the average academically "impartial" and seemingly neutral theologian whose brain was not epileptic. Was the epilepsy responsible, so to speak, for certain nuanced details in his thought and in generating in him, to a degree, the conditions within his mind that gave him a more dynamic and truer understanding of the eschatological reality that humanity occupies, and the judgment that we all will face? More pertinently, did the condition of his brain allow the triune God to impart to him, to generate in his mind, a sounder eschatological understanding than many cossetted Western academics? This inevitably raises questions about Dostoevsky's understanding of the supernatural, and his flirtation with spiritism, which we must consider.

This will be followed in Part Two by an analysis of his theological anthropology—the human condition before God—evident in his novels, in particular *Crime and Punishment*, *The Idiot*, and *The Brothers Karamazov*. This will involve a comparison between the Western— essentially Augustinian—understanding of the human, defined by original sin and the *fall*, as compared to the Russian Orthodox understanding, which excludes, to a degree, a claim for the transmission of original sin. This will lead into an understanding of forgiveness and mercy as evident in the works from Dostoevsky's mature period.

In Part Three we will look at two major subjects: first, an analysis of Dostoevsky's use of dialectic in his theology and novels; second, an analysis of his dialectical criticism of religion in the service of the gospel (seen through a short story entitled *The Dream of a Ridiculous Man*). We will then focus on *The Brothers Karamazov* and in particular on its anti-hero, Ivan Karamazov, and Dostoevsky's prose poem *The Legend of the Grand Inquisitor*, demonstrating how true faith is achieved often through a struggle against dark forces, which may ensnare and destroy the human, but may also be escaped, so that the human may emerge into the true light of heaven, sanctified and saved.

2. EXPLANATIONS, QUALIFICATIONS

A few terms do need to be explained before we proceed. Some readers may not appreciate the full meaning and use of the terms used here; indeed, some terms are used with widely different meanings according to which church denomination uses them, or for that matter, which tribal grouping within a particular church or congregation. It is important to remember that the Russian Orthodox Church did not undergo the fragmentation that was the Reformation in the West. There is a unity of purpose and aim to the religion that Dostoevsky was raised in and to which he returned after his overtly politicized missspent youth. Professionals familiar with these terms may still gain some understanding of the context in which they are used in this book.

i. o/Orthodox

The term orthodox can have, here, two meanings. When cited with a lower case initital letter—orthodox (originally middle English, from Greek **orthodoxos**, from **orthos** *straight* or *right*, with **doxa**, *opinion*)—this, in essence, defines beliefs as conforming with traditional or generally accepted ideas or doctrine, and thus in accord with what has been established. When cited with an upper-case initial letter, the term Orthodox refers to the Russian Orthodox Church specifically (though may refer to Orthodox Judaism or other Eastern Orthodox Churches).

ii. Scripture

Following on from his incarceration in a Russian *gulag* in Siberia, Dostoevsky placed a very high value in his mature years on Scripture, specifically the New Testament. What value, what status, indeed what ontology, do we assign to Scripture? Despite a century or more of critically analytic Bible study the truth of much of Scripture still survives, but amidst the hermeneutic of suspicion that has driven this academic venture there is often one major casualty: authority. What authority do we assign to the Bible? True the books that constitute it were written with often differing intentions, and all can be seen as belonging to differing genres, but if the Bible tells us something, what authority can we legitimately give it? Dostoevsky is highly selective. He in effect ignores the Old Testament, and is discriminating as to what he accords value to in the New Testament. For this study I accord a traditional ontological authority to Scripture: the Bible as a whole, and its individual books, have an authority which is God-given and which we ignore at our peril, regardless of how we believe the books may have been composed. If we analyze—archeologically—how a building, say a house, was constructed, how its use has changed over decades or centuries, how it has been extended, or demolished and rebuilt, this does not invalidate the function, purpose, and use of that building today. The same is true of Scripture: let us suppose that several authors over decades or centuries wrote and constructed the Book of Isaiah: it is still the Word of God and has prophetic authority as to God's one true revelation in Jesus Christ. Sometimes the Bible has been misused and its authority has been used as a weapon, but this misuse does not invalidate the fundamental ontological authority of the Bible. This study of Dostoevsky's works is grounded in a traditional, orthodox, concept of the Bible. Much of the evidence will be from Dostoevsky's own copy of the Russian New Testament given to him on his way to exile and imprisonment, and annotated by him in the prison camp.

iii. Trinity

Dostoevsky is orthodox (lower case "o") in that he acknowledges the Trinity. Central to the theological framework we can read from his works is the centrality of Jesus Christ the God-man. Using the Gospel of John as evidence of Christ's divinity, he did find difficulty in conceiving or knowing of God outside of Christ. The immanent was all-important to him. As we shall see, at times Dostoevsky so believed in Jesus Christ as God that he lost any understanding or idea of God's transcendence, as in the Father in heaven. Dostoevsky therefore accepted the transcendence of God axiomatically whilst grounding the knowability of God in Christ. Any encounter with the Holy Spirit would then be perturbing, puzzling, and certainly not conforming to the cognitive and epistemological expectations of humanity as demonstrated by the immanent: sacred Scripture was the measure and test of any perception/encounter. In addition, the second person of the Trinity was often perceivable for Dostoevsky through ordinary people, and distinctly through suffering.

iv. The Supernatural: Spiritualism/Spiritism, and Spirits

Establishing Dostoevsky's respect for and understanding of the Trinity as a ground rule for this study leads into a consideration of his stand towards the supernatural and spiritualism/spiritism. Spiritism (a form of religion that grew out of spiritualism) was codified in the nineteenth century by the Hippolyte Léon Denizard Rivail (1804–69, pseudonym Allan Kardec), and religionized into the Kardecist Spiritualism Doctrine, which was based on the study of the origin and nature of spirits, and speculated on the ultimate end of the human, and the relationship between the human as spirit and the physical world. A basic dogmatic premise in this thought system is that humans are in essence immortal spirits that only inhabit physical bodies on a temporary basis. (This reflects a Docetic incarnation, also Hindu avatars are a closely related religious idea.) This physical *residing* may occur for several "incarnations," whereby the spirit, to attain moral and intellectual improvement, moves towards perfection; such spirits, through mediumship, may have an influence on the physical world.[1] Spiritism was highly popular in St Petersburg society in the mid-nineteenth century.

v. . . . and Deliver Us from Evil

Dostoevsky's novels, his belief system, is centered, in many ways, on deliverance from evil. This raises the question, what concept of evil is Dostoevsky working with? Evil is clearly manifold and present and active in his novels. But is it *real*, and what do we mean by real? For Dostoevsky evil is a spiritual force manifest in the corporeal, but it is not Manichean: it is not equal to God's goodness, it is goodness turned away from God, it is corrupted good, in many varying degrees, descending deeper and deeper, taking the human ever further from God's goodness, destroying the human. Evil, like demons, is not an abstract idea, even though such evil is clearly expressed psychologically in Dostoevsky's most depraved characters. Evil for Dostoevsky is real, but it is a transcendent actuality, the flip side of a coin: good and evil are states each and every human can rise to, or descend into. Dostoevsky's novels are full of demonic motifs, but does such evil, for him, have a supernatural component, *actual* demonic powers exerting influence? There do appear to be real demons operating behind people, pulling their strings, so to speak, but Dostoevsky is ambiguous, and he falls safely on the line that evil may simply be bad politics, bad human actions within a hermetically sealed, closed-off world. So is evil solely psychological? Whether this transcendent actuality is "real" or not, many of his characters are a reflection of actual people: these characters are possessed by evil and go on to possess and destroy others (unless at the final moment in their lives, they turn!). So in this work references to evil are according to how Dostoevsky saw it: sometimes as a noun, sometimes as subjective verbs or adjectival criticism, though it is important to remember that Dostoevsky does sometimes regard good and evil as simply relative and comparative, subjective, seeking to avoid

---

1 See, Alexander Moreira-Almeida, *Allan Kardec and the Development of a Research Program in Psychic Experiences.* Cited on Wikipedia, https://en.wikipedia.org/wiki/Spiritism, accessed Jan. 16, 2016.

(as with the question of demons) the question of the ontological nature of this transcendent actuality.

vi. The Fall / Original Sin

From an Eastern Orthodox—specifically Russian—standpoint there is no concept of original sin comparable to the Western tradition. This distinguishes the East from the West, in particular with regards to a theological anthropology. In addition, there is no need for a Marian doctrine of immaculate conception, or a doctrine of *total* depravity, penal substitution, and related atonement theories, and so forth; these do not feature in the way they do in the West. Humans are therefore, from an Eastern perspective, not born with Eve and Adam's guilt. Therefore, Eastern Orthodoxy, specifically Russian Orthodoxy, does not comport with Augustine's doctrine of original sin: human nature is *fallen*, humanity is depraved, to a greater or lesser degree, but not *totally* depraved. Ancestral sin is accepted, but not ancestral *guilt*. We are all affected by Eve and Adam's sin: we are all sinners, and exercise little control over our ability to sin, however, from the Orthodox perspective, Eve and Adam's *guilt* is not assigned to humanity. Writing on the doctrine of John Cassian—who influenced both the East and the West on this point—Casidy notes, "[Cassian] boldly asserts that God's grace, not human free will, is responsible for everything which pertains to salvation, even faith."[2] Dostoevsky's work reflects this Russian Orthodox tradition on the question of the *fall* and original sin, but is also, albeit implicitly and only to a degree, influenced by the Western tradition. We see this often as some of his most evil characters descend deeper and deeper into total depravity from which there appears to be no return, no redemption: unless they somehow turn at the last minute and repent.

vii. l/Liberal and Modernism

Dostoevsky's writings are set against the background of cataclysmic political, cultural, and social change in Russia specifically, Europe generally, in the nineteenth century. "Liberalism" is often seen as a contentious and problematic word—often it appears to generate an emotional response, may be considered pejorative, and may also be invoked in an equally subjective manner. Here the words "Liberal" and

2 Casiday, *Tradition and Theology in St John Cassian*, 103.

"Liberalism" with an initial capital letter are used strictly in the context of theological Liberalism in the church: this is a position that more often than not denies (but not always) the incarnation and resurrection, seeking to promote the idea of Jesus of Nazareth as an ordinary human being, furthermore, a Liberal theological position may not believe in God (with a capital "G") but happily allow people to believe in "gods" of their own making, their own invention (this is a position that can be identified with some l/Liberals in the nineteenth century, as well as in the twentieth and early twenty-first centuries).

Having been an avid supporter of Western European Liberalism in his heady youth, Dostoevsky reacted against what he had seen and read of this liberalism, both theological and socio-political. Therefore Dostoevsky reacted against this modernist tendency in his middle and mature years, having been beguiled by the proto-communism of French intellectuals in his youth. Theological Liberalism since the eighteenth century had claimed freedom not only from traditional dogmas and creeds but also in the analysis of and value accorded to Scripture. Such theology was to a large degree formulated in the light of what were considered advances in the natural sciences and philosophy—the spirit of the Age of Reason and the Enlightenment. In this work, when cited with a lower case initial letter ("liberal"), the term refers to liberalism in politics, society, and culture generally, in ethics and morality, in the nineteenth and twentieth centuries. Therefore a distinction needs to be drawn between Liberalism as a theological movement or belief system and what is often euphemistically called a liberal perspective in nineteenth-century Russian society generally. Dostoevsky regarded the term "Modernism"/"Modernist" very much in the same context as Liberalism; he was often scathing about Modernist tendencies associated with the proto-communist anarchistic groups who threated both Russian society and the Russian Orthodox Church, tendencies that were often essentially grounded in theological Liberalism, and philosophical atheism.

viii. Atheism–Theism

A common misconception with the characters in Dostoevsky's novels is that there is no actual difference between theists (Christians) and atheists (often anarchists, proto-communists, anti-monarchists of sorts, and so forth). This has led some to argue that all are saved, all are acceptable before God: beliefs make no difference to the final outcome of a human life. Dostoevsky posited a paradox, something of a puzzle: at times the person may claim to be atheistic, yet exude a sound understanding of God and eternity; at other times the individual may proudly believe and scorn atheists, but exhibit a religious pride that appears to place him or her far from the love of God. At times the person will claim atheism and die far from God (and from a traditional Western perspective face condemnation and an eternity in hell); at other times the person may exhibit sound faith and be saved. What Dostoevsky posits is the risks of religion: bad religion condemns; good religion saves, proclamations of belief/unbelief may not always point to the final destination of each human. The pertinent question when we come across a declaration of atheism by a character in one of Dostoevsky's novels is, *which* God does the character not believe in? Likewise we may ask, which "god" is it that such-and-such a person claims to believe in, and will swear absolute allegiance to?

ix. Bourgeois/Bourgeoisie

Though normally associated with left-wing revolutionaries, the term bourgeois often crops up in translations of Dostoevsky's works as a criticism of the comfortable indulgence of the wealthy classes in nineteenth-century Russia who claimed—superficially in Dostoevsky's view—to be Christian. Dostoevsky is as scathingly critical of these people as he is of the revolutionaries and the nihilists. (*Bourgeois*, also *bourgeoisie*, is then an adjectival criticism of lifestyle characteristics of the so-called middle classes, especially in having materialistic values or conventional attitudes.) Dostoevsky's life and sufferings set him apart from the comfortable bourgeois classes—as he saw them—particularly in St Petersburg, often considered at the time to be the most European and French of Russian cities.

3. DOSTOEVSKY AS THEOLOGIAN

From the time of his incarceration in a Siberian prison camp, through his exiled years, and into his mature years as a writer and prophet, Dostoevsky was as astute a theologian as the most qualified academic. We will see flaws and holes in his theological scheme, as compared to the Christian theological tradition, but these notwithstanding, he is a light blazing in the firmament of nineteenth-century skepticism. This volume is therefore intended as a relatively brief study of Dostoevsky's understanding of the eschatological reality that his theology pointed him towards. This reality attests to the truth that every person is, throughout his or her life, ever moving towards judgment and eternity: that is, towards heaven or hell (though a veiled universalism can be read from Dostoevsky's work). With death comes the final judgment on the individual; the resurrected Christ is the arbiter and judge, death merely brings into sharp focus the actual state of the person and what he or she will be for eternity. Therefore, from reading the works of Dostoevsky we can postulate how this dialectic demonstrated the movement of the individual toward salvation . . . or toward damnation. In Dostoevsky's view, every individual human being holds his or her future in his or her hands, the individual person decides: through beliefs and actions. What humanity does in the here-and-now echoes through eternity. I shall argue that it was to this eschatological reality that the works of Dostoevsky consistently attest, even if at times obliquely.

::

PART ONE

::

FYODOR MIKHAILOVICH DOSTOEVSKY, WRITER AND PROPHET

::

"Very truly, I tell you,
unless a grain of wheat falls into the earth
and dies, it remains just a single grain;
but if it dies, it bears much fruit."

JOHN 12:24

::

quoted by Dostoevsky after the title page
of *Братья Карамазовы,*
(*Bratia Karamazovy*—*The Brothers Karamazov*)

::

1

Ideas and Ideology, Eschatology and Possession

1. A BEGINNING

Following his father's wish, Fyodor Mikhailovich Dostoevsky (1821–81) was trained as an army engineer (to enlist as an officer in the army was the custom of the day for a son amongst the wealthy and educated— the middle and some of the aristocratic classes). Therefore, the young Dostoevsky attended the St. Petersburg Academy, and served in the Russian military; his life being mapped out like thousands of other young men from a similar background. However, his life was far from conventional. As a young man he was exiled for sedition, imprisoned for revolutionary views. The man that returned to European Russia was in many ways very different to the young army officer who had been exiled: he had rediscovered Russian Orthodox Christian faith, and went on to carve out a career as a writer of essays, novels, and short stories, and also as a philosopher. Dostoevsky's writings are deeply psychological, but also deeply Christian. They are highly critical of the arrogant delusions of the revolutionary, but also—as Dostoevsky saw it—of the superficiality of the Russian establishment, which gave only passing acknowledgement to the church and therefore to the gospel. For Dostoevsky, many of the wealthy in the Russian establishment used Christian morality judgmentally, effectively ignoring the reality of the gospel. Dostoevsky saw no bounds in exploring the human psyche. His writings are set against the tumultuous developments—socio-political and cultural—of Russia in the nineteenth century.

Born in Moscow on November 11, 1821, Dostoevsky was brought up in a devout Russian Orthodox home, to relatively well-off parents.[1] However, his home was in the grounds of the Mariinsky Hospital for the Poor, where his father worked. The young Fyodor grew up playing with the children of the poorest of the poor. This notwithstanding, Dostoevsky had a conventional education and upbringing. His mother introduced him to literacy from the age of four. She taught him to read using the Bible (a relatively common practice throughout most pre-modern European societies), and provided whatever books he desired. Dostoevsky commented later in life how his imagination was brought alive by his parents reading aloud in the evenings.[2] From early on Dostoevsky's health was described as delicate, and he was considered stubborn and quick-tempered. His formal education took place at two boarding schools. However, this ceased with his mother's death from tuberculosis when he was fifteen years of age. Shortly after her death he left schooling to enroll at the Nikolayev Military Engineering Institute (the St. Petersburg Academy). However, he disliked the military; his inclinations were literary and artistic, and even at this early stage his espoused an interest in the Russian Orthodox faith to the extent that he was nick-named by his fellow military students, "Monk Photius."

2. PUBLISHING . . . AND DEBT

Dostoevsky graduated as a military engineer. He attended concerts, operas, plays, and ballets, ingratiating himself with the wealthy bourgeoisie of St. Petersburg. He combined his army work with the beginnings of a literary

1   Dostoevsky gives some autobiographical material in his letters—*Pis'ma* (several volumes; English trans., Dostoevsky, *Fyodor Mikhailovich Dostoevsky: Complete Letters*), and in the *Diary of a Writer* (published throughout the 1870s). A valuable source is from his second wife, Anna Grigoryevna, who prepared a volume from journals and diaries (collated and prepared 1911–16) before she died in 1918 (the publication was delayed by the Soviet revolution, which later banned Dostoevsky's work)—Anna Grigoryevna Dostoevsky, *Dostoevsky Reminiscences*, English translation by Beatrice Stillman (1975).

2   See, Breger, *Dostoevsky: The Author as Psychoanalyst*, 72f., and, Sekirin, *The Dostoevsky Archive*, 108. See also, Bloom, *Fyodor Dostoevsky*. For biographical detail see also, Frank, *Dostoevsky: A Writer in His Time*; Frank, *Dostoevsky: The Seeds of Revolt, 1821–1849*; Frank, *Dostoevsky: The Years of Ordeal, 1850–1859*; Frank, *Dostoevsky: The Stir of Liberation, 1860–1865*; Frank, *Dostoevsky: The Miraculous Years, 1865–1871*; Frank, *Dostoevsky: The Mantle of the Prophet, 1871–1881*; Kjetsaa, *Fyodor Dostoevsky: A Writer's Life*; and, Lavrin, *Dostoevsky*.

career. He translated French books into Russian and published his first novel, *Poor Folk* (1846). Dostoevsky had developed what can only be described as a lavish and indulgent lifestyle, and an addiction to gambling. Writing began to generate funds for this lifestyle. Dostoevsky was a European-orientated *literatus*—something of a dilettante. *Poor Folk* was followed by *The Double* (1846), both stories present relatively superficial characters who seek to avoid any trouble in life. *Poor Folk* presents two nice people who are poor and simply exchange correspondence over a distance. These early works echo the calm optimistic world of the St. Petersburg bourgeoisie. Over the next two years Dostoevsky published several short stories in *The Annals of the Fatherland*, including, *A Weak Heart, Mr Prokharchin, White Nights*, and *The Landlady*. If writing was intended to solve his financial troubles, the lack of success and the adverse criticism left Dostoevsky in deeper debt, with his health worsening. *Netotchka Nezvanova*, a novel, was left unfinished in 1849. Alongside his early attempts at writing, Dostoevsky left the army, and became more and more involved with small proto-socialist groups, inspired by the French Revolution.

3. EPILEPSY . . . AND RELIGION

A history of mild "seizures" culminated in Dostoevsky's teen years in a diagnosis of epilepsy; the first written record is from 1839 when he was an eighteen-year-old cadet at the military academy. These early-diagnosed seizures are from the time of his father's death. The idea that these seizures were caused by the stressful impact of his father's death—a common argument by critics in the nineteenth and early twentieth centuries (including Sigmund Freud)—is now considered wide-of-the-mark by neurologists.[3] The stressful impact of his father's death, three years after his mother had died, could have exacerbated an already latent tendency towards seizures in the brain, but a sudden onset of epilepsy is most often caused by a head injury. Anecdotes and speculation as to the cause of epilepsy in historical figures are considered unreliable: there is simply not enough actual evidence to determine the cause. However, Dostoevsky

---

3   See, Reik, "The Study on Dostoevsky," 158–76. Freud's analysis (that Dostoevsky's epilepsy was not caused by a physical flaw in the brain, but was a *pseudo-epilepsy*, the symptoms being brought on by stress and guilt, also hysteria) is now considered speculative and inaccurate. See also, Rosen, "Freud on Dostoevsky's Epilepsy: A Revaluation," 107–25.

was certainly an epileptic; he suffered from seizures, and wrote about seizures, for example, in *The Idiot* (1869).

Contrary to the view of most scholars that his epilepsy was an unfortunate illness that occasionally troubled Dostoevsky, a consideration of epilepsy and the profound effect the condition has on the mind of an epileptic is crucial in understanding the eschatological theology that can be read from his writings, indeed that undergirds his *corpus*. Epilepsy is crucial to understanding Dostoevsky and the dialectical foundation of his theological views. Seizures may be caused by an injury to the brain, or sustained substance abuse (including alcohol). A diagnosis may issue from the culmination of very mild seizures during childhood—moments of frozen expression, absent mindedness, losing all sense of continuity and place just for a second—which often indicate an underlying latent epileptic condition before the onset of actual and noticeable seizures or fits. Seizures may be focal or generalized. Focal seizures are caused by a small area of scar tissue in the brain; generalized seizures offer no focal point. In Dostoevsky's case, there came a point in his teens where he collapsed with a major seizure. As he progressed through his adult years the seizures became more severe. This is a predictable development. Seizures cause minute damage in the brain, and therefore leave scarring. Such scarring then triggers further seizures of increasing intensity, because at its most basic epilepsy is simply a minute electrical malfunction in the brain's wiring, in the synaptic pathways that provide the conditions for thought. (From a reductionist perspective these electro-chemical events are taken as the sole manifestation of "thought," but the functioning synaptic pathways do not so much *constitute* our thoughts, as provide a *vehicle* for our thoughts.) As the scarring increases, the number and intensity of the seizures increases.[4]

---

4   Here I must own to a personal involvement and understanding comparable to Dostoevsky's, and his wife's. My wife of thirty-three years, Hilary, has been epileptic all her life. For the last twenty years the condition has been severe. As Hilary's full-time carer I not only watch for and care for the condition on a daily—hourly—basis, but have researched it in minute detail, including modern theories and treatments, which, apart from modern anti-convulsants, offer little more in the way of understanding, treatment, and cure than could the medical profession in the mid-nineteenth century. In the late twentieth century, highly detailed "keyhole" surgery to remove the scar tissue causing seizures offered hope; but this necessitated cutting out and thereby generated fresh scar tissue. There is therefore, with the human brain, no restoration to the original condition.

How recurrent epileptic seizures affect the precise nature of theological beliefs in one such as Dostoevsky is an open question yet to be examined. Epilepsy may under certain circumstances be considered to be eschatological because epilepsy can foster dualistic, binary thinking, and as such has an inclination towards an eschatological way of seeing the world; in addition, there is a sense in many epileptics of the need for urgency in decision making, in dealing with a crisis, a sense that everything is coming to a head, that judgment is coming (these thoughts often precede a seizure of varying intensity). This may be considered a particular interpretation of eschatology when most people do not concern themselves with the crisis of life and the risk of eternal judgment. Epilepsy can lift people out of a worldly complacency. Dostoevsky's beliefs are profoundly eschatological and, to a degree, dualistic: light and dark, heaven and hell, good and bad, ecstatic and nihilistic, either-or: in a word, *dialectic*. Dualism, issuing from the epilepsy, accounts—in part— for his dialectic. Epilepsy is not an inconvenient illness that occasionally disables the individual. An epileptic brain operates differently from a so-called "normal" brain. Epileptically conditioned beliefs significantly alter the superficial religious background (characterized by a relatively trite theological anthropology). Why? Epileptics are often forced into the position of outsiders. Dostoevsky demonstrates this in his novels: for example, Prince Myshkin (*The Idiot*) is often politely ignored, shunned, subtly omitted from social interaction for risk he may have a fit or damage something precious! People around him fear a seizure, not just because they do not know how to cope with it, but it un-nerves them—they fear losing their own mind, not being in control, and they fear the risk of death (SUDEP: sudden unexplained death from epilepsy). Outsiders, like lepers in the biblical world of Jesus, or the blind, the lame, the disabled, who are ostracized from the Jerusalem temple cult and religion, either love Jesus, or loath him: the gospel sees such matters in terms of light and dark, either-or, angels or demons, heaven or hell. Such is the case with epileptics, even if the condition is relatively well controlled. It may be speculated that this is why the marginalized, the afflicted, the suffering outcasts, saw Jesus and responded strongly, either one way or the other. In 1862 Dostoevsky visited clinics in Western Europe to try to find either a cure, or ways of stabilizing his epilepsy. There was no cure.

4. EPILEPSY . . . AND CHRISTLIKENESS

Dostoevsky aligns the position of the suffering outsider with Christlikeness. This is starkly presented in *The Idiot* (1869). Myshkin, the Christlike figure, fails in his efforts to save Nastasya Filippovna because he is human and not divine. As Eduard Thurneysen notes, "The Idiot, Prince Myshkin, an epileptic, returns to Russia from a nerve clinic in Switzerland without being cured."[5] Myshkin ends up returning to the clinic after suffering his destruction at the hands of murderers, libertines, and the proud cultured classes in St. Petersburg. The world still remains the same, but there has been a change in people: this is movement, either the movement *towards* salvation or, for some, a movement *away* from salvation into damnation. Dostoevsky's faith was characterized by an existential eschatological crisis, which was conditioned by his epilepsy, but also by other factors in his life, in particular the mock execution he faced in response to his revolutionary activities as a young man. Dostoevsky's suffering was to a degree (but certainly not always) a form of Christlikeness that separated him from the polite social etiquette of the St. Petersburg religious classes. His wife, Anna Dostoevsky, noted a state that almost led to a seizure, which defines this outsidership:

> On the way to Geneva we stopped overnight in Basel, with the object of viewing a painting in the museum there which someone had told Fyodor Mikhailovich about. This painting, by Hans Holbein, depicts Jesus Christ after his inhuman agony, after his body has been taken down from the Cross and begun to decay. His swollen face is covered with bloody wounds, and it is terrible to behold. The painting had a crushing impact on Fyodor Mikhailovich. He stood before it as if stunned. And I did not have the strength to look at it—it was too painful for me, particularly in my sickly condition—and I went into other rooms. When I came back after fifteen or twenty minutes, I found him still riveted to the same spot in front of the painting. His agitated face had a kind of dread in it, something I had noticed more than once during the first moments of an epileptic seizure. Quietly I took my husband by the arm, led him into another room and sat him down on a bench, expecting the attack from one minute to the next. Luckily this did not happen. He calmed down little by little and left the museum,

5   Thurneysen, *Dostojewski*, 22/ET: 25–26.

but insisted on returning once again to view this painting which
had struck him so powerfully.[6]

Dostoevsky understood the height of the intensity of beauty and joy
in an aura in the minutes before an epileptic seizure possesses (such an
aura is not experienced by *all* epileptics), and how these may be moments
of true knowledge of God and of humanity's existence, only to be followed
by the destructive nihilism of the seizure: this is "to push the paradox
to the limit . . . wherein God is seen."[7] This can be seen in the depths
of negation and nihilism, illness and suffering that allow the epileptic
to gain deep knowledge out of the moment of near death. Thurneysen,
again, "Humanity can be true to the real meaning of this life only in
those great negations of all human standpoints and possibilities."[8] These
negations are like a premonition of the *eschaton* because they generate
the crisis of judgment. In *The Idiot*, the unworldly Myshkin, the epileptic,
unnervingly speaks the truth and never partakes in the games of status,
power, and sexual politics that other people do, but he eventually returns
to the asylum as the result of *status epilepticus* (continuous epileptic
seizures over several hours with the resulting brain damage that in most
instances causes death) having effectively been destroyed by the people he
was trying to save. Myshkin is only understood truly for what he is—as
an example of Christlikeness—by the outcasts in society, the outsiders:
in Myshkin's case, by a harlot (Nastasya) and a murderer (Rogozhin).
The Swiss theologian Karl Barth noted of Myshkin's character in *The
Idiot*, "Why can we work up no indignation against Dostoevsky's daring
to make Christ pass as an idiot in society and the real understanding of
him begin with the murderer and the harlot?"[9] Jeannette Stirling notes
that this psychotic murderer (Rogozhin) and this victim of child abuse,
turned into a sex slave (Nastasya), "are also fragmented characters,
their emotional fragility manifesting from time to time as 'convulsive'
and 'hysterical' behaviors."[10] Perhaps it is that those outside of what we
take to be the church (leastwise, the visible manifestation of the church)
are sometimes in receipt of a deeper, greater, and more profound (and

6   Anna Grigoryevna Dostoevsky, *Dostoevsky Reminiscences*, 134.
7   Thurneysen, *Dostojewski*, 24/ET: 27.
8   Ibid., 48/ET: 53.
9   Barth, "Der Christ in der Gesellschaft," 61.
10   Stirling, *Representing Epilepsy: Myth and Matter*, 97.

therefore *truer*) understanding of the human and its relationship to God than clerics and religious. The ranks of clergy and religious professionals may perceive something of this knowledge, but their witness is hampered and compromised by their religious status.

Dostoevsky describes epilepsy, that is seizures and the effect of seizures on the human being, through characters in his novels: more pertinently, he describes how the condition of epilepsy marks the epileptic as different to the rest of the herd of humanity, how the condition sets the individual apart. Some of Dostoevsky's accounts are first-hand, drawing on his own recollections of the seconds and minutes leading up to a seizure (often for him an *ecstatic aura*), and the state of confusion afterwards (i.e., *post ictal confusion*). No epileptic has a sound reasoned memory of the actual seizure, it would be like a camera trying to take a picture of itself, or a computer trying to analyze itself when it is switched-off! Many of his descriptions are from his wife's observations, and those of various doctors. These descriptions are then projected onto characters in his novels: Kirillov (*The Demons*); Smerdyakov (*The Brothers Karamazov*); Nellie in (*The Insulted and Injured*); Prince Myshkin (*The Idiot*).

In *The Idiot*, Dostoevsky portrays Myshkin in the half-hour or so leading up to a seizure, wandering; this preamble is not so much confused or aimless, but without consistent purpose. Myshkin is focusing on small irrelevancies, obsessive details, in what to some may seem an autistic manner.

> For some time the prince wandered about without aim or object
> .... Towards six o'clock he found himself at the station of the
> Tsarsko-Selski railway.... He was tired of solitude now; a new rush
> of feeling took hold of him, and a flood of light chased away the
> gloom, for a moment, from his soul. He took a ticket to Pavlofsk,
> and determined to get there as fast as he could, but something
> stopped him; a reality, and not a fantasy, as he was inclined to
> think it. He was about to take his place in a carriage, when he
> suddenly threw away his ticket and came out again, disturbed
> and thoughtful. A few moments later, in the street, he recalled
> something that had bothered him all the afternoon. He caught
> himself engaged in a strange occupation which he now recollected
> he had taken up at odd moments for the last few hours—it was
> looking about all around him for something, he did not know

what. He had forgotten it for a while, half an hour or so, and now, suddenly, the uneasy search had recommenced.[11]

The lack of focus and the wandering continue and he begins to question reality:

> But he had hardly become conscious of this curious phenomenon, when another recollection suddenly swam through his brain, interesting him for the moment, exceedingly. He remembered that the last time he had been engaged in looking around him for the unknown something, he was standing before a cutler's shop, in the window of which were exposed certain goods for sale. He was extremely anxious now to discover whether this shop and these goods really existed, or whether the whole thing had been a hallucination. . . . He remembered that at such times he had been particularly absentminded, and could not discriminate between objects and persons unless he concentrated special attention upon them.

Myshkin then realizes that he may be drifting into a seizure:

> He remembered that during his epileptic seizures, or rather immediately preceding them, he had always experienced a moment or two when his whole heart, and mind, and body seemed to wake up to vigor and light; when he became filled with joy and hope, and all his anxieties seemed to be swept away forever; these moments were but intuitions [forebodings?], as it were, of the one final second (it was never more than a second) in which the fit came upon him. That second, of course, was inexpressible. When his attack was over, and the prince reflected on his symptoms, he used to say to himself: "These moments, short as they are, when I feel such extreme consciousness of myself, and consequently more of life than at other times, are due only to the disease—to the sudden rupture of normal conditions. Therefore they are not really a higher kind of life, but a lower." This reasoning, however, seemed to end in a paradox, and lead to the further consideration:—"What matter though it be only disease, an abnormal tension of the brain, if when I recall and analyze the moment, it seems to have been one of harmony and beauty in the highest degree—an instant of deepest sensation, overflowing with unbounded joy and rapture, ecstatic devotion, and completest life?" Vague though this sounds, it was perfectly comprehensible to Myshkin, though he knew that it was but a feeble expression of his sensations.

11   This an subsequent extracts are from *The Idiot*, Pt. 2, ch. 5, 139–41.

What Dostoevsky is describing is the *aura* prior to a seizure (*prodromal* or *pre-seizure*), the dark nihilistic destruction that follows on he cannot describe, he will only know of the sheer destruction in his mind after the seizure is over: the *post ictal confusion*. During the last twenty years of his life Dostoevsky kept a record of the number of seizures he experienced in his notebooks. This is a total of 120 (which is actually a relatively low number: an average of one every two months). Jeannette Stirling, in *Representing Epilepsy: Myth and Matter*, considers Dostoevsky's condition:

> One of Dostoevsky's friends wrote that the author often spoke of his prodromal, or pre-seizure, phase as a period of ecstasy. He claimed to have experienced:
>> . . . a contentedness which is unthinkable under normal conditions, and unimaginable for those who have not experienced it. At such times I am in perfect harmony with myself and the entire universe. Perception is so clear and so agreeable that one would give ten years of his life, and perhaps all of it, for a few seconds of such bliss.[12]
>
> Many of these aspects of cerebral paroxysm, as well as the darker and more difficult sensory changes, are written into the characterizations in Dostoevsky's fictional works. In *The Idiot*, Prince Myshkin's pre-seizure states sometimes elevate him to a "lofty calm" where "his mind and heart were flooded with extraordinary light;"[13] however his seizures also plummet him to to the lowest mode of existence.[14]

Dostoevsky therefore focuses on the pre-seizure aura, often termed ecstatic epilepsy, and the nihilism of the post seizure, or *post ictal* period of recovery, where the brain slowly "reboots" and recovers, where perception and understanding needs to gradually re-ground in reality.

An interesting point he projects into his epileptic characters is the primordial scream immediately prior to a seizure:

> Myshkin's seizures, like those of Yelena in *The Humiliated and Insulted*, are preceded by a "frightful, unimaginable scream":

12 Stirling, *Representing Epilepsy: Myth and Matter*, 95 and 127. Stirling notes, "The quote is attributed to Strakhov, cited in Henri Gastaut, 'Fyodor Mikhailovitch Dostoevsky's (1821–1881)'. *Epilepsia*, Vol. 19, 1978, p. 188."

13 Stirling is here quoting from Dostoevsky's, *The Idiot* (trans. Constance Garnett) 219.

14 Stirling, *Representing Epilepsy: Myth and Matter*, 95.

> In that scream everything human seems obliterated and it is
> impossible, or very difficult, for an observer to realize and
> admit that it is the man himself screaming. *It seems indeed*
> *as though it were someone else screaming from within the*
> *man.* That is how many people at least have described their
> impression. The sight of a man in an epileptic fit fills many
> people with positive and unbearable horror, in which there is
> a certain *element of the uncanny*.[15] (My emphasis.)
>
> In an indexical turn, Dostoevsky describes Myshkin as having
> "that strange look from which some people can recognize at the
> first glance a victim of epilepsy."[16]

Dostoevsky, quoted here by Stirling, appears to be invoking something
beyond the rational, beyond the immediate reductionist diagnosis of
epilepsy; so what is going on here?

5. EPILEPSY AND DEMONS . . . EVIL AND POSSESSION?

i. Epilepsy . . . and the Demonic?

The standard reductionist (i.e., "modern"/"scientific") approach to
epilepsy reflects the closed-off world of Kantian philosophy. Epilepsy is a
brain disease, a malfunction in part of the matter/flesh that is manifested
by the synaptic pathways and brain cells. Any spiritual dimension is simply
where the sensation in a person's mind leading up to a seizure may, under
certain circumstances and according to the individual's background (has
s/he been introduced to "religious" ideas?), be given a "religious" gloss.
Feelings of warmth, light, contentment, pleasure, heightened awareness,
and so forth—these are considered by psychologists and neurologists to be
"religious" (though without an accompanying definition and explanation
of what being "religious" actually is). Thus, epileptic seizures, where there
is consciousness of the pre-seizure or actual seizure in the epileptic,[17]

---

15   Stirling is here quoting from Dostoevsky's, *The Idiot* (Constance Garnett
trans., Melbourne: Heinemann, 1961, 228–9). Note, descriptions of Yelena's seizure can
be found in Dostoevsky, *Humiliated and Insulted*, 191f.

16   Stirling, *Representing Epilepsy: Myth and Matter*, 95.

17   A *simple partial seizure* involves a degree of conventional consciousness by the
epileptic; a *complex partial seizure* involves no conventional consciousness, but *altered
consciousness*, as the individual will still walk, try to talk, bump into things, but have no
more understanding of the world and its dangers around her/him that a ten-month old

are often considered "spiritual," but this is a no more than a comment upon the *epileptic's* interpretation of the event. The psychologists and neurologists themselves do not make sense of the event in terms of such categories. They may indeed deny the reality of any spiritual dimension to the world that transcends the psyche of human beings.[18]

Things are different with the Bible. The biblical world is invisibly peopled by angels and demons: spirits that underpin and influence the actions and beliefs of people. To the biblical authors, these spiritual beings were not to be considered abstract ideas; angels and demons were not to be seen as psychological projections. They were to be seen as *real*—as real as people are; invisible, perceived by their sway, their influence on humanity.

What did Dostoevsky himself believe? He accepted and valued the Bible and it is clear that many of his characters are defined by what appears to be angelic goodness or demonic evil, but also that they have the freedom to move between the states of good and evil. Did Dostoevsky realize or acknowledge that we cannot dismiss the influences of good or bad spirits on the human mind? If he did, did he learn this from his epilepsy? Or did he avoid the question? The concept that we may be influenced in our thinking, in our beliefs and actions, by angels and demons is not, to Dostoevsky, an abstract idea, a concept underpinned by his respect for the Bible, specifically the New Testament. The protagonists in Dostoevsky's novels are heroes or anti-heroes, the behavior of many of these characters is "demonic", "hellish," as in *The Demons* (1872), and in the character of Raskolnikov (*Crime and Punishment*, 1866). But we must be clear that Dostoevsky does not assert actual real spiritual demons behind the evil behavior of humans. Dostoevsky is very coy about the biblically asserted spiritual realm, a point we will consider in relation to his flirtation with, and then rejection of spiritism.

This dualism may define the human condition, but it does not define God and God's economy with creation. It is of paramount importance to note that in traditional Christian theology the devil is not a parallel "god," equal to God, uncreated, co-existing from eternity. Rather, the devil, the

---

child just beginning to walk (a state of *complex partial seizure* can sometimes be similar to advanced dementia). The depth of a *complex partial seizure* may lead into a full-blown seizure with total loss of consciousness and the risk of brain death.

18   See Coles, "Temporal Lobe Epilepsy and Dostoevsky's Seizures: Neuropathology and Spirituality"

arch-leader of demonic evil forces, is a *creature:* Lucifer. Lucifer was good, in some ways the highest creation, the brightest of angels. But Lucifer rebelled, set himself up as "god," and attempted to parallel God. Lucifer could not coexist in heaven, in eternity, and fell. He was expelled. This rebellion and its consequences are mirrored in Dostoevsky's anti-heroes, the depraved and fallen characters who move ever deeper into a "hell" of their own making, eventually losing all traces of a God-given humanity. Madness and suicide await them; unless at the last moment they turn and repent. This is a recurring theme in Dostoevsky's mature period novels. However, it is important to note that according to conventional interpretation Dostoevsky appears to use the biblical notion of devils, demons, and hell, as a motif and theme, he sees this reality from the Bible played out in the *fall* of human characters. That, however, is not at all the same as seeing actual evil spirits at work as part of the world of the novel.

Epilepsy may help to generate this "either-or" dualism in Dostoevsky's understanding of the human condition, but Scripture bears witness to a deeper understanding of the relationship between seizures and the world of angels and demons: an epileptic seizure (or for that matter cramp in the leg!) may, or might not, be triggered by the influence of a spiritual being— invisible, but outside our control. This is a world that characterizes and underpins Dostoevsky's novels, but he was not necessarily asserting that the evil anti-heroes in his books were manipulated by actual, real, demons. Is this a weakness in his work, and in his own life's belief system? Again, we will consider Dosteovesky's own beliefs in relation to his interest in spiritualism and spiritism.

ii. Possession and Possessors

In *Demons* (*Besy*, 1872; often translated as *The Devils*, or wrongly translated as *The Possessed*, where, *The Possessors* would be a more accurate translation) Dostoevsky explicitly invokes this world of demonic influence whereby ideas are the main weapons that are used in the downfall into evil of seemingly altruistic and idealistic people. The novel draws on actual events, the assassination of opponents of revolutionaries in Moscow, St. Petersburg, and other places. Rowan Williams comments,

> Fyodor Dostoevsky was already a major figure in the Russian cultural scene when he published *The Devils*, the third of the four great novels of his maturity. By this time, he had returned to

Christian faith and practice, and saw himself as called to defend this faith in his writing. But this did not mean that he wrote improving stories on religious subjects. His way of defending Christianity was to try and show how it could cope with the most horrific and extreme of human situations. He never gives easy answers, but expects his readers to face the worst the world can offer so that the scale of God's grace becomes even more astonishing.[19]

Williams notes how the two key figures in a proto-socialist (armchair) revolutionary group are presented as demonically-driven: "Verkhovensky is a brilliant manipulator . . . Stavrogin is intelligent, wildly independent, mysterious and charismatic, a 'messianic' figure." Based on an actual incident, the murder of one member of the group binds all the others together.

Here, Williams understands how it is through willful decisions, many tiny, little decisions, and the influence of those we live with, decisions that allow us to accept the courting of demons or angels—which will ensure our progress towards the eschatological judgment that none of us can escape, but also how that judgment permeates back into time as the individual becomes ever more evil, or good:

These two diabolical characters don't come from nowhere. Their parents also figure in the book. Pyotr's father is a vain and silly old man, who loves to think of himself as a daring revolutionary writer; Nikolai's mother is an equally silly woman, caught up in a whole complex of self-deceit. . . . The message is clear: the demonic evil of the two younger men comes from this sterile, fantasy-ridden atmosphere, full of large talk about change and progress, but with absolutely no spiritual or moral substance. One generation's flabby fashions become destructive horrors in the next generation. You can see why Dostoevsky's novel was so unpopular with progressives in Russia at the time.[20]

Williams asks the pertinent question, "Can there be redemption for people like these, people whose emptiness invites the devil in?" Dostoevsky explores this possibility, the openness of redemption, towards the end of the book, but both characters walk away from the public confession and

19   Williams, *The Archbishop on Dostoevsky's "Devils."* http://rowanwilliams.archbishopofcanterbury.org/articles.php/2003/the-archbishop-on-dostoevskys-devils., para 1.

20   Ibid., para 5.

utter repentance that is required for salvation. Both are too demonically possessed to move to God. *Demons* was profoundly influenced by Dostoevsky's reading of The Book of Revelation. It is an explicitly political and eschatological text. Revolutionary forces were highly active in Russia in the second half of the nineteenth century (only coming to power with the revolution in 1917). However, already in Dostoevsky's day, competing ideologies fought each other for power and control. Dostoevsky is highly critical of these radical proto-communist idealists, who presented their beliefs and ideas—their politics—as quasi-religious; indeed Dostoevsky saw the very foundation and ground of these ideologically motivated beliefs to be inherently evil.

iii. Evil as a Tangible Transcendent Actuality

We cannot avoid the question, in relation to Dostoevsky's works, what do we mean if we refer to evil as "real"? In defining evil as real, is this an attempt to acknowledge that evil exists and is more than just an opinion about behavior that offends and is considered to be bad? Is evil no more than a judgment made by people to distance themselves from something they don't like and don't approve of? If evil is a turning away from God, is such evil supernatural, issuing from *actual* demonic powers (beings created good by God, but who have turned from God and embraced evil?) exerting influence in the here-and-now? Are the demonic motifs in Dostoevsky's writings an adjectival judgment, used to interpret and criticize political powers, or do they represent an interference, and at times perhaps even a possession, of the human by *actual* evil? Dostoevsky *does not* go down the latter path, of actual, tangible, real, and concrete evil, though for some readers his use of the demonic is ambivalent, it seems to call for acknowledgement of evil as a *transcendent actuality*. The allusion can be seen as Pauline in the sense that the New Testament speaks of principalities and powers and many biblical scholars debate whether these principalities and powers (Eph 6:12) are spiritual or political, as the original Greek text appears, for some, to be indecisive. Or are Paul's (and Dostoevsky's) spiritual powers "real" but operative through earthly powers. The Pauline texts show this well, and so does the Book of Revelation; however, are these powers to be understood as individual demonic beings or something akin to actual evil spiritual forces, a transcendent actuality, or are they simply psychological—a mental manifestation in a closed-off universe?[21] And what biblical background can we read between the lines of Dostoevsky's works? Dostoevsky is ambiguous, though he considers evil to be bad politics, bad human actions (where humans exercise power and authority). For Dostoevsky evil issues from bad ideas, and as such is worse than brawling fisticuffs, or sexual sins: pride and arrogance issue from corrupt beliefs, bad principles, twisted and convoluted dogma, that lead to the turning away from God. Dostoevsky does not appear to posit real demons operating behind people, pulling their strings, so to speak, yet the evil we can read from his novels is analogous to a *tangible transcendent actuality*, and appears to exist without of the human, even though this was in all probability not Dostoevsky's intention.

iv. Evil as Politics

The imperial Russian establishment is presented by Dostoevsky as inept, toothless, and in many ways complicit through its failure to refute the arguments of the revolutionaries, but not necessarily evil. F. Derek Chisholm, assessing Dostoevsky understanding and use of the "demonic" and eschatological, but also assessing the Russian and Soviet history that follows on after Dostoevsky's death and into the twentieth century, comments:

> The novel *Demons* accurately applies New Testament texts from Luke's gospel and Revelation on the demonic to Russian political extremism and the foundations of Russian communism. Second, that the formation of Russian communism by Lenin and Stalin provides an insightful case study of the demonic in politics. . . . Dostoevsky's copy of the New Testament indicates that he believed the Book of Revelation was an eschatologically prophetic book that was being fulfilled within late nineteenth-century Russia.[22]

Furthermore, Chisholm notes how,

21 See, for example, the works of Walter Wink: *Engaging the Powers: Discernment and Resistance in a World of Domination* (1992); *Naming The Powers: The Language of Power in the New Testament* (The Powers : Vol. 1, 1959); *Unmasking the Powers: The Invisible Forces That Determine Human Existence* (The Powers, Vol. 2, 1986);

22 Dostoevsky explicitly uses Revelation, chs. 10 and 13. Chisholm, "Dostoevsky as Political Prophet: *Demons* as Prophecy of Lenin, Stalin and the Foundations of Russian Communism," para. 1. Accessed online Nov. 28, 2013, www.fyodordostoevsky.com/essays/d-chisholm.html.

Verkhovensky is modelled after the beast that rose out of the earth in Chapter 13 of the book of Revelation. Snakes rise out of the earth and have an association with Satan and the perpetration of evil that goes way back. Stavrogin is modelled after the beast from the sea described in Revelation 13:11–18. Stavrogin is described as being a "beast of prey" that has "ungovernable wildness" and "superhuman strength." In the book of Revelation the beast that rose out of the earth prepares the way for the beast that rose out of the sea. In the novel Verkhovensky prepares the way as Stavrogin's subservient follower.[23]

The conclusion that we can infer from these allusions to Revelation in *The Demons* is that politics can be demonically controlled: is this the conclusion Dostoevsky draws? Indeed, are all politicians, to a greater or lesser degree, demonically inspired and sometimes even controlled? Are they possessed by evil and then become—in a true translation of *Besy*—"*possessors*"? Dostoevsky offers no comforting nuances here, no grey, confused middle ground: politics rules and governs our lives and politics is either-or: politicians are for God or against God, angelic or demonic: but they, the politicians, the rulers, the movers and shakers, those who set trends and generate the political ideology that rules people (as Raskolnikov vainly believes of himself in *Crime and Punishment*) are the real *possessors* of the ordinary people, playing them like puppets. But we err if we believe we can lump all demonic influence on politicians alone, leaving all other human activities free from demonic manipulation. Perhaps the reason Dostoevsky focused so much on the politics of revolutionaries, and its demonic foundation, was in a way to repudiate the flirtation he had with political radicals during his misspent youth: the Franco-inspired revolutionaries that he came to be the self-styled leader of. William J. Leatherbarrow notes, "[t]his pattern of biblical motifs, imagery and allegory drawn from the apocalyptic revelations of St. John occupy a particularly significant place, and reveal much about the nature of Dostoevsky's Christian vision. This apocalyptic coloring emerged suddenly in Dostoevsky's works of the 1860s, and appears to be linked to his increasing awareness of the nature of Western European society."[24] We

23   Chisholm, "Dostoevsky as Political Prophet: *Demons* as Prophecy of Lenin, Stalin and the Foundations of Russian Communism," para. 16, quoting Kjetsaa, *Fyodor Dostoevsky: A Writer's Life*, 253–56. Chisholm accessed online Nov. 28, 2013, www.fyodordostoevsky.com/essays/d-chisholm.html.

24   Leatherbarrow, "Apocalyptic Imagery in *The Idiot* and *The Devils*," *Dostoevsky*

cannot deny that the apocalyptic in Dostoevsky's work from the time of the writing of *Crime and Punishment* is in all probability also linked to the worsening of his epilepsy. Therefore, Dostoevsky understood how the real risk in serious assaults by demons lay not in, say, an inept demon needling him by triggering an epileptic seizure, but in the way such evil spirits, whether understood as actual spiritual beings or as personifications of the lower aspects of our fallen natures, whispered ideas into the minds of people, gradually bringing about their downfall, their *possession*, and their *servitude* to this personified evil.

This raises the question for his readers: to whom do you belong? To Satan, the prince of evil; or to God, the Lord? Or do you subsist in the delusion that you belong only to yourself, that no one or no one thing lays claim to you?

Epilepsy defines frailty. Dostoevsky understood this from observing people in the world, but also from his own epilepsy. It lays open our vulnerability. If the mind can be subject to forces from outside of what we take to be perceivable reality then not only bad forces but also good forces could act upon the mind, and in turn upon the brain. And good forces, good spirits, could trigger an epileptic seizure in one who is prone to such attacks in the same way that more tangible triggers may cause an attack. If the brain, or part of the brain, has a weakness then something, even with good intention, may act as a trigger. Consider the account of Saul on the road to Damascus: a Spirit-enabled encounter with the risen and ascended Christ had a dramatic and cataclysmic effect on him (Acts 9:1–18). His symptoms are like a partial epileptic seizure (phasing between *simple* and *complex*, between consciousness and altered consciousness) both in the attack on the road and in the details given at the point of his healing at the hands of Ananias: Saul/Paul's temporary blindness (an extended period of *post ictal confusion*?) indicates the possibility of a seizure in the rear of the cerebral cortex (the outer layer of the brain), which processes information from the eyes before sending it to the temporal lobes at the front of the brain for interpretation, recognition, and so forth.

Modernist liberal philosophies and lifestyles do not insulate from demonic influence. It is simply that this reality of spiritual influence is more open, more noticeable, in epileptics. And it is a reality of spiritual influence that characterizes the theological veracity of Dostoevsky's novels.

Studies 3, 1982, 44. Accessed online Nov. 28, 2013, www.utoronto.ca/tsq/DS/03/043.shtml.

This eschatological reality is to be seen as a characteristic of Dostoevsky novels, and it is a reality that epilepsy bears witness to, an understanding that epilepsy may generate, as I believe it does, with Dostoevsky's writings. Proximity and commitment to Christ, the incarnation of God, should alleviate such a danger. It is a question of to whom we belong: personified evil, or to God? Who are we exposed to? What influences us?

This spiritual protection can be seen in many of the characters of Dostoevsky's novels, for example, Father Zossima in *The Brothers Karamazov*, or Sonya's younger sister in *Crime and Punishment*, the innocent and charismatically holy child, Polenka. Grace will surround and protect holy individuals from the wiles of the devil, and from the subversive influence of demons. This is not favoritism; the potential is there for all humanity, and to all of Dostoevsky's characters. It comes down to a question of faith and proximity. Christians may have epileptic seizures (a physical breakdown in the wiring—the synaptic pathways— in the brain) and still be insulated by God's Holy Spirit from the demonic world. It comes down to the relationship between the individual and God—which brings us back to the characters in Dostoevsky's novels: the promise of spiritual protection.

What is important is that two of the main epileptic characters in Dostoevsky's work—Myshkin and Smerdyakov—are in some way diametric: Myshkin, the innocent fool, who fails through his humanity to be truly Christ-like; Smerdyakov, the scheming murderer who flirts with evil till it possesses and destroys him. Both suffer from seizures, which may or may not be thought to result from "demonic" interference (though Dostoevsky does exclude the *actual* demonic from causing them), therefore it is not the seizures *per se* that are of concern, but the ethical teleology: what impact on the moral character did the seizures have, and how did the person develop and progress after the seizure? What do we say of demons and epilepsy?—that is, the impact of demons on the minds of Myshkin and Smerdyakov's (and Dostoevsky). The aim of such demons—if we follow the biblical paradigm—is to ensure the downfall of an individual by whispering ideas into the person's mind. [25] Demons may, or may not, have triggered epileptic seizures in Dostoevsky's brain, but they did not necessarily cause him to *fall*; where demons had been

25   In Mark's Gospel, the boy who manifests epileptic seizures is in his right-mind, and morally sound before God after the seizures. Demons did not need to trigger seizures in Judas, Pilate, or Herod, to ensure their *fall*, only whisper ideas into their minds.

successful was in whispering revolutionary *ideas* into the mind of the young Dostoevsky, encouraging him down this path. These demonically-driven ideas nearly led to Dostoevsky's execution, at a point where he had not repented of his youthful (political) mistakes. In his later life he was much more morally sound before God: despite being plagued, racked, and broken by the seizures: he held to his right mind and a right judgement before God.

6. ANGELS AND DEMONS,
THE BIBLE AND THE SUPERNATURAL

If we are to acknowledge a distinction—sometimes blurred—between the natural and the supernatural, then we must ask what was Dostoevsky's approach to the supernatural, and how did he regard his epilepsy? To answer this question we must examine, first, Dostoevsky on the influence of the resurrected Christ on humanity, the *imago Christi* and the *imitatio Christi*, and the question of atonement, then, second, his approach to the New Testament, that is, in essence his doctrine of Scripture (however implicit his approach to dogma and doctrine was). Dostoevsky's beliefs on both have a profound effect on the structure of his work and the characters he invents (drawn, to a degree, from a theological observance of people around him): the influence of the resurrected Christ is a supernatural influence on people; likewise, how we regard the references to angels and demons in the Bible raises questions about the supernatural. *We can then consider the question of Dostoevsky's beliefs about the supernatural and its influence, or not, on humanity.*

2

Formation and Influences

1. *IMAGO CHRISTI–IMITATIO CHRISTI*

A hallmark of Dostoevsky's struggle with faith, and the promise of protection for some of the characters in his novels, is the *imago Christi* (the image of Christ). Dostoevsky approaches the *imago Christi* apophatically—it is un-named. The characters and events in his novels are realistic. Many, indeed, were based on actual people and events that he was aware of. But his gift for portraying the human condition was more than mere borrowing from life. Often he was so successful in his characterizations that, however implausible a character's beliefs and actions might appear to be, real people and events could be found to correspond to them in the immediate years after the publication of the novel. For example, Dostoevsky was something of a prophet in the crime/trespass of Raskolnikov (*Crime and Punishment*, 1866). In November 1869, three years after the book was published, a young student at the Petrovsky Agricultural Academy in Moscow was murdered by a revolutionary group headed by Sergei Nechaev[1] for the supposedly humanitarian aims of radical ideology, or what Dostoevsky would have described as rational egoism: just like the character of Raskolnikov— killing for anarchic reasons. The characters in Dostoevsky's novels are ever moving towards the reigniting and fulfillment of the *imago Christ*, or they are moving away from the *imago Christi*.

---

1   Sergei Nechaev (1847–82), a Russian revolutionary nihilist who advocated the single-minded pursuit of revolution by any means necessary, including violence: the end justified the means.

If the *imago Christi* (essentially issuing from the cross and the resurrection) is, at its simplest level, the imprint of the true humanity that was masked and nearly obliterated by the *fall* into original sin, then humanity's appropriation, for Dostoevsky, of the cross and resurrection brings this image back. The restoration is gradual, its pace varies from person to person, and such a re-establishment might occur at different points in the human life, and at times may appear to be destructive more than restorative, but it is—through sanctification—the goal of each human life: failure (according to an traditional/orthodox reading of Scripture) leads to hell. Dostoevsky knew this. The *imago Christi*, for Dostoevsky, was not about being super-religious, or developing a career as a religious professional. In this he is both orthodox (traditional) and Orthodox (Russian). If the characters—based on Dostoevsky's observations of those around him—allow the Holy Spirit to work in them, they will be brought back to this true image, they will become more and more Christ-like, whatever the cost, whatever it takes.

If we speak of "image" we must avoid the contemporary Western obsession with personal appearance, with projecting a lifestyle image. The *imago Christi*—this is clear from Dostoevsky's novels—is not an affectation we project for the benefit of others, it does not issue from our vanity, it is the essential nature and character that is deep within us, it is the ground from which everything that constitutes us emerges. From a general Christian perspective, implicit to read from Dostoevsky's novels, and codified to a degree in Russian Orthodoxy, we can note that prior to the *fall* this image was complete and untainted: we were as God intended. After the *fall* it becomes corrupted, tarnished, prey to evil, self-justifying in its corruption. But it is not lost completely. Christlikeness, issuing from the atonement wrought for us by the blood of Jesus, will gradually restore us by drawing out the *imago Christi*, buried deep beneath the evils of the person, the self-justifying willful egotism of the postlapsarian human.

Christlikeness is not about mimicry: only Christ can be truly Christ. Dostoevsky's characters who try, *through pietism*, to be Christ-like simply end up as laughable, pretentious, and judgmental (for example, Madame Yepanchina, in *The Idiot*). It is clear from Dostoevsky's character portraits that we cannot achieve Christlikeness for ourselves by our own efforts: for example, Prince Myshkin, in *The Idiot*. However, people can in a haltingly limited way, through being in Christ, begin to be drawn into Christlikeness: beauty of character, graceful compassion, self-denying altruistic love, joyous yet suffering, they may radiate an inner Christlikeness despite manifold difficulties and oppression. In his mature writings, Dostoevsky focuses at length on the *imago Christi*—but does not name or mention this Christlikeness explicitly. We are left to discriminate, to discern, to identify and admire, if admiration leads us to seek the re-igniting of the *image* in us. In Dostoevsky's world it is the broken and damaged, the willful and bad, it is the murderer and the prostitute who can see, perceive, and recognize, but that recognition does not make them good, though in humility it may be the beginning of sanctification.

This raises importance questions about the *imitatio Christi* (the imitation of Christ), which relates closely to the *imago Christi*, though the two are not synonymous. Often the *imitatio Christi* issues from the *imago Christi*; however, any imitation of Christ must be unselfconscious, or it is likely to be feigned. How does the Holy Spirit recover the *image of Christ* buried deep within us? Our feeble halting imitation, if it is conscious, can only, perhaps, be Christlike when it involves self-denial, and leads us to self-sacrifice, which every fiber of our being rebels against, yet we must submit gracefully. The *imago Christi*, is therefore part of the *imago Dei* (the image of God), as Christ is the second person of the Trinity. The *imago Dei*, a fundamental concept in a doctrine of creation (Gen 1:26–27; 5:1–3; 9:6[2]), asserts that human beings are created in the image God and have intrinsic worth, importance, and significance, *in addition* to their purpose or meaning, which distinguishes them from the other animals in creation. If the human is created in the image of God, then the debased and depraved behavior that Dostoevsky identifies and presents so accurately is a denial of what we are and should be. This all concurs with Russian Orthodox theology.

As Dostoevsky demonstrated in *The Idiot*, epileptic seizures may wipe the mind, damage the brain, only for the person to recover. In a moment faith will go, belief will be annihilated . . . only to return. But if what is left of the mind in and after a seizure fails to perceive God or believe in God, this does not deny God's "existence." The moments of apophatic nihilism, of apparent loss of faith, immediately after a seizure may help by clearing out false ideas about God. Such a denial may refute, to a degree, the depraved egocentricity of the *fallen* human and in the shriven humility of recovering from the seizure, the reigniting of the *imago Christ* may or

---

2   For a Christian perception about the *imago Dei* see, Heb 1:3; Col 1:13–15; 1 Cor 11:7; Rom 8:29; 2 Cor 3:18; 4:4–7.

might—indeed *should*—take up the space, the emptiness. Such nihilism simply points to the human condition, but because of Christ's sacrifice such nihilism may serve Christ's purposes.

2. ATONEMENT

Dostoevsky is no theologian, yet his works are theological. As his faith— post Siberia—developed he found himself drawn more and more into the Russian Orthodox Church. He absorbed and drew on an Orthodox doctrine of atonement, which—having its formulation and roots in the early and patristic church—reflects a consistency that the atonement theories of the Western church have lacked over the last one thousand years.

The early church in the years after the resurrection developed theories as to *how* Christ's sacrifice saved us (to be ordered and codified by subsequent generations into a doctrine of atonement or salvation) and the resulting model of atonement has been adopted consistently in the Russian Orthodox Church. This early-church model has remained at the core of salvation theory in Russian Orthodoxy. The church, as it developed into the patristic church, formulated the "classic atonement model," often referred to as the "ransom theory."[3] This model is heavily eschatological, it is reflective, and is existential in that it lays emphasis on the crisis in which humanity finds itself since the *fall* into original sin (though it is important to note that an acceptance of the essentially Western doctrine of original sin in Russian Orthodoxy is not universal, often outright rejected or acknowledged with some limited reluctance, and not as systematically expounded as compared with Augustine's exposition). The *fall* enslaved the first humans and their progeny, indeed all of humanity, to the devil, to personified evil through rebellion. In order to *redeem* humanity, God descends in Jesus of Nazareth, the Christ, as a "ransom" or "bait."[4] As such the devil brings about Jesus Christ's death, unaware that the righteous innocent one could not be destroyed perpetually; through Christ's resurrection the devil loses the *right* to

3   Aulén, *Christus Victor: An Historical Study of the Three Main Types of the Idea of the Atonement*, chs. II and III, 16–60.

4   Ransom, from the Latin, *redemptio*; redemption, to redeem. See, Aulén, *Christus Victor*, 20f.

humanity: Christ is the victor! This is a monumental spiritual battle acted out in time, and outside of time (Rev 12:7).

Gustav Aulén argues that some theologians lay too great an emphasis on the "ransom" motif as a payment, ransom, or debt: "The work of Christ is first and foremost a victory over the powers which hold mankind in bondage: sin, death, and the devil . . . the victory of Christ creates a new situation, bringing their rule to an end, and setting men free from their dominion."[5] What could be seen as a financial transaction becomes a liberation: the motif of *Christus Victor* eases an overemphasis on the financial model by uniting the human Jesus with God (reuniting the incarnate Christ into the triune Godhead) through the cross; in so doing the devil is subverted.[6] The liberation component, over the financial, makes sense in a modern concept where a child has been kidnapped and held hostage, and the mother offers herself in place of the child, or more pertinently an older sibling offers itself in place of the younger children, with the parents agreement and anguish: Jesus offers himself to the powers of darkness in the place of fallen humanity; he is a part of humanity though the incarnation. Entering into humanity is crucial. This is a story more than a philosophical, rational account of atonement.

Irenaeus (130–202 AD) advanced a theory of "recapitulation" whereby Jesus became what we are so that we could become what he is; this was further developed by Athanasius (c. 297–373 AD) in his *De incarnatione verbi Dei* (*On the Incarnation of the Word of God*),[7] which advanced atonement through the descend-to-reascend motif: God descends to redeem humanity, in the flesh, dying to be resurrected, then to reascend to heaven with humanity. In the early centuries after Christ's resurrection this "classic" atonement model was recognized by all the churches; however, the Western (Latin) church developed this theory into recognizably different models. Initially the medieval church developed the "satisfaction/substitutionary/debt model," as laid out initially by Anselm of Canterbury (1033–1109) in *Cur Deus homo*:[8] Christ agonized and suffered on the cross as a substitute for humanity, in the place of

5   Ibid., 20.

6   Ibid., 22–28.

7   *St. Athanasius: The Incarnation of the Word. Being the Treatise of St. Athanasius, De incarnatione Verbi Dei*, trans. Sr. Penelope CSMV (1944).

8   Anselm of Canterbury, *cur Deus homo*, (*Why the God Man* or *Why is God Man?*)

rebellious humanity, as the weight of humanity's sin weighed down and crushed him: Jesus is the innocent substitute for humanity that satisfies God's honor and justice, thereby bringing in a judicial element: hence the language of debt/objectivism and the legal. During the Reformation many Protestants (in particular John Calvin) developed this "satisfaction/ substitutionary/debt model" into a "penal substitution" model whereby Christ is a substitute, taking the place of humanity on the cross. As with the Anselmian model, the emphasis is on satisfaction: justice through punishment. The Anselm's model is often seen to be about an offence to God's honor, which does not damage God's honor, but damages us. God can demand either punishment from us (which in this case would be infinite) or satisfaction. But to make satisfaction to the infinite honor we have insulted we must offer a gift of equivalent value (i.e., infinite value). We are not in a position to do that. Christ, however, can and does, thereby setting things right. For Calvin the image is of a legal penalty due that justice demands the payment of. Christ pays it. The difference is that for Anselm Christ is not paying the penalty for our sins—instead, he is offering his life as a freely given gift of satisfaction to undo the insult to God's honor. For Calvin, on the other hand, Christ is paying the infinite legal penalty. Both models can speak of justice and satisfaction but they do not mean exactly the same thing when they use those terms.[9]

Forgiveness flows from this act: the barrier between God and humanity is removed through the cross because it assuages God's need for justice.[10] Elements of "penal substitution" are to be found in some

---

9   My thanks and acknowledgement are to Dr. Robin Parry for assisting with the subtlety of difference between Anselm and Calvin.

10   We can acknowledge a later Western development, the "subjective theory of atonement," also referred to as "the moral influence model" (see Aulén (*Christus Victor*, 133–42 and 145) whereby the passion of the Christ was an act of exemplary obedience that profoundly alters, changes, and lifts up whoever comes to know about it. Essentially this relates closely to a form of pietistic religion (for example, as practiced by successful Victorians—a few good works of charity, complemented by respectable church attendance), and by, for Aulén, Enlightenment philosophers, and in the nineteenth century, neo-Protestant Liberals. But is this little more than humanity admiring the martyrdom of a "good" person? Therefore, the subjective model marginalizes the incarnation: the emphasis is on the individual's religious response. Being religious develops a new relationship for the individual with God. This is in effect reconciling, but is subjective and moralistic. There are characters in Dostoevsky's novels that admire Jesus and wonder if they might follow him, but this is not seen as an explanation for how the cross works.

patristic writers, but this is not their dominant theory or emphasis. The Russian Orthodox Church has consistently through its history remained wedded to the ransom/recapitulation theory, the "classic" model—Christ as the victor over Satan and death. Hence, Dostoevsky's characters live on a knife-edge: To whom do they belong? Who do they serve? Certainly not to themselves when their ideas and actions, their beliefs and behavior point to their ownership either by God or by the devil. Their ownership is defined, to a degree, by their service, beliefs, and actions. And a life is eventually defined eschatologically: by death, by culmination and completion.

At any given moment the most depraved and evil of persons in Dostoevsky's novels can turn and, through personal sacrifice, re-establish allegiance to Christ—God. (Or they may not: perceiving the *potential* for repentance and salvation in a depraved sinner does not guarantee an eventual redemption, but merely the possibility.) As was seen with the two thieves crucified next to Jesus (Luke 23:39–43), one turned, the other did not. Therefore, at any given moment a saint can throw away his or her salvation (though, governed we may argue by the re-development of the *imago Christi*, this is not always probable). Such is the eschatological view that underpins Dostoevsky novels: the reality of the eschaton is being worked out minute-by-minute in the here-and-now; when we die it will be obvious what we have become and where we are bound for. The "classic" model of atonement defines the characters and their relation to God in Christ . . . or to Satan. So, how did this framework in his novels come about? This eschatological and atonement framework defines his middle period and mature works—written after his return from imprisonment and exile in Siberia, convicted for subversion and revolutionary activities.

3. DOSTOEVSKY THE REVOLUTIONARY

As a young man at the St. Petersburg Academy Dostoevsky fell in with a revolutionary/socialist group under the aegis of the editor and writer Vissarion Grigorievich Belinsky (1811–48). Belinsky was active and influential in Russia, and then in continental Europe. He was primarily a literary critic, however, he was expelled from the University of Moscow for his revolutionary views, taking up work as a journalist. He is generally considered the father of radical intellectuals in Russia and was highly respected by the Soviets in the twentieth century. Belinsky died in 1848, a year before the authorities arrested the members of a crypto-political group—the Petrashevsky circle—named after its founder (Mikhail Butashevich-Petrashevsky, 1821–66), who was a self-confessed atheist, humanist, anti-Czar, proto-socialist. In 1847, through contact with Belinsky, Dostoevsky joined a secret political group headed by Petrashevsky. The group was a forum for political debate characterized by naïve socio-political action, such as attempting to run a printing press; however, more serious aims followed, for example, the founding of a commune in Petrashevsky's own village. The group took inspiration from, and was centered on the writings of, two leading figures in the French revolution: Jean-Baptiste Joseph Fourier (1768–1830) and Auguste Comte (1798–1857). Fourier initially trained for the priesthood, but took no vows. He was torn by an inner conflict, that is, whether he should follow a religious life or one of mathematical research. However, in 1793 he became involved in politics and joined the local Revolutionary Committee. He argued that the natural ideas of equality should be developed so as to conceive the sublime hope of establishing a free government without kings or priests, and to free the people from ancient burdens and yokes. Fourier was unhappy about the terror that resulted from the French Revolution and he attempted to resign from the committee, but fell afoul of the revolutionary authorities and was nearly executed. Comte was an initiator of sociology and scientific ethics (in effect, a representative of French-utopianism) who often referred to the "Great Discovery of 1822"—the plan of *The Scientific Operation Necessary for the Reorganization of Society* as he termed it. Between 1830 and 1842 he worked on the foundation principles of Positive philosophy.[11]

The Petrashevsky Circle, or group, met between 1845 and 1849 at its namesake's St. Petersburg home. Members included minor officials and junior officers, writers, and students, who were interested in the teachings of the French utopian socialists. Their primarily objective was the future transformation of society into a federation of self-supporting communes in which human labor and other activities were organized in such a way as to allow the free play of human passions and therefore the fulfillment of all. The Petrashevsky group publicly criticized the autocracy of Nicholas I's Russia and called for rights such as free speech along with press and legal reforms. By 1849 Dostoevsky was regarded by the authorities as the leader

---

11   Comte's political philosophy culminated in a six-volume *Cours de Philosophie Positive*. See also, *The Positive Philosophy of Auguste Comte*, 3 vols.

of the Petrashevsky Circle. Inevitably Dostoevsky was arrested, and with many of the others, convicted of sedition, sentenced to death by firing squad, but was reprieved at the last second just as the firing squad had taken aim and had cocked their rifles. William J. Leatherbarrow notes:

> Nicholas I was persuaded to commute the death sentences to imprisonment with hard labor, but he was determined to teach the conspirators an unforgettable lesson: they were kept in ignorance of the judgment of the court until the day of execution. Early in the morning of 22nd December, Dostoevsky and his fellow prisoners were transported to Semyonovsky Square, a regimental parade ground, where they were confronted with solemn priests, a black-draped scaffold, empty coffins, a line of armed soldiers and other signs that they were to be subjected to immediate execution. The original sentences were read and the first three prisoners, including Petrashevsky, were led to the stake. At the last moment, as the order to fire was about to be given, a messenger galloped into the square with news of the Tsar's "gracious" clemency. One of the prisoners lost his mind, and Dostoevsky himself was to be radically altered by this grim charade, which he later described in striking detail in his novel *The Idiot*.[12]

This experience had a profound effect on Dostoevsky—it was the experience of being born again, of resurrection. This theme of resurrection was to dominate his mature novels and he was to project this near-death experience onto his characters on more than one occasion.[13] With the sentences commuted to transportation and imprisonment, Dostoevsky, along with his co-conspirators, was imprisoned and exiled in Siberia for ten years (1849–59). As convicts they were transported to Omsk in central Asia in shackles (riveted into place before they left Moscow and not removed till they were released four years later) for the journey of over 1,700 miles to the prison camp. For four years they were imprisoned in diabolical conditions with examples of humanity that the cultured classes of St. Petersburg tried their best to forget about. Upon release he completed his sentence by serving in the army in Siberia as a common soldier for a further six years and was banned from returning to European Russia. After much pleading and corresponding with the authorities he was allowed to resign the army and return to Moscow and St. Petersburg

12   Leatherbarrow, "Introduction," in *Crime and Punishment*.
13   See, for example, Dostoevsky, *The Idiot*, Part 1, chapter 2.

ten years after he had left. The significance of the trial, mock execution, and the ten-year Siberian sentence are of profound importance to anyone who wishes to understand Dostoevsky's theological beliefs.

4. DOSTOEVSKY AND THE NEW TESTAMENT

The New Testament is of crucial importance in Dostoevsky's rediscovery of his Christian faith and as the source and basis for the beliefs underlying his novels.[14] On route to Siberia an elderly woman thrust a copy of the Russian New Testament into his hands, which helped to rekindle his faith and was, arguably, the most precious of possessions to him during his imprisonment.[15] The elderly woman was the widow of one of the Decembrists, an aristocratic uprising (December 14, 1825 old calendar, December 26 post-revolution calendar) in St. Petersburg, which wanted to outlaw serfdom and in some cases the monarchy; she thrust the copy of the New Testament into his hand as the convicts marched in shackles through Tobolsk in Siberia. The widows/wives of the Decembrists often gave copies of the New Testament in Russian to individuals in prisoner convoys. This particular widow would have had no idea who Dostoevsky was, only that he was a convict in exile, and heading for almost certain death in prison or in the cold of the Siberian winter. Dostoevsky's experience in prison and exile would have been very similar to Aleksandr Isayevich Solzhenitsyn, especially as recounted in *One Day in the Life of Ivan Denisovich* (1962). Conditions in the prison camps in the 1850s were no different from the 1950s. This copy of the Russian New Testament helped him to reaffirm his commitment to Christian principles, as embodied in the traditions and spirituality of the Russian Orthodox Church (though he was always wary of ecclesial power and authority). He kept this New Testament[16] until his

14   References to the Old Testament are extremely rare in Dostoevsky's notebooks, diaries, journals, and drafts—however, the importance of the Old Testament is seen in the profound impact he says that the book of Job on him in his childhood and youth (see *Diary of a Writer*).

15   See Dostoevsky's *Memoirs from the House of the Dead* (1862).

16   Chisholm, "Dostoevsky as Political Prophet..." Online: www.fyodordostoevsky. com/essays/d-chisholm.html. See, GBL, fond 93/I, K. 5b./1. *Evangelie. Gospoda nashego Iisusa Khrista Novyj Zavet*. Pervym izdaniem. Sanktpeterburg. V tipografii Rossijskogo Biblejskogo Obshchestva 1823.

See: Kjetsaa *Dostoevsky and His New Testament*. The work is dual language: English and Russian text of the marked passages from Dostoevsky's New Testament, with an introduction in English. Dostoevsky's New Testament is in the manuscript division of

death, reading John's Gospel on a daily basis, annotating it and writing his theological thoughts in the margins.[17] From the evidence of the annotations, the following books were of most importance to him: The Gospel according to John, The Epistles of John, then The Revelation to John.[18] Twenty-one of the twenty-seven books of the New Testament are marked—however, The Gospel of Mark is annotated only in two places, Luke in seven; by contrast there are fifty-eight annotations in The Gospel of John. The teachings of Christ and the passion are heavily marked and annotated. The short First Epistle of John is heavily marked and annotated in six places; The Revelation to John sixteen places.[19] By contrast The Sermon on the Mount, respected and used by Lev Nikolayevich (Leo) Tolstoy, is largely ignored. (This may be due, in part, to Dostoevsky's fear of any abstract ideological system resulting from his experiences with the Petrashevsky circle and studying at the feet of Belinsky.[20]) Even after his return from Siberia he regularly consulted, annotated, and wrestled with what were to him key passages marking in ink, pencil (even finger-nail indentations whilst in prison, when no pen or pencil was available—these marking are forcefully engrained); the practice of wrestling with what he termed "Sacred Scripture" continued even until the day before his death.[21] Therefore, The Gospel according to John and The First Epistle of John are by far the most important foundational basis for his belief system during the post Siberian period of his life.

To understand Dostoevsky's complicated life and beliefs we need to look at his appropriation of The Gospel of John. The greatest number

---

what used to be the Lenin Library. Kjetsaa writes, "It is also indeed with strange feelings that one sits today in the Manuscript Division of the Lenin Library, leafing through Dostoevsky's dirty copy of the New Testament. Countless fleas and lice have crawled over the dark covers of the book. From the writer's bunk it witnessed din and uproar, the rattling and jangling of shackles, cursing and coarse laughter, shaven heads and branded faces, degradation and misery. But it was precisely in this earthly inferno that the book was to have such importance for the writer's spiritual rebirth. . . . As a guest of the Gor'kij Institute of World Literature (IMLI) I was given the opportunity in the summer of 1982 to study the book, and in this connection I should like to express my sincere thanks to the head of the Manuscript Division, L. V. Tiganova." Kjetsaa, *Dostoevsky and his New Testament*, 6 and 80

17   Kirillova, "Dostoevsky's Markings in the Gospel of St. John," 41–50.

18   Ibid., 43.

19   Ibid., 48.

20   Fears expressed later in life in *The Diary of a Writer*.

21   Anna Grigoryevna *Dostoevsky, Dostoevsky Reminiscences*, 375.

of markings in John's Gospel relate to the divinity of Christ, and the relationship between the Son and the Father.[22] Irina Kirillova notes, "like no other of the Evangelists John sees the miracle embodied in the Christ who preached love in an evil world."[23] This can be seen in the heavily marked passages from both The Gospel according to John and The First Epistle of John, which deal explicitly with love—from the new commandment passages in the Gospel through to the comments in the Epistle dealing with the nature of love between people.[24] Irina Kirillova notes that as a religious type, Dostoevsky is a "Thomas the Doubter who needs to confront Christ in his own way."[25] A large group of markings relate to resurrection—one of Dostoevsky's central concerns.[26] These annotations emphasize that belief and life were inseparable—in Russian *zhivaia zhizn'* (living life). The resurrection of Lazarus was central to his faith—the passage is heavily marked in his New Testament. In addition, it is the central biblical passage in *Crime and Punishment*.[27] Overall, Irina Kirillova notes, The Gospel of John was of particular significance to Dostoevsky, more than any other book in the New Testament:

> The Gospel of St. John has particular significance for Dostoevsky because, more than any of the other New Testament books, it enables him to affirm his faith in the divine Son of God through the affirmation of Christ's Sonship made manifest in the "theology of love" that is so central to both The Gospel of St. John and the First Epistle of John. Dostoevsky's profession of faith had to overcome not so much the claims of nineteenth-century Natural Science as the tragic, insoluble contradiction between belief in an omnipotent and merciful God and the cruel, bleak reality of innocent suffering. The luminous revelation of love in the person of Christ enables Dostoevsky to believe that it is possible to resolve the terrible antinomy of innocent suffering and divine mercy through faith in Christ, the God-Man, who is both innocent victim and Redeemer. [28]

22   Kirillova, "Dostoevsky's Markings in the Gospel of St. John," 48–49.

23   Ibid., 49.

24   Dostoevsky's annotations are: John 13:34 and 15:12; and 1 John 2:10; 4:7, 12, 19–20: see also, Kirillova, "Dostoevsky's Markings in the Gospel of St. John," 50.

25   Kjetsaa, Geir, *Dostoevsky and his New Testament*, 45.

26   John 6:54; 8:51–52; 11:26; 12:32.

27   Dostoevsky, *Crime and Punishment*, Bk 4, ch. 4

28   Kjetsaa, *Dostoevsky and his New Testament*, 50.

This antinomy between divine mercy and apparently innocent suffering presented by the dialectical contradiction between the idea of an omnipotent and merciful God and the reality of suffering and death here on earth is reconciled only in the Lordship of the Son of God. This is the central dialectic in Dostoevsky's beliefs and in the theology presented in his novels. All other examples of Dostoevsky's dialectics flow from this resolution of the contradictions of faith and life in the God-man—hence *zhivaia zhizn'*.

5. DOSTOEVSKY AND SPIRITUALITY/SPIRITUALISM?

Spiritism was something of a fashionable preoccupation amongst the wealthy and leisured classes in St. Petersburg, particularly in the 1840s and 1850s. Thomas Berry notes, "From the reign of Catherine the Great to the Revolution of 1917, Russian society and literature were affected by the relationship between Western spiritualism with its séances and mediums and an ancient folk tradition with its superstitions and fancifulness. The common Russian belief in spirits, combined with the Western occult science, brought charlatans into the highest court circles throughout the last hundred and fifty years of the Romanov's rule."[29] These were people who considered themselves Christian but dabbled with séances and mediums, the occult and psychic phenomena, in particular, what they considered to be communication with the dead, all framed by religious interests and practices that denied fundamental Christian doctrine. Considered an innocent playtime, many were drawn into a much darker world than they expected, becoming infatuated with these gatherings. As a young army officer Dostoevsky was involved in such séances, flirting with the pronouncements of mediums, and so forth. As such Dostoevsky's seduction by spiritists is interlinked with the military society he moved in, then with the fashionable bourgeois world of his early novellas where he is a sceptic but plays with spiritist ideas as an innocent pastime, and then—ironically—with his politicization through revolutionary Franco-ideologues: "Dostoevsky was aware of the literary tastes of the period and his own writing reflected his effort to appeal to the public's taste for the esoteric."[30] In *The Landlady* (1847), Dostoevsky flirts with the idea that the

29   Berry, "Dostoevsky and Spiritualism," 43.
30   Ibid.

heroine is possessed by the devil, but narrates that this is psychological imbalance; the early Dostoevsky weaves some ideas from Russian folklore into his short stories and novellas, for example, a violinist possessed by evil powers when he plays the instrument (*Netochka Nezvanova* 1848).

Post-Siberia he embraced Orthodox Christianity and rejected spiritism. Post-Siberia his understanding of the supernatural is related to this rejection of spiritualism/spiritism; this rejection then effects, to a degree, his reading of the New Testament. It also shaped his theology generally, his eschatology specifically, creating apparent anomalies and flaws, contradictions in his otherwise traditional/orthodox theological framework. Fundamental to this question is whether the "other," the supernatural, exists, and is acknowledged; that is, a spiritual dimension: good and bad, holy and evil, angelic and demonic. Does such a reality exist in a way not reducible to the physical world we occupy? A Naturalistic position considers the material world to be all there is. Spiritualism, specifically spiritism as a form of transdimensionality, was rejected by Dostoevsky post-Siberia, at a time when it was even more highly fashionable amongst the leisured classes in St. Petersburg. Dostoevsky is critical of spiritualism/spiritism as a system of belief or religious practice based on supposed communication with the spirits of the dead, especially through mediums in séances. But does this rejection also involve a denial of the reality of the supernatural as attested to in the Bible?

Implying, in philosophical terms, the doctrine that the spirit exists distinct from matter, or that spirit is the only reality (OED), spiritism can be considered to be, for many, gnostic and heretical, raising serious questions about the incarnation, and the value of the corporeal. Aware of the "tremendous popular regard for the occult science"[31] during the 1860s and 1870s, Dostoevsky does weave into his major novels some examples, but walks a fine line between belief and skepticism, for example, "the dual nature of Russian spiritualism from the folkloric devils in many of his works to the sophisticated devilish phantom of Ivan's dream in *The Brothers Karamazov*."[32]

If in his major novels he tries to steer a path between belief and skepticism with regard to the influence the supernatural might exert on us in the here-and-now, he ends up with an hermetic world where any

---

31   Ibid.

32   Ibid.

sense of the supernatural is to be considered psychological. However, in his personal life he toyed with the idea of a spiritual reality that can exert influence on us.

Although skeptical of demons and spiritism, Dostoevsky was aware of what we may term the action, the enigmatic presence, of the Holy Spirit in his life, of unusual, nigh impossible, coincidences.

> In his personal life, Dostoevsky gave evidence of his curiosity about psychic phenomena. Doctor Janovskij, who treated the author, reported that Dostoevsky believed in premonitions and related the following incident. During the second year of their acquaintance, the doctor lived in Pavlovsk, returning to St. Petersburg three times a week for his medical practice. One day a strange urge convinced him of the necessity of returning to the city for an unscheduled visit. In a remote area he accidentally ran into Dostoevsky who had no money to pay a petty debt demanded of him by some military clerk. When the writer saw the doctor, he shouted, "See! See who will save me!" Later Dostoevsky called the incident remarkable and every time he would remember it, he would say, "Well, after that, how could one not believe in premonitions!"[33]

Saved from punishment under the law for this debt by this unexpected, unpredictable, encounter, Dostoevsky saw this as a form of divine intervention, though he fails to identify and acknowledge the triune, pneumatological nature of the encounter. Premonitions, for Dostoevsky, equal the enigmatic presence of the Holy Spirit, though he fails to distinguish, or test, the spirits.[34]

Although there are sometimes references to devils/demons/evil imps in his novels (as distinct from *the* devil as a dark personified evil force),[35] he states explicitly that he does not believe in such devils/demons/evil imps: "My whole trouble is that I, too, cannot believe in devils/demons; this is really a pity, since I have conceived a very clear and most remarkable theory of spiritism, but one exclusively based upon the existence of devils: without them, my whole theory comes to naught of its own accord."[36]

33   Quoted in ibid., 44.

34   "Dear friends, do not believe every spirit, but test the spirits to see whether they are from God." 1 John 4:1f. See also, Rom 8:16, Acts 10:30–32, 1 Thes 5:21–22.

35   For example, in *Crime and Punishment*, the conversations between Svidrigailov and Raskolnikov about ghosts, and hauntings, often generated by a guilty conscience.

36   Dostoevsky's theory was that the apparent revelations and encounters that

If we check through Dostoevsky's New Testament, examining the annotations, there are no marks against any passages in the Synoptic Gospels describing demons, demonic encounters, demonic possession, exorcisms, or the supernatural generally. He clearly selects the parts of the New Testament he feels comfortable with. There are likewise no annotations or markings against the episodes of exorcising of humans possessed by demons where the possession appears to be responsible for epileptic seizures.[37] Dostoevsky nowhere questions the cause of his epilepsy, or considers the possibility of supernatural interference as a trigger for seizures (whether good or evil—we noted earlier the possibility of pneumatological interference triggering a type of epileptic seizure as part of Saul/Paul's Damascus Road encounter/experience).

Assessing Dostoevsky's annotations to the New Testament, The Gospel according to John and The First Epistle of John, both with the emphasis on the figure of Christ and what is termed in Eastern Orthodoxy the "Theology of Love"[38] are by far the most important foundational basis for his belief system during the post-Siberian period of his life. It is pertinent to note that there are no exorcisms in John. There is the devil, but "its" influence is mediated through the darkness of the world. The devil is also mediated through the darkness in and of an individual like Judas Iscariot; indeed, this is the self-destructive darkness that starts initially with ideas, maybe one seemingly innocent idea that progresses through a manifold till the darkness engulfs the individual, condemning him/her. Such darkness ensures the demonic behavior, and the intolerance and persecution, the destruction and chaos, which Dostoevsky saw at its worst in bad politics. Dostoevsky wrote, in 1876, in his mocking criticism of spiritism (and associated demons), of the dangers of a theological debate:

> Naturally, I have been jesting and laughing from the first word to the last; yet this is what I wish to express in conclusion: if one were to regard spiritism as something carrying within itself a new creed (and virtually all spiritists, even the sanest among them, are a bit

---

appeared to happen in séances were demons/evil spirits toying with susceptible people, but he denies the existence of such spiritual phenomena and thus he concludes that what is happening can be explained psychologically. See Dostoevsky, *The Diary of a Writer*, Vol. 1, Ch. 3, §. 2, 'Spiritism. Something about Devils. Extraordinary Craftiness of the Devils, if only these are Devils,' 190–96, quote, 191.

37   For example, Mark 9.

38   See Lossky, *The Mystical Theology of the Eastern Church*.

inclined toward such a view) . . . [then] for this reason, may God speedily bring success to a free investigation by both sides; this alone will help to eradicate, as quickly as possible, the spreading stench, and this might enrich science with a new discovery. But to shout at each other, to defame and expel each other from society on account of spiritism—this, to my way of thinking, means nothing but consolidating and propagating the idea of spiritism in its worst sense. This is the beginning of intolerance and persecution. And this is precisely what the devils are after![39]

So evil/the devil is, under certain qualified conditions, real, but demons may be psychological creations of our imagination, though still result from the action of this dark personal force. Did Dostoevsky, in effect, retain the closed-off world of a Kantian philosophy from his youth, a concept of the world that denied the supernatural and was *de rigueur* amongst the proto-communist revolutionaries and anarchists he scorned, post-Siberia? And it is perhaps important to note that we do not dictate the conditions under which the Holy Spirit acts on us and in us (if we try to, we end up inventing impish demons and spirits, the idea of which is generated by real personified evil). Rhetorically, we may ask, did Dostoevsky, post-Siberia, have, in effect, a phobia about demons and the supernatural, which colored his understanding and acceptance of the real spiritual world of heaven and hell, the triune God and salvation/damnation? Was this how he dealt with the sins of his youth—specifically, his flirtation with spiritism which he had be involved in at the same time as his politicization into Franco-Russian revolutionary ideas and praxis? Dostoevsky noted, "I don't believe in spiritualism, but besides that, I don't want to believe."[40]

39   Dostoevsky, *The Diary of a Writer*, Vol. 1, 196.

40   Ibid., 139–40.

::

PART TWO

::

DOSTOEVSKY'S
THEOLOGICAL ANTHROPOLOGY

::

"Then Jesus told his disciples,
'If any want to become my followers, let them deny themselves
and take up their cross and follow me.'"

"Then he said to them all,
'If any want to become my followers,
let them deny themselves and take up their cross daily
and follow me.'"
LUKE 9:22

::

3

Dostoevsky, Writer and Prophet

1. RETURN

On return from exile in Siberia Dostoevsky carved out a career as a novelist; later in life he was feted as a genius and a hero of Russia—and as a *Prorok* (*prophet*).[1] But he regarded such fame as transitory and illusory. He wrote about the human condition with a level of psychological understanding that has rarely been surpassed. He wrote about the dangerously alluring power of evil. He wrote, in addition, of the threat, as he saw it, of Roman Catholicism and socialism (he regarded the two as synonymous), but also the dangers of individualism—indeed of any philosophy, religion, or human culture, that did not give God God's rightful place, and did not recognize the salvific value of suffering. (He suffered from many physical ailments from his years in the prison camp in Siberia in addition to the epilepsy, treatment of which was neglected during his imprisonment). Dostoevsky was no systematic theologian;

---

1   This occurred at the unveiling of a statue to the Russian poet and hero Pushkin—festivities, June 6–8, 1880: Dostoevsky gave "The Pushkin Lecture" on the last day. Dostoevsky's speech was received with an outburst of public acclaim. The audience— as did the Russian public—regarded his words and works as prophetic. Writing to his wife, Anna Grigoryevna, he said, "When at the end I proclaimed the universal oneness of mankind, the hall seemed to go into hysterics, and when I finished I cannot tell you the roars and yells of enthusiasm. . . . For half an hour they kept calling out and waving their handkerchiefs. . . . 'A prophet, a prophet! [*Prorok*]' cried voices in the crowd. . . . 'You are a genius, more than a genius,' they told me . . . .": Letter to Anna Grigoryevna Dostoevsky, dated June 8, 1880 in Frank and Goldstein (eds.) *Selected Letters of Fyodor Dostoevsky*, translated by Andrew R. MacAndrew.

he did not write works of philosophy or theology exhibiting what many regard as genius as a creative writer. The nearest he approached to outlining elements of his theology is in *The Diary of a Writer*.[2] The diary, published over a number of years towards the end of his life, set out directly many of his beliefs (as compared to the indirect exposition through the characters in his novels). His greatest theological comment is in the mature existential novels: *Crime and Punishment* (1866), *The Idiot* (1868), *The Devils/The Possessed* (1871), and *The Brothers Karamazov* (1879–80). A central aim in his mature work is to bear witness to God, essentially seen through God's salvific actions towards humanity. In *The Brothers Karamazov* Ivan Karamazov warns that without God anything is possible, there are no constraints on human behavior. In his notebooks for *The Brothers Karamazov* and in *The Diary of a Writer* he states that it is only self-interest that then acts as a restraint on atheistic individuals, or in a social context, the protectionism of the most powerful and influential group: he knew the language of the socialist from his involvement with Belinsky and the Petrashevsky group—but turned it round on them much in the same way that George Orwell did with *Animal Farm* (1945) and *Nineteen Eighty-Four* (1949), though Orwell remained a socialist.

2. DOSTOEVSKY'S WORKS

Dostoevsky's career as a writer spans a thirty-six year period: 1845–81. If, in effect, we categorize the novellas and short stories from the pre-Siberian period as the writings of a different man, then his middle- and mature-period writing career is really only a little over twenty years— from his return from Siberia in 1859 to his death in 1881. Prior to his conviction for sedition and exile/imprisonment in Siberia he produced a small number of articles, short stories, and two novels, which we have noted were poorly received. If he had died in exile/imprisonment (which, given the mortality rate in the unsanitary wooden huts, with no glass in the shuttered windows, was very possible) then on the basis of these early works he would, in all probability, not be remembered today, or at best be categorized with a plethora of minor, obscure, nineteenth-century writers regarded as of no consequence. The writings we need

2   Dostoevsky, *The Diary of a Writer*, published in 1873, 76, 77–78, 80 and 81. The *Diary* was an open-ended vehicle and was used for the expression of the widest range of views. In the *Diary* he freely expressed all of his theological, philosophical, and political doubts and convictions

concern ourselves with are from the middle and mature period: after his Siberian exile/imprisonment. Initially, in 1861, he published a relatively short work, *The Insulted and the Injured* (*Unizhennye i oskorblyonnye*), sometimes translated as *Humiliated and Insulted*. A number of central themes in this work, which occurs in subsequent works, were moral degradation, childhood trauma, adult perversion, and human depravity, thereby establishing a central theme in Dostoevsky's work, that of the atoning value of suffering, through expiation, but also the incalculable risks of damnation dialectically set against salvation. This was followed by *Notes from the House of the Dead* (*Zapiski iz mertvogo doma,* 1862), based on his prison camp experiences; *Notes from Underground* (*Zapiski iz Podpol'ia,* 1864), which established his critique of humanist ethics; then come the extensive and much-acclaimed novels, which explore the relationship between humanity and God: *Crime and Punishment* (*Prestuplenie i nakazanie,* 1866), *The Idiot* (*Idiot,* 1868), and *The Demons—or Devils—* (*Besy,* 1871–72—often called, *The Possessed,* or *The Possessors*). *The Dream of a Ridiculous Man* (*Son smeshnogo cheloveka,* published 1878 in *The Diary of a Writer—Dnevnik pisatelia*) is relevant to our considerations as is the *magnum opus* of his entire career—*The Brothers Karamazov* (*Brat'ia Karamazovy,* 1878/9–80, published initially in serial form). Despite his criticisms of European intellectuals he went on European tours (often to escape creditors, as he struggled for years to master his gambling addiction). His first marriage to a widower, Maria Isayeva, did not work out well, and he took a mistress; his wife died in 1864 from tuberculosis. After a difficult period trying to raise his stepson, write, and manage his debts, he married his stenographer, the youthful Anna Grigoryevna Snitkina, in February 1867, who helped him master his gambling addiction, looked after the finances, and organized his work, besides raising his stepson and their children. Without her it is doubtful, given his ill health and the epilepsy, that he would have produced the works of his mature years. Dostoevsky's life and creativity did not come easily.

3. DEVELOPMENT

Once he returned from Siberia, Dostoevsky wrote at length and depth (his middle-period works), having abandoned his naïve socialistic beliefs and the cultured urban niceties of his indulgent youth. These new works by contrast are dark, despairing, and any sense of the goodness in humanity is so buried as to seem lost: but there is just enough of the *imago Dei* left to be rekindled. Only with maturity do we find a balance between light and dark, goodness and evil, hope and desperation. The pessimism of his understanding of the human condition in the middle years, following the return from Siberia, culminates in the more balanced approach to the human predicament in his mature years—as characterized by his *magnum opus, The Brothers Karamazov.*

4. THEOLOGICAL ANTHROPOLOGY

Dostoevsky's works have the reputation of being psychological—indeed of plumbing depths that many psychotherapists rarely encounter (or have the intellectual framework to cope with). The psychology of his novels can sometimes mask the theology: that is, if we regard theological beliefs as divorced from the nature of humanity—of God's creation. If we do not, then we need to establish Dostoevsky's precise understanding of the human condition, that is, his theological anthropology.

So what theological anthropology can we read from Dostoevsky's novels? He may not have been a theologian expounding an explicit doctrine, but he created characters that exude and conform to a particular anthropology. As distinct from a scientific or a humanist anthropology, theological anthropology is essentially the human condition as defined in relation to God, and relative to the crucified and resurrected Christ, the creator and redeemer. Theological anthropology is the relationship between humanity and God, where humanity must realize the full depravity of its sinfulness. It must be prepared, facing this crime (the *fall,* original sin, and the selfish human history that issues from it), to accept forgiveness given in judgment, forgiveness given as a free pardon by Christ, because without this forgiveness humanity is fallen, corrupt, and irretrievably lost. The *fall* radically alters the actual ontological nature of humanity. Humanity's understanding of its theological anthropology varies: sometimes naively confident and optimistic, other times darkly despairing and pessimistic. God did not create the fallen human condition. Humanity took the natural God-given creation and corrupted it: humanity is responsible for the condition it has willed upon itself. Humanity—not God—is responsible for the corrupted creation. Yet there is hope through the cross and resurrection; but can humanity turn?

Or, can individuals—one by one—sometimes in isolation, sometimes in community (the church) turn? The turn to repent is often the hardest part. A true and sound theological anthropology states the utter necessity of the cross and resurrection as the solution to the human problem, to the contagion of original sin: the answer and solution is in God. A doctrine of original sin has been an explicit building block of Western theology, but it is less influential and much more implicit in Russian Orthodoxy. That we are all sinners, and have no—or little—control over our decisions to sin is inherent if sometimes unspoken in Russian Orthodoxy. However, from the Orthodox perspective, Eve's (and Adam's) guilt is *not* imputed to all their progeny; the classic Western tradition asserts that all are justly punished for what the proto-human's did. The East does not claim this. Theological anthropology (the condition) is therefore measured by theological existentialism (the relationship), which is about the association and affiliation between human existence and God. It is only from without—God's understanding of us—that any *sense* of the human condition can be gleaned; any future for humanity is in the relationship of sin (inward) and grace (outward, from without). Individuals must come to face Christ, and in this pneumatologically-generated encounter, through the conscience, they must accept the depravity and delusions that their selfishness has brought about—in a word, sin—and in the judgment, often perceived as a terrifying judgment, they will be forgiven.

4

The Human Condition before God

1. DOSTOEVSKY'S UNDERSTANDING OF HUMANITY

The effectiveness of Dostoevsky's beliefs as projected into his novels revolves around his theological anthropology. Within this there is one central question: how much good remains in humanity? The answer to this question for Dostoevsky is defined by the condition of humanity. Theologians and philosophers have not agreed on this matter. Some, such as John Calvin, will claim that through original sin humanity is depraved, corrupt, evil. Calvin refers to an "hereditary depravity and corruption of our nature."[1] By contrast, C. S. Lewis argued that if we were indeed *totally* depraved we would, logically, not realize this or know it: there is, there must be, some fragment of God's goodness left in humanity.[2] That is, enough goodness to at least know or perceive the Good, even without being able to do it (Romans 7).

Dostoevsky considered Eve and Adam's sin as having affected all in the sense that people cannot stop repeating their sin, their arrogant mistake (he does not appear to tackle the question of transmission). Dostoevsky was neither working with nor against the Western theological tradition engendered by Augustine, but he was working *against* an understanding of human sinfulness as perpetrated in Western Europe in the eighteenth and nineteenth centuries from the Age of Reason and the Enlightenment, which saw humanity in a very different light. The

1   Calvin, *Institutes* II.i.8
2   Lewis, *Problem of Pain*, ch. 4, 50.

primacy of rationalism and idealism, the rise of the historical-critical method for analyzing biblical texts, also the development of a theory of evolution through natural selection, all had the effect of undermining the central Christian doctrine of the *fall* and original sin. Dostoevsky was not concerned about the questions of whether or not Adam and Eve had existed, whether or not these specific individuals had *fallen* from grace. What Dostoevsky concerned himself with was what he saw around him and what he understood of the human heart: an existential reading for him pointed to the effects of the *fall*, of the reality of the corrosive effects of sin. The question of the historical authenticity of Genesis 1–3 was to a large degree irrelevant to him. All around him and in his own heart he saw the effects of a corrupt will. Dostoevsky's theological anthropology pivots on the inner conflict presented in Romans 7: try as hard as we can, we mere humans are weighed down and fail to do the good we wish to;[3] our good intentions are always compromised by the weight of a corrupt will. This was not just mere selfishness, there was for Dostoevsky, as with Calvin, a strong element of evil for its own sake in the human condition. Dostoevsky saw evil as a noun. Evil was real, tangible, transcending our selves. It infiltrated and infected, so to speak, the human soul causing it to move further and further away from God. Evil courted and seduced the human so that individuals became ever more immune to the depravity of their own actions.

By contrast it can be generalized that Western intellectuals were seeing evil as a verb (or an adjective)—one of a panoply of actions, behavioral traits in the human psyche to be defined relatively (for example, Comte, Freud). Dostoevsky is one of a few outsiders in this period who did not see humanity as innately good, but as corrupted and flawed, albeit still capable—just—of some good, *if they turned*. Dostoevsky's position is in contrast to the majority of intellectuals in the nineteenth and twentieth centuries who claimed that human nature was innately benevolent and kind, as Rousseau would have us believe.[4] At the heart of Rousseau's belief

---

3   Rom 7:14–20

4   Jean Jacques Rousseau (1712–78): see, in particular, *Discours sur les sciences et les arts* (Paris, 1750), a prize essay in which he set forth the paradox of the superiority of the savage state of humanity and proclaimed his gospel of "back to nature"; also, *Du contrat social* (Amsterdam, 1762), which became the text-book of the French Revolution. See, Rousseau (ed. Victor Gourevich), *Rousseau The Discourses and Other Early Political Writings: Vol. 1.*

system is the idea that individuals are innately good and that it is *society* that is bad, or other people make them evil. Thus, if we create the right sort of humanist society, evil will go away (for example, the utopian-socialist communes of the Petrashevsky group inspired by Fourier's theories). The Age of Reason, seemingly supported by natural science in the nineteenth century, raised a third option (as compared to Rousseau or the traditional Christian view): that humanity was born neutral, that a single man or woman was born neither malevolent or benevolent (a proposition often exemplified by the work of John Locke). To Dostoevsky the nature of humanity before God was fundamental: the moral nature of humanity was of fundament importance to his work. Each human was a battleground between good and evil; such an individual could turn to Christ; or to evil: prior to the crucifixion and resurrection humanity was innately driven deeper into evil; after the crucifixion and resurrection humanity is rebalanced: it can be for the good, or it can be for the evil.

2. DOSTOEVSKY'S
THEOLOGICAL ANTHROPOLOGY

What was informing Dostoevsky in his beliefs about the human condition? He centered his beliefs on the New Testament. He believed that the Christian understanding of humanity was the only sound understanding, further, that the view of Russian radicals, centered as it was on Western influences, would destroy Russia (a prophetic view, given the history of the Soviet Union). His early, pre-Siberian works present characters that are considered shallow, meek, and fearful of any trouble in life; as a student and into his mid-twenties in St. Petersburg he was, in his own words, "a European liberal."[5] Whilst in prison and then exile in Siberia his understanding of humanity underwent a radical transformation (see figure 1, Dostoevsky's theological anthropology, overleaf). In prison he was living day and night not just with criminals, but with men who were deranged and who positively reveled in the excesses of their crimes— torturing and abusing children, chopping up women; he came across the nihilism of a people that had abandoned all restraint, while he was learning holy restraint. Most of these prisoners showed little respect for Dostoevsky and his comrades from the Petrashevsky circle, regarding them, as Dostoevsky recounts, as naïve little boys who were caught playing

5   Dostoevsky, *Diary of a Writer* (1880), II, 984.

with fire.[6] But he also saw a spark of hope and goodness flicker sometimes even in the most deranged and lost of souls—the times when one of these men would do a small act of goodness at no gain to himself, even for his loss. However, what is important for the development of his theological anthropology is that he came to the conclusion that those who were in prison were no worse than those in polite society in St. Petersburg, and the latter were no better than those who were convicted and incarcerated. While the European "enlighteners" were flattering humanity about its innate goodness, he saw much of its worst. While the remains of the Belinsky circle were plotting to Westernize Russia, Dostoevsky was languishing in the hell of Siberian winters in a prison that consisted of large wooden barracks, followed by exile from all that he had known and loved. During this time he realized that all his thinking in his youth had been wrong:

> He began to recognize how unutterably false, indeed how dangerous, were the premises and promises of Belinsky and the Fourierist members of the Petrashevsky circle who had influenced his youthful years. If he were to come to the truth about life, then he would have to accommodate his thinking to a vastly more realistic estimate of human nature than he had done heretofore. It was still to be some time, however, before he addressed himself seriously to the question, which later most occupied him, namely, if man is by nature so inclined to evil, then how can civilization be preserved?
> ... [C]learly, Dostoevsky will not henceforth be hoodwinked by the sentimental vaporings of intellectuals carrying on about the natural goodness of man.[7]

It is this question of what is going to save humanity from itself that he tackles to the greatest depth in his last work, *The Brothers Karamazov* (see figure 1), centered as it is on the assertion of Ivan Karamazov that without God there are no constraints on human behavior,[8] and voiced as a question by Dmitri Karamazov whilst he is in prison awaiting trial:

---

6   See, Dostoevsky, *Diary of a Writer*; also Anna Grigoryevna Dostoevsky *Reminiscences* (1925, ET: 1975).

7   Trace, *Dostoevsky and the Brothers Karamazov*, 16.

8   Dostoevsky, *The Brothers Karamazov*, Bk. V Pro and Contra, ch. 7. It's Always Worthwhile Speaking to a Clever Man.

Fyodor Mikhailovich Dostoevsky (1821–1881): Key Works and their Relationship to the Development of his Theological Anthropology

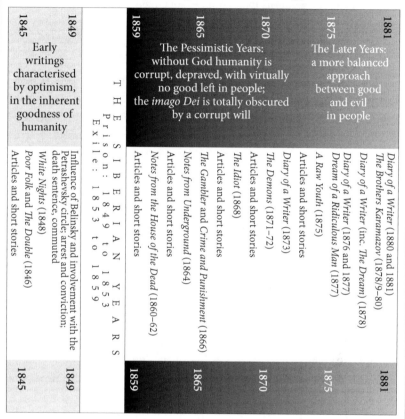

Figure 1. Dostoevsky's Theological Anthropology

The major works are shown chronologically in relation to the period of Siberian exile and the changing nature of Dostoevsky's theological anthropology, from the naivety of his early novellas and short stories, through the pessimism of his understanding of the human condition in the middle years, culminating in the more balanced approach to the human predicament in his mature years—as characterised by *The Brothers Karamazov*.

> What if *He* [God] doesn't exist? What if Rakitin's right—that it's an
> idea made up by men? Then if *He* doesn't exist, man is the chief
> of the earth, of the universe. Magnificent! Only how is man going
> to be good without God? That's the question. I always come back
> to that. For whom is man going to love then? To whom will he
> be thankful? To whom will he sing the hymn? Rakitin laughs.
> Rakitin says that one can love humanity without God. Well, only a
> sniveling idiot can maintain that. I can't understand it.[9]

During his Siberian years and gradually as his work progressed in
the 1860s he came to see the Christian gospel as the only way forward
for humanity. However, as the words he projects into Dmitri illustrate, he
could see no other answer to these questions other than God's revelation.
For Dostoevsky, "Sacred Scripture" becomes, for him, a primary—indeed
the only—source of truth.

So what was Dostoevsky's understanding of humanity? His early,
pre-Siberian works, for example *Poor Folk* and *The Double,* present—as
we have seen—characters that are superficial, and to a degree neither
good nor bad. His first publications at the age of twenty-four years were
confident and professional, but reflected the calm optimistic world of
the St. Petersburg bourgeoisie. In the short stories there is sometimes a
naïve, even over-romantic, understanding of humanity, though it is fair to
say that these stories do reflect the immaturity of youth. In *White Nights*
and *Netotchka Nezvanova* (both serialized in 1848 and 1849 respectively)
we find humanity characterized by little good deeds, but like his
Enlightenment forbears Dostoevsky did not ask himself at this time where
goodness came from, neither, it appears from these early short stories, did
he recognize that there was evil in human hearts. His belief system was
nurtured by the influence of French and German philosophers, poets,
novelists, all in the Enlightenment mold. The experience of Siberia was an
education for him. Up to this point in his life he had been raised in relative
comfort and security; student days had been in St. Petersburg, the most
Westernized of Russian cities, he had an army career (engineer, initially
as a Lieutenant) ahead of him and he had seen little to give him any doubt
about an innate goodness in humanity. Post Siberia Dostoevsky picked
up the threads of his fledging career as a writer, but now his anthropology
was characterized by a recognition of the evil that infected the nature
of humanity. Within a few years of returning to Russia in 1859 he had

9   Dostoevsky, *The Brothers Karamazov*, Bk. XI Ivan, ch. 4. A Hymn and a Secret.

published a few short stories and articles, and produced *Notes from the House of the Dead*, based on his experience of a Siberian prison camp, and *Notes From Underground*. Scholars of Dostoevsky often refer to this period as his dark period. This period culminated in the writing and publication of *Crime and Punishment* (1866) and *The Idiot* (1868). Dostoevsky is at his most pessimistic during this period.

Dostoevsky's theological anthropology is therefore defined by uncontrolled freedom. The human cannot help itself, even when it develops what it regards as repulsive amoral behavior. The human has taken this freedom onto itself, it has defined itself by this freedom. But this is not the freedom of God, which is balanced by a right judgment on behavior and beliefs. A person finds it can do something, an act or action, that initially it might have regarded as repugnant, even abominable; then it finds it enjoys this act, then it realizes it can no longer stop doing it. Such a person then develops justification for this act, even religious theories to justify such fallen willfulness: such an action is often abuse, whether physically and mentally violent, or sexual. Often, the person's involvement in these actions cannot be reconciled with the beliefs—religious or otherwise—that it has held, and with the perception of an external morality, so that the tension may lead to suicide. All sins can be forgiven; but suicide is perhaps the worst manifestation of the sin against the Holy Spirit of which Jesus warns us. Suicide rejects God's forgiving judgment; the person simply passes judgment on him- or herself with all the consequences of that action. Therefore, Dostoevsky's theological anthropology is about the dark side of humanity, the dark side of desire, the corruption of love: that is self-love, generated by pseudo-divinized protectionism. The worst thing humanity can do in this situation is to invent religious justification for its depravity.

In *Crime and Punishment* Dostoevsky does not totally lose sight of the goodness in human nature, the flawed remnant of the *imago Dei*, but his people are characterized by weakness—the drunkenness of Marmeladov (Sonya's father), or Pulkheria Alexandrovna's (Raskolnikov's mother) desire for the easy life. This weakness leads men and women (and children) to desire and enact more and more what is wrong, then evil, simply so as to protect themselves—or champion themselves as little "gods." It is this latter desire that is at the heart of Raskolnikov's desire to murder Alena Ivanovna, the elderly pawnbroker whom he describes as a louse to be crushed under foot. It is this triumph of the insidiousness of evil in Raskolnikov that leads him to believe that he is a superman in the mold of Napoleon, that such men can trample over others and redefine human law because they are "extraordinary," they are above the ordinariness of most of humanity. Therefore, he murders Alena Ivanovna, stealing a few trinkets, convincing himself that he is a truly extraordinary human to have rid the world of this "louse" of a pawnbroker. But he does not control life in the way he believes. He is forced to kill Alena's sister, Lizavéta, who returns early only to discover Raskolnikov with the body of her murdered sister. He kills her in the same manner as Alena—but this time not as a Napoleonic superman, but so as to cover up the first murder. It is possible to see this as a worse crime than the murder of Alena (who is portrayed as a hard hearted and evil extortionist and money lender), because Lizavéta is seen as relatively innocent, as foolishly holy (an example of an *iurodivaia—a holy fool*), as one who submits to her sister's domination and abuse, then quietly goes out in the evening to do Bible study with Sonya the prostitute! Raskolnikov then nearly loses his mind over the next few weeks as his conscience troubles him. But the *imago Dei* is not totally lost in Raskolnikov—in an act of pure charity he gives all his money to Sonya's mother, Katerína Ivanovna, to feed her children when he witnesses the death of the drunken, unemployed Marmeladov, her husband. Raskolnikov gains nothing from this act—indeed at this point he is unknown, even by name, to Sonya (whose prostitution has fed the family). For Dostoevsky it is an act of pure charity. In relation to his atheistic superman beliefs it is illogical—a dialectical paradox. He is only saved by the relationship he then forms with Sonya—who reads to him the resurrection of Lazarus.

In *The Idiot* (1868) Dostoevsky continues this portrait of *fallen* humanity—it is a searing psychological portrait. With the exception of Prince Myshkin, who is not of this world, as he is portrayed as a Christ-like figure, the book is a study of people's self-destructive tendencies. The only difference between the violent debauchery of Rogozhin and the pious sanctimony of Madame Yepanchina is the veneer of culture and civilization: Rogozhin knows his faults; Madame Yepanchina does not. Religion can give people false illusions. Religion, therefore, can work against the gospel. By the time we come to his last work, *The Brothers Karamazov,* Dostoevsky presents a more balanced understanding of the human condition. A balance between good and evil is expressed in a constant battle within the soul of each person pulling that person either one way or the other so that what is left at the culmination of a person's life is truly fitted for either heaven or hell (it is important to remember that there is no concept of purgatory in either Russian Orthodox theology or Dostoevsky's thinking). But this is not the balance between good and evil that issues from the enlightened revolutionary liberals (whereby the human is born neither good nor evil, but in effect a moral blank canvas); no, this is where the human is born mired in sin but Christ's death and resurrection resets the human to it prelapsarian state so that it can choose to be for God or for personified evil. That choice is enacted countless times during a human life, ever moving the individual either towards God and eternity or into its own self-generated and self-willed hell. Arthur Trace sums up this development quite succinctly:

> In short, in his early works [pre-Siberia] he tended to believe that man is better than he is; in his post-Siberian works he tended to believe that man is worse than he is, until in *The Brothers Karamazov* he finally came to an understanding of how good and how bad they really are, that is, that there is good in man, but not nearly enough to enable him to get along without God.[10]

This battle between good and evil impulses within the human will is dialectical. But first we need to examine Dostoevsky's understanding of the human condition in more depth.

What Dostoevsky disagrees with in the "enlighteners" is their naïve faith in human nature, not necessarily their emphasis on human reason. Humanity is not only rational, it is also perverse, disjointed, and contradictory in its desires and aims. The human is therefore chaotically destructive. Free will has become corrupted. Altruistic impulses vie with sado-masochistic desires, despair competes with hope, malice with concern. Nothing that humanity can offer can prevent a character like Nastasya Filippovna *(The Idiot)* from reliving and reveling in the years of abuse she underwent as a girl and adolescent, despite her desire to forget the past. By contrast Myshkin appears incorruptible in an almost prelapsarian sense—but he is human and the strain of trying to save these people from themselves, from their own self-destruction, destroys him. Within five years of returning from Siberia, as evidenced from *Notes from Underground* (1864), Dostoevsky has arrived at the dialectic that humans have a divine soul that separates then from the beasts, yet all their natural

10   Trace, *Dostoevsky and the Brothers Karamazov*, 11.

instincts drive them to be beasts. It is clear from this work that he had concluded that if there is no God then we are no more than beasts—i.e., not moral agents. If we are no more than beasts then we delude ourselves with moral sufferings, stemming as they do from the illogical sacrifices of attempting to live righteously. Virtue becomes senseless, unless there is a God; a God who places value on moral suffering. The idea of a virtuous beast is, to Dostoevsky, a nonsense. Dostoevsky construes from all this that faith and Christ are the only answer—*we are* more than mere beasts and the existential observations he made in prison in Siberia proved it to him. This is the conclusion he came to in *Notes from the Underground,* a conclusion he uses as the center of *The Brothers Karamazov,* in particular the relationship between the four brothers. This raises the question of the sacredness of life—murder is often the central theme of his stories, or its conclusion. If we are mere beasts then murder is no problem—the natural science feted by the "enlighteners" illustrates the onward march of species with no concern for others, the genetic drive to procreate. Survival of the fittest knows no moral constraints—kill or be killed. But Dostoevsky emphasizes the sacredness of life, not primarily because we are all fellow creatures, though this is important for him, but because we are all God's creatures. Murder is a violation of God's law as well as an offence against humanity. Where does he get this conclusion? Is this from reason? No— from revelation; God's revealedness. In *Crime and Punishment* he shows that if a person's value is imputed to him/her by other people then it is equally valid for another to take away that value—which is exactly what Raskolnikov does. He invents his theory that there are extraordinary people, like Napoleon and himself, who have the right—who have invented the self-generated right—to raise themselves above the common herd and shatter conventional law to impose their own rules.[11] But when he tries to live by this heretical observation he fails. Why is his conscience so troubled? Why does he desire to revisit the scene of his crime? Why does he provoke the police with taunts about his possible guilt? Why does he not feel the elation he expected, the elation of a Napoleon? Why in the end does he give in to Sonya's pressure to confess his crime publicly? The answer to these questions is that he has transgressed divine law—not just human mores. What Sonya teaches him is that truth is not in his mind, but in the Bible she and Lizaveta study together. Thus, the novel

11   Dostoevsky, *Crime and Punishment,* Bk 3, ch. 5

ends with resurrection: he is imprisoned and exiled in Siberia where the change effected by Sonya slowly takes growth in him.

> Thus the theorizer of socialism, the believer in the natural goodness of man, the one who had believed that there is no God, or only an indifferent God, comes to recognize that his ideas have been wrong all along, and that he has himself been the instrument of spreading them. In the end he comes to the light of Truth in the only place in which the light of Truth is to be found, the Bible, and most clearly visible in the New Testament. And so Dostoevsky is telling us, once again, that the perfection of truth lies not in man's reason but in God's revelation and that without that, there is not enough love, of the merely theoretical, unguided, random, inconstant, human sort for humanity itself to long endure.[12]

Resurrection is at the heart of Dostoevsky's work. Yes, bodily, physical resurrection (the so-called general resurrection), to follow on from the resurrection of Jesus Christ, but Dostoevsky also saw resurrection, as here in the case of Raskolnikov, as the radical transformation and reordering of the person. In Raskolnikov's case, his beliefs, attitudes, morals, everything about his life, have to change. The source of this, like the story of the resurrection of Lazarus, comes from John's Gospel: the encounter between Jesus and Nicodemus.[13] Resurrection for Dostoevsky is also about being reborn in this world. Such a rebirth is linked to and the result of the resurrection of Jesus Christ. This is not a humanist change of mind, a cultural reorientation; for Dostoevsky it is initiated by and rooted in God. This focus on resurrection very likely stems from his near-death experience at the hands of the firing squad, the mock execution. This radical reordering in Raskolnikov's conversion is due not primarily to the religious beliefs of Sonya (though it is fair to say that he gradually develops a respect for her beliefs), but in submitting to her way of thinking, the abandonment of his theories about extraordinary Napoleon-like figures who claim the right to transgress the law; in addition, his submission to the will of the investigating authorities and acceptance of trial, conviction, and imprisonment/exile in Siberia. Sonya follows him and takes work as a seamstress in the nearby town. She abandons her life as a prostitute, which was only done to provide money with which to feed her step-brothers and step-sisters (her father being an unemployable drunk, her step-mother

12   Trace, *Dostoevsky and the Brothers Karamazov*, 39.
13   John 3.

consumptive); once they are provided for financially (by money willed to them by the suicide of Svidrigailov!) Sonya watches and waits as the resurrecting transformation takes place in Raskolnikov.

> He did not know that the new life would not be given him for nothing, that he would have to pay dearly for it, that it would cost him great striving, great suffering. But that is the beginning of a new story—the story of the gradual renewal of a man, the story of his gradual regeneration, of his passing from one world into another, of his initiation into a new unknown life. That might be the subject of a new story, but our present story is ended.[14]

3. FORGIVENESS AND MERCY IN THE DOCTRINE OF GOD IN DOSTOEVSKY'S THEOLOGY

Dostoevsky's theological anthropology raises a question. If our understanding of humanity is to be so pessimistic, if the account of the *fall* in Genesis 3 gives an accurate diagnosis of humanity and the human condition, if Paul is correct in Romans 7 that even when we try to do the good we fail, then *what hope* is there for humanity? The answer lies in the grace relationship between God and humanity: when humans (individuals in a communal context) come to see their depraved nature and total need for forgiveness and mercy then they can accept in humility God's love and mercy and forgiveness *and live thereafter for God in repentance*. This may involve the conscious religious knowledge of Christ's crucifixion and resurrection, or not—according to temporal and geographic understanding of Christian salvation history. If they do not know about Christ's sacrifice, its effects will still work on them, if they allow God to act on them pneumatologically. This is the grace/mercy of a criminal class characterized by a free pardon, benevolently given—it is legalistic, forensic, and above all, biblical (again, reminiscent of Paul's Epistle to the Romans). This is why so many of Dostoevsky's characters are criminals—and only when such a person is prepared to acknowledge his or her depravity and guilt publicly can s/he begin to live the forgiven life. There is no grace and mercy from God without judgment.

---

14   Dostoevsky, *Crime and Punishment*, Epilogue, ch. 2.

4. The Human Condition before God

i. Judgment and Forgiveness

This judgment prefigures, in many ways, the eschaton. The eschaton for Dostoevsky was about death, judgment, heaven, and hell. Judgment and hell were very real for Dostoevsky (judgment and hell have been elided in many instances from the eschaton in Western liberal theologies). But he also preached, through his novels, about the overwhelmingly unlimited scope and power of God's love and mercy and forgiveness, like free grace bestowed on a criminal. This is particularly well presented in *The Idiot*: Myshkin is driven by altruistic love for Nastasya; he wants to save her from herself and will do anything for her, even pledge marriage (and this is not a proposal based upon *eros*). This, for Dostoevsky, is the measure of God's infinite love for humanity; like Myshkin and Nastasya, at the heart of Dostoevsky's soteriology is the picture of God simply waiting for us to turn and accept him, in our humility and repentance. (But if we fail to turn, then we may perceive God as wrathful, as rightly judgmental and condemnatory.) Let us look at two examples: Marmeladov's adaptation of the Parable of the Sheep and Goats from *Crime and Punishment*; and the story of Grushenka's Onion from *The Brothers Karamazov*.

ii. The Last Judgment

Marmeladov is the drunken unemployed former civil servant who fathered Sonya in his first marriage and now lives with his second wife, the consumptive Katerína Ivanovna. They live in desolate and squalid rooms shared with other paupers in a ram-shackled tenement in the poorest district of St. Petersburg. He has three little children by his second marriage (Pólya, Lída, Kólka) but spends on drink any money he can lay his hands; Sonya works as a licensed prostitute to earn money to feed the children and pay the family's rent—given her background and abode no other work is available for her. Near the beginning of the novel Raskolnikov encounters Marmeladov in a pub. The latter is drunk and they enter into conversation. Amidst his shame and self-pity Marmeladov voices Dostoevsky's understanding of forgiveness and mercy to the landlord:

> "Why am I to be pitied . . . I ought to be crucified, crucified on a cross, not pitied! Crucify me, oh judge, crucify me but pity me!
> He will pity us Who has had pity on all men, Who has understood all men and all things, He is the One. He too is the

71

judge. He will come in that day and He will ask: 'Where is the daughter who gave herself for her angry, consumptive stepmother and for the little children of another? Where is the daughter who had pity upon the filthy drunkard, her earthly father, undismayed by his beastliness?' And He will say, 'Come to me! I have already forgiven thee once . . . I have forgiven thee once. . . . *Thy sins which are many are forgiven thee for thou hast loved much* . . . .' And he will forgive my Sonia, He will forgive, I know it . . . I felt it in my heart when I was with her just now! And He will judge and will forgive all, the good and the evil, the wise and the meek. . . . And when He has done with all of them, then He will summon us. 'You too come forth,' He will say, 'Come forth ye drunkards, come forth, ye weak ones, come forth, ye children of shame!' And we shall all come forth, without shame and shall stand before him. And He will say unto us, 'Ye are swine, made in the Image of the Beast and with his mark; but come ye also!' And the wise ones and those of understanding will say, 'Oh Lord, why dost Thou receive these men?' And He will say, 'This is why I receive them, oh ye wise, this is why I receive them, oh ye of understanding, *that not one of them believed himself to be worthy of this.*' And He will hold out His hands to us and we shall fall down before him . . . and we shall weep . . . and we shall understand all things! Then we shall understand all! . . . and all will understand, Katerína Ivanovna even . . . she will understand . . . Lord, Thy kingdom come!" And he sank down on the bench exhausted, and helpless . . . ." [15]

[my emphases]

This is explicitly based on the Parable of the Sheep and the Goats (Matt 25:31-46). In addition, as Boyce Gibson notes, "Marmeladov's outburst [is] gorgeously decorated with fragments of Church Slavonic. . . . The only version of Christianity which appeals to him [Dostoevsky] at all is that which includes the wastrels and scoundrel . . . ."[16] Dostoevsky is very tolerant of thieves and ruffians, libertines and villains—people who commit wrongful actions but may not necessarily suffer from bad ideas in the philosophical sense: "as long as one is content to use fists and axes, there is always the possibility of continued life in Dostoevsky's world."[17] This parable of the Last Judgment is spoken by a character

15   Dostoevsky, *Crime and Punishment*, Bk. 1, ch. 2 (Constance Garnett translation).

16   Gibson, *The Religion of Dostoevsky*, 93–94

17   Kjetsaa, *Dostoevsky and his New Testament*, 11

(Marmeladov), but it is also Dostoevsky's innermost conviction—it is indirect theology. However, is this universalism? No. For Dostoevsky, not everyone appears to be saved (which is also broadly in keeping with Russian Orthodox soteriology). This is reminiscent of the declaration in the York Mystery Plays from the scene dealing with the Parable of the Sheep and the Goats: "All this I suffered for thy sake; say, man, what suffered thou for me?"[18] On the surface, those used to a puritanical/Protestant ethic in the West will expect the drunkards and prostitutes to be condemned by God. However, if this is so, such condemnation is not in keeping with the Gospels. Dostoevsky is saying that they are forgiven, that the all-powerful merciful God who watched and knew all forgives them. Why? Because "not one of them believed himself to be worthy." Worthy of what?—worthy of forgiveness by God. Not unworthy before respectable society, not unworthy within a humanist ethic, but unworthy to face God—the otherworldly God of Dostoevsky's dialectical doctrine of God. Why are they loved even when they are unworthy before God?—because "thou hast loved much." Sonya sins are great—as a prostitute. But her love and suffering for her family are also great. This does not make her prostitution right before God, but when Christ has died for all so all may be forgiven their sins there is still the question, for Dostoevsky, of God's justice: justice is measured by the amount someone has loved, and that love is measured by Christ.

iii. Grushenka's Onion

The scope and power of the forgiveness of God is presented further in the story of Grushenka's onion in *The Brothers Karamazov*:

> "You see, Alyosha," Grushenka turned to him with a nervous laugh. "I was boasting when I told Rakitin I had given away an onion, but it's not to boast I tell you about it. It's only a story, but it's a nice story. I used to hear it when I was a child from Matryona, my cook, who is still with me. It's like this. Once upon a time there was a peasant woman and a very wicked woman she was. And she died and did not leave a single good deed behind. The devils caught her and plunged her into the lake of fire. So her guardian angel

18   York Cycle, Play 47: "The Mercers, The Last Judgment, Christ speaking in Judgment," lines 275–76, circa fourteenth century: Happé (ed.), *English Mystery Plays*, 642. Online text, University of Michigan:
       http://quod.lib.umich.edu/c/cme/York/1:50?rgn=div1;view=fulltext.

stood and wondered what good deed of hers he could remember to tell to God; 'She once pulled up an onion in her garden,' said he, 'and gave it to a beggar woman.' And God answered: 'You take that onion then, hold it out to her in the lake, and let her take hold and be pulled out. And if you can pull her out of the lake, let her come to Paradise, but if the onion breaks, then the woman must stay where she is.' The angel ran to the woman and held out the onion to her. 'Come,' said he, 'catch hold and I'll pull you out.' He began cautiously pulling her out. He had just pulled her right out, when the other sinners in the lake, seeing how she was being drawn out, began catching hold of her so as to be pulled out with her. But she was a very wicked woman and she began kicking them. 'I'm to be pulled out, not you. It's my onion, not yours.' As soon as she said that, the onion broke. And the woman fell into the lake and she is burning there to this day. So the angel wept and went away. So that's the story, Alyosha; I know it by heart, for I am that wicked woman myself. I boasted to Rakitin that I had given away an onion, but to you I'll say: 'I've done nothing but give away one onion all my life, that's the only good deed I've done.'"[19]

There is some profound psychology and theology here: God/Christ appears to be prepared to allow the old woman into paradise, at the intercession of the angel, but the measure is the one good deed she did in her bleak, mean-spirited life. (This apparent concession Christ offers to the angel could be because Christ, foreknowing the result, is teaching the angel a lesson.[20]) Yet even this one deed—the giving away of an onion— appears to be sufficient as the angel begins to pull her out. But the onion is not enough to contradict the mean-spirited evil in her character. This was, as it is chillingly portrayed, all there was to this woman at the point of death. And her mean-spiritedness causes the onion to break. She is lost to heaven. What is important here is not the bad she has done during her life—this has been erased by the atoning sacrifice of Christ on the cross. Indeed, she may have done the other villagers little harm. But she has

19 Dostoevsky, *The Brothers Karamazov*, Pt. III, Bk. VII Alyosha, ch. 3 An Onion (Constance Garnett translation). This is actually an old Russian folk tale included by Dostoevsky. A variation on this story in the folk tradition is that the onion given away to the beggar woman by the wicked old lady was rotten—too rotten to eat—hence when the guardian angel used it to try to pull the woman out of the lake of fire the old woman's hands slip on the putrid onion, and the onion breaks, and so she falls back into the lake of fire. The actual nature of her supposed good deed condemns her.

20 Comment by Brendan Wolfe, former president University of Oxford C. S. Lewis Society.

done no good to them—save the free gift of an onion. This gift apart there would have been little discernible impact on the world she inhabited had she never existed, never lived, never been born. This is what condemns her: judgment is subtractive—take away the sins, the bad, the evil, and what is left? In her case virtually nothing. However, she is offered a free pardon by God. She accepts but then throws it away by her actions. She had not the *grace* to behave generously to the other hell-bound sinners. Why? because she had refused, preveniently, this grace during her life (this is reminiscent of the sin against the Holy Spirit[21]). This woman's life was characterized by negative decisions. By exercising mean-spiritedness all her life her chief fault was the sin of omission—she failed to love her neighbor. The fact that God is prepared to extend to her a free pardon at the behest of the angel is not universalism. It is not her faults, her sins that have condemned her. It is the omission to love that has condemned her. For Dostoevsky it is often sins of omission that are more serious than bad actions. This elderly woman displays the chief characteristic that Dostoevsky believed condemned people: bad ideas. Dmitri (*The Brothers Karamazov*) never loses his faith—but it gets submerged beneath the welter and confusion of drunken debauchery. His immorality is wrong—and he damages other people through his actions—but he does not suffer from bad ideas as his brothers Ivan and Smerdyakov do. Marmeladov is the same—he knows he is unworthy, but relies totally on God's forgiveness and mercy. This emphasis on the insidiously evil nature of bad ideas (produced by a corrupt will) is reminiscent of Kierkegaard's anti-intellectualism. Critical of Hegel and the claims of German Idealism, Kierkegaard argued for a connection between thought and life—an active engagement with truth within the confines of concrete, finite existence.[22] This is what many of Dostoevsky's characters that are saved do, they may get pulled down by life, but they do not indulge in the abstract intellectualism that had been characteristic of German Idealism. Dostoevsky saw this at the heart of the "Westerners" and the "enlighteners" deriving the foundation of their beliefs from their own rational faculties. Their rubric was, "Think hard enough about life and the universe and you will solve the problem, find all the answers."[23]

21   Mark 3:29
22   Kierkegaard, *Philosophical Fragments, Johannes Climacus.*
23   Comment by Dr Steve Holmes, St. Mary's College, University of St. Andrews; formerly of King's College London.

::

PART THREE

::

**DIALECTIC AND A CRITIQUE OF RELIGION
IN THE SERVICE OF THE GOSPEL**

::

"For those who want to save their life
will lose it,

and those who lose their life for my sake,
and for the sake of the gospel,
will save it."

MARK 8:35

::

5

Dialectic and a Critique of Religion

1. DIALECTIC, PARADOX, AND ANTINOMY

Dialectics may be considered to be the art of investigating or discussing the truth of propositions, or opinions. It may be an enquiry into metaphysical contradictions and their solutions, which implies the reality of opposing concepts. Or "dialectic" may be an adjective relating to paradoxical ambiguity, what may be termed apparent illogical contradictions. From the Middle English, originally derived from Old French *dialectique* and the Latin *dialectica*, theological dialectic is ultimately from the Greek *dialektikē* (*tekhnē*), the art of debate, from *dialegōmai* (the verb for debate). Theological dialectics postulate apparent or seemingly contradictory propositions—often in pairs—each of which must stand. However, one form of dialectic is to draw a distinction between complementary and supplementary dialectics. If two opposing or contradictory concepts or propositions stand equally opposing each other, with no recourse to resolution, then the dialectic is complementary, indeed often one concept can't exist or be justified without the other; they stand existing in complementarity. Supplementary dialectics are when one concept, proposition, or actuality will be subsumed into the other. For example, creation, the world, will cease, and will be subsumed into eternity—but not annihilated. Creation will be re-created, which is the promise of resurrection. Whatever dialectical contradictions we may identify in Dostoevsky's work, they stand as supplementary dialectics. One will be subsumed into the other in eternity, this is reconciliation, and is defined by resurrection. The antinomy (sixteenth century, from the Latin *antinomia*, from the Greek, *anti*, against, with *nomos*, law), the apparent paradox, must be lived with. Therefore we now need to look at Dostoevsky's use of dialectic in his work. This goes much deeper than merely a literary style— something is reflected that is fundamental to his beliefs about humanity's relationship to God. Initially we will look at a general understanding of dialectic in Dostoevsky's work; then we will examine specific examples in greater depth.

2. DIALECTIC IN THE WORK
OF DOSTOEVSKY

Dostoevsky's theology is characterized by four propositions: a dialectic between revelation and reason (often seen as Scripture as compared to the Western Enlightenment); paradox (often in the sense that some atheists *might* have a clearer understanding of the gospel than religious people, though neither atheism nor religion guarantees salvation); a devastatingly pessimistic theological anthropology issuing from the *fall*, Gen 3 and Rom 7 (the legion of delusions the human hides in, the result of going-it-alone, defining right and wrong in its own image); and a severe criticism of ecclesiastical abuse and power (The Legend of the Grand Inquisitor in *The Brothers Karamazov*).

Dostoevsky knew that the agony of unbelief might be the first step towards belief—troubled atheists could cross to faith if they only asked the right questions, which involved a criticism of human religion. He therefore identified many types of atheist. Dostoevsky is rightly considered a prophet—he warned of the dangers of modernism; likewise he is often perceived as crying out from the darkness of the human condition that the only option, the only path for humanity, is to turn back to God.

Dostoevsky's novels are heavily dialectical, indeed they *may* be considered dualistic, to a degree, on account of the extremes of life that are presented. There is likewise great emphasis on light and dark—or better put, light *or* dark, saved *or* damned, good *or* evil, faith *or* unfaith, belief *or* unbelief. However, nowhere does he set out or analyze this dialectic. (For that matter, the subject has not been set out systematically by any Dostoevsky scholars, though occasionally there is a reference to a particular dialectic or antinomy in a particular novel.[1]) For Dostoevsky, his work was an illustration of the dialectical truth of the gospel. Dostoevsky

---

1   Trace, *Dostoevsky and the Brothers Karamazov*, ch. 3; also and Kirillova, "Dostoevsky's Markings in the Gospel according to St. John," 41–50.

proclaimed the gospel indirectly by creating characters (sometimes alter egos into whom he poured his doubts, frustrations, and beliefs) framed by a story that promoted the truth of the human condition before God. Because he wrote and published in the form of the novel, Dostoevsky is essentially speaking indirectly. Often this is through the third person. The exception is *The Diary of a Writer* published during the 1870s till his death;[2] in *The Diary* he spoke clearly and confidently of his own views). However, this technique of projecting beliefs through the form of a novel was in part a way of circumventing the Czar's official censor—it is easier to argue that the views expressed are those of a character and are necessary for the story and are not those of the author (he argued this successfully over *Crime and Punishment*). When setting out his theological beliefs explicitly in a novel he often uses the technique of parable: The story of Marie in *The Idiot* (1868), or *The Dream of the Ridiculous Man* (1878), or The Legend of the Grand Inquisitor in *The Brothers Karamazov* (1878–80) are key examples. This indirect technique is very well suited to conveying dialectical paradox and apparent contradiction. Why? Because antinomies and dialectical paradoxes prevent us from seeing matters to do with faith as clearly as we would desire: many will accept the idea of a paradox in a parable more easily than in real life, or in matters of faith about God's involvement in the world (such as, the incarnation and the resurrection). Presenting theological truths indirectly (that is, through novels or parables) prepares us to see the fundamental existential truths of the gospel analogically and therefore ontologically. In the case of the Grand Inquisitor Dostoevsky is projecting the beliefs of a frustrated logical atheist onto Ivan Karamazov. He knew and owned these arguments during the pre-Siberian period in his life; beliefs that he subsequently repudiated following his return from Siberia.[3]

There are many types and uses of dialectic in Dostoevsky's works, though as has been stated already they all flow from one central dialectic: the antinomy between an omnipotent and merciful God and the cruel, bleak reality of relatively (relative that is to the *fall*) innocent suffering. This can also be seen as the *diastasis* (separation) between divine mercy and suffering. Dostoevsky's dialectics are rooted in theodicy: *Si Deus justus—unde malum?*: If God is righteous, good, and omnipotent, then

---

2   Dostoevsky, *Diary of a Writer*, 1873, 1876, 1877, 1878, 1880, and 1881.

3   This indirect technique of Dostoevsky is similar in many ways to the way Kierkegaard wrote in pseudonyms.

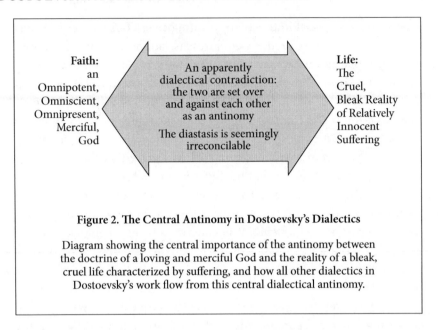

Figure 2. The Central Antinomy in Dostoevsky's Dialectics

Diagram showing the central importance of the antinomy between
the doctrine of a loving and merciful God and the reality of a bleak,
cruel life characterized by suffering, and how all other dialectics in
Dostoevsky's work flow from this central dialectical antinomy.

why is there evil and the suffering that flows from it? This is the concern
of Ivan Karamazov in his long conversation culminating in the Legend
of the Grand Inquisitor. At this juncture in the story Ivan is not a logical
atheist, he does not examine everything in life in terms of a denial of
the existence of God and a denial of any meaning in life. His beliefs
are summed up by the title of the central chapter in this debate with
Alyosha—"Rebellion."[4] It is his perception of suffering in the world that
causes him not to deny the existence of God, but to refuse to *acknowledge*
God or God's creation. In consequence, it is this dialectic which is at
the heart of Dostoevsky's theology as expounded in his mature novels,
the irreconcilable dichotomy between the concept of a good and loving,
all-powerful and merciful, God and the cruel randomness of suffering
in this reality. It is in this context that we can understand how many of
Dostoevsky's characters, even though they are seemingly irreligious, can
perform an act of faith that points towards a closure of this antinomy.
For Dostoevsky a perfect act of faith is a dialectical paradox. What saves
many of the lost and evil characters in his works is a perfect act of faith:
for example, Raskolnikov (*Crime and Punishment*). Why? Because when

4   Dostoevsky, *The Brothers Karamazov*, Bk. 5, ch. 3 The Brothers Get Acquainted,
ch. 4 Rebellion and ch. 5 The Legend of the Grand Inquisitor.

all the obstacles are removed, where the only remaining witnesses to the truth of their criminal folly have committed suicide, there is no earthly reason why they should confess. If there is no God, no eschatological judgment, as they believe, then what we do here counts for nothing—yet they do go ahead and confess. For Dostoevsky this is a perfect act of faith. This is an example of a dialectical paradox.

3. TYPES OF DIALECTIC
IN THE WORK OF DOSTOEVSKY

We can broadly identify eight areas/types of dialectic in the work of Dostoevsky generally, the mature novels specifically: all of these dialectics flow from the central dialectical antinomy between faith and life (see figure 2, opposite):

> i. Dialectic in Dostoevsky's Doctrine of God
>> ~ Dialectic in Dostoevsky's Doctrine of God:
>> Separation, Distinction, and Disjuncture
>> ~ Dialectic in Dostoevsky's Doctrine of God:
>> Transcendence and Immanence
>> ~ Dialectic in Dostoevsky's Doctrine of God:
>> Russian Orthodoxy and Eastern Platonism?
>> ~ Dialectic in Dostoevsky's Doctrine of God:
>> Trinitarian Considerations
>
> ii. Dialectic between Revelation and Reason
>
> iii. Dialectical Theological Anthropology
>
> iv. Dialectical Paradox Regarding the Weak and Vulnerable
>
> v. Dialectic between Bourgeois Religion and Piercing Atheism
>
> vi. Dialectic between Religion and Faith
>> ~ Dialectic between Religion and Faith:
>> European Nihilism
>> ~ Dialectic between Religion and Faith:
>> Dostoevsky, "The Idea," The Tower of Babel,
>> The Crystal Palace, and The Ant Heap
>
> vii. Dialectic between Goodness and Comfort
>
> viii. Dialectical Eschatology

This list of sub-divisions is not exhaustive, but encompasses, broadly speaking, the nature of Dostoevsky's use of theological dialectics.

i. Dialectic in Dostoevsky's Doctrine of God

~ Dialectic in Dostoevsky's Doctrine of God:
   Separation, Distinction, and Disjuncture

Dostoevsky's doctrine of God is not stated explicitly, this is because he is a novelist and not a systematic theologian. However, if we accept the central importance of the antinomy between the doctrine of a loving and merciful God and the reality of a bleak, cruel life characterized by suffering, and that all other dialectics in Dostoevsky's work flow from this central dialectical antinomy (see figure 2) then there is an implied separation, distinction, even disjuncture between God and life as experienced by humanity. Throughout all his post-Siberian works generally, the mature novels specifically, there is a dialectic based upon the seemingly irresolvable/unbridgeable gulf between human understanding/knowledge of the divine on the one hand, and God as transcendent, on the other. In his days as a "European liberal" (as he referred to his student days in St. Petersburg[5]), he read, via Belinsky, the German theologian Feuerbach and took on board the man's atheism. In many ways, his entire writing career after Siberia is about coming to terms with how to justify faith in God. The only way Dostoevsky could claim faith in God was by stressing God's transcendence and otherness—beyond the world of Feuerbachian religious atheism. Therefore, there is a dialectical distinction between God and creation, an irresolvable dialectic from a human perspective.

~ Dialectic in Dostoevsky's Doctrine of God:
   Transcendence and Immanence

If there is resolution of the dialectic it is in Jesus Christ, the God-man: Dostoevsky used the Gospel of John and annotated/underlined the passages to do with Christ's divinity in the Siberian prison camp, continuing to annotate once he returned to European Russia. Boyce Gibson has noted how Dostoevsky seemed to ground God in Christ and had difficulty conceiving of God as transcendent such was the importance, existentially, of the immanent to him.[6] At times Dostoevsky so believed in Jesus Christ as God that he lost any understanding or idea

---

5   Dostoevsky, *Diary of a Writer* (1880), II, 984.

6   Gibson, *The Religion of Dostoevsky*, 166.

of God's transcendence—the Father in heaven. However, Dostoevsky appeared to accept the transcendence of God though he was not able to conceptualize it whilst grounding the knowability of God in the human Jesus of Nazareth.

~ Dialectic in Dostoevsky's Doctrine of God: Russian Orthodoxy and Eastern Platonism?

Russian Orthodox Mysticism: Russian Orthodox beliefs never attempted to close the separation, the distance, between the human Jesus and the transcendent Godhead in the way that, it may be argued, it was closed by theologians and philosophers in nineteenth-century Liberal Protestantism and in the religion of feeling of Schleiermacher; furthermore Orthodox epistemology stated that we mere humans could not know God completely, directly, but any encounter with the Holy Spirit would be with and from God. Such an encounter would be perturbing, puzzling, and certainly not conforming to the cognitive and epistemological expectations of humanity. Further, any mystical experience must be measured against "Sacred Scripture."

Dostoevsky was a Slavophile and in his middle age and mature years a passionate supporter of the Russian Orthodox Church. This raises the question of whether the theological beliefs inherent in Dostoevsky's work are a reflection of the beliefs of the Russian Orthodox Church. Dostoevsky was committed to the Church—warts and all. So what of Russian Orthodox theology generally, and an Eastern understanding of soteriology specifically? Are the theological beliefs undergirding Dostoevsky's work a fair reflection of the doctrine of the Russian Church he came to love more and more in his middle age?

Though one of its more public supporters (as he immersed himself in the doctrine of the Russian Church) he was also prepared to be one of its severest critics. What was the ground of Dostoevsky's faith and therefore his theological beliefs? Answer: the New Testament. Upon being convicted of sedition, reprieved from execution at the last second, shackled then imprisoned and exiled in Siberia, it was a theocentric (or biblical) mindset that informed him in his conversion back to faith: the Russian New Testament that was given to him whilst in a prison convoy being marched to central Asia. Dostoevsky's works are imbued with Russian Orthodox beliefs implicitly and an Eastern understanding of

Christian soteriology specifically (as in *Crime and Punishment*); this is biblical and patristic.

Dostoevsky's presentation of some elements of Russian Orthodoxy are crucial to his reawakened faith whilst imprisoned; this faith sustained him and inspired and influenced his middle and mature period works. Fundamental to Dostoevsky's recovery of faith was the role of the New Testament, studied when he was imprisoned in Siberia in the context of the fellow prisoners around him: some who were open to faith and the grace and forgiveness of God, others who withdrew into the hardened, deranged, and criminally perverse world they had created for their own self-justification. The world of the prison camp in Omsk was in this sense "biblical" and "patristic." This is all underpinned by Russian Orthodoxy. It is important to remember that the Russian church never went along the path of Feuerbachian religious atheism, or liberalism, which can be seen in some elements of the neo-Protestant doctrine of nineteenth-century Liberal Protestantism in Germany and to a lesser extent in Switzerland. Eduard Thurneysen, writing in 1920/21, noted how Dostoevsky, "bore in himself the deepest mistrust toward a Christendom that had become church, and he loved in his Russian church just that which is not church in it—the reminders, still preserved pure, as he believed, of the early history of Christendom, free from compromise."[7]

But what do we make of what we may call, Eastern Platonism? Plato and Platonic concepts are naturally important here. We have seen enough already to see that there is something of a Platonic distance between humanity and God in Dostoevsky's middle and mature period works. In a Platonic context, Dostoevsky states that there is another reality to be taken into account, that we are in relation to this otherness, as Plato's world of shadows (the changing world we see, hear, feel, smell, and taste) relates to the truer reality (the world of forms). It is important to steer clear of a well-established past generalization that the Eastern church was Platonic, other-worldly, and mystical; the Western church Aristotelian, this-worldly, and efficient.[8] Such a distinction is often reductively dualistic and indeed we must be wary of identifying such a dualism in Dostoevsky.

---

7   Thurneysen, *Dostojewski* (1921), 6/ET: 10

8   A generalisation from the past echoed by Lossky, *The Mystical Theology of the Eastern Church*, and Parry, *et al.*, (eds.) *Blackwell Dictionary of Eastern Christianity*, both of whom repudiate the generalisation.

Yes, Dostoevsky's doctrine of God can be said to be analogous with a Platonic doctrine, but that is only a comparison.

Dostoevsky is primarily influenced by the theocentricity of the New Testament; however, his invocation of a specifically Russian Christ—rooting Christ in the Russian peasants and serfs—is sometimes questionable. It can be argued that this is an element in Russian Orthodoxy and may be from his cultural upbringing, from his childhood. But he did develop a healthy suspicion of much institutionalized religion and religious practice. For example, whilst in Siberia, Dostoevsky read and studied the New Testament when he could, but he endured the hard physical labor of a prisoner during the day and slept alongside deranged men, murderers, and child rapists at night. There, he mistrusted the priests and formal religious services that they were obliged to attend. Instead, he valued the *sobornost* of togetherness as he rekindled his faith with his fellow convicts who were Christian. For example, Vrangel, a "good Christian" whom Dostoevsky befriended when the latter was released from prison to serve the remainder of his sentence in the army, observed, "he [*sc.* Dostoevsky] was rather pious, but did not go often to church, and disliked priests, especially the Siberian ones . . . ."[9] Vrangel linked this "spiritual revival" to his Bible reading, which he preferred to the formalities of public religion. But this was not individualistic piety—he shared his Bible reading with sympathetic fellow prisoners, they were his congregation, his church. Here he discovered true *sobornost*—the spiritual togetherness of Christians in which the ego is both submerged and enhanced, the spontaneous togetherness of a congregation at the moment of worship which is then carried over into everyday living. Dostoevsky wrote on this period of his life, "From the people [*sc.* in prison] I received again into my soul Christ, whom I had known in the family home when still a child, and nearly lost when in my turn I was transformed into an European liberal."[10] In correspondence from Siberia he commented on his repudiation of "Schillerism" (a term he coined, along with endarkeners/endarkenment; the later as a euphemism for all that he now saw was wrong with European liberalism, and European philosophers and politicians grounded proudly in their "Enlightenment")

---

9   See, Dostoevsky, *Memories from the House of the Dead*, 214f.

10   Dostoevsky, *Diary of a Writer* (1880), II, 984.

and admitted that he had "believed in theory and utopia."[11] In a famous and often quoted letter he sent in 1854 to a Christian living in Siberia named Madame Fonzina,[12] he commented:

> I am a child of the age, a child of unbelief and doubt, up till now . . . this longing for faith, which is all the stronger for the proofs I have against it . . . I thank God for the times when I can love and believe I am loved . . . .
>
> In such moments I have formulated my creed, in which all is precious and holy to me . . . there is nothing lovelier, deeper, more appealing, more rational, more human and more perfect than the Savior . . . not only is there no one else like him, there never could be. . . . If anyone could prove to me that Christ is outside the truth, and if the truth really did exclude Christ, I should stay with Christ rather than with the truth.[13]

In spite of this, truth (as distinct from certain religious practices) began to be of supreme importance to him. And religion? The public show of religion that was sometimes required of the prisoners left him very uncomfortable. Whilst in Siberia he realized that his period as a "European liberal" had also been a search for truth—but a mistaken, misguided search whereby he arrived at "wrong truth," the relativistic truth of the man-god. Christ and truth became synonymous to him. This, however, was very Russian in the sense of *pravda*: a word that combines both "truth" and "justice." And it is in keeping with Russian tradition, including the Russian Orthodox Church, to seek not simply *pravda* reduced to *istina* (theoretical truth), but *pravda-spravedlivost*—truth as righteousness, righteousness as truth.[14] For Dostoevsky, God in Christ was primarily about truth, righteousness, and justice, religion was a vehicle, a form of human expression of love and worship. Dostoevsky attempts to articulate something like this in his mature writings. In looking at some of these we will understand his criticism of religion—that is, a criticism of religion where such religiosity worked against the gospel. This is a critique of religion and the church seen as human culture, piety seen as social respectability. Dostoevsky's ecclesiology as such was then the result of this biblical faith brought about whist in the prison camp

11   Dostoevsky, *Fyodor Mikhailovich Dostoevsky: Complete Letters*, I, 178.

12   Ibid., I, 142; see also, Murray, *Fyodor Dostoevsky: A Critical Study*, 77–78.

13   Ibid., I, 142.

14   Edie *et al.*, *Russian Philosophy*. See Vol. II, 175.

at Omsk. It was uncompromising in its criticism of religion and church when they were self-serving, but was also colored by his childhood love of the Russian Orthodox rituals. It must be considered as formative for the rest of his outlook. Church and religion were regarded ambivalently to a degree by Dostoevsky, but God was everything—the God revealed specifically by the Christ of John's Gospel.

~ Dialectic in Dostoevsky's Doctrine of God:
   Trinitarian Considerations

Dostoevsky saw the first person of the Trinity as wholly transcendent and other. This is highly reminiscent of Kierkegaard's often quoted proposition that there is an infinite qualitative distinction between *time* and *eternity*, also between *humanity* and *God*. There is no evidence that Dostoevsky knew of or read Kierkegaard's work; he took his theology from Russian Orthodoxy—often going to stay in monasteries. This distinction of his is not just grounded in the separateness and independence of creation from God, but is the result primarily of the *fall*. A *fall* initiated by humanity. Humanity is lost, *fallen*, separate, distant from God—humanity must turn to God and make a decision to live for God and not for itself. As Eduard Thurneysen notes,

> The question of God is the question of all his works: God, the root of all life, and the basis of the world, which gives everything its basis, but also its abrogation, its torment, its "dis-ease," the enigmatically unreal in all that is real, the unearthly, toward which all that is earthly aspires. The dialectic of this paradoxical truth is the dialectic of all Dostoevsky's men and women. They all have God as their goal, they are all moved and driven by him from the beginning on. They press toward him in the insatiability of their longing for life, in the search for final answers, and yet no step leads over from man, for how would God still be God if man could become "god"?[15]

Despite this gulf, which is unbridgeable by humanity, we can, through an act of directing our will, turn to God and know God: this is pneumatological and issues from the crucifixion and resurrection of the Christ. Despite this dialectical disjuncture, it is fair to consider Dostoevsky's doctrine of God as Trinitarian, though not in so many

15   Thurneysen, *Dostojewski* (1921), 37/ET: 42–43.

words. There is the distance, the unbridgeable gulf, between humanity and the Father, with the Father only known through the Son. For example, in Dostoevsky's New Testament we have seen already the heavy emphasis on John's Gospel. Within John's Gospel there are the passages annotated/ underlined relating to how the Father is in the Son and how those who know the Son know the Father—"Jesus said to him, "I am the way, and the truth, and the life. <u>No one comes to the Father except through me. If you know me, you will know my Father also</u>. From now on you do know him and have seen him"[16] (this passage is marked "N.B." in the margin, with verses 6b and 7a underlined as shown here); also "Believe me that I am in the Father and the Father is in me; but if you do not, then believe me because of the works themselves,"[17] which is marked in a similar manner. The atoning sacrifice of the Son bridges this divide. Further, the second person of the Trinity is knowable, for Dostoevsky, to ordinary people through suffering. The existential decision to turn to God is then an experience of the Holy Spirit often characterized by prevenient grace leading to the denial of will—this pneumatological immediacy is paradoxical in the sense that it appears to contradict the distance/distinction between humanity and God. This can seem abstract when projected into the lives of his characters in the context of a novel: for example, Dmitri in *The Brothers Karamazov* or Raskolnikov in *Crime and Punishment*, but the relationship—however nebulous and intangible—is there, and is real and concrete. Each soul appears to be a battleground between this triune action on the one hand and the insidious overtures of personified evil on the other. The litmus test is, as always with Dostoevsky, "Sacred Scripture": how the problems of existence measure against the Bible. Therefore, as we shall see, the struggles of his characters to live either for the good or for self is a reflection of an existential gospel.

ii. Dialectic Between Revelation and Reason

Dostoevsky recognized the utter inability of science, reason, and the Western (so-called) Enlightenment to explain the important questions about human existence. (He referred to this movement in the West as an "endarkenment" in his notebooks; the pillars of the age of reason, the

---

16   John 14:6–7. See, Kjetsaa *Dostoevsky and His New Testament*, 39.

17   John 14:11. See, ibid.

French revolution, the Enlightenment philosophers were parodied as "endarkeners."[18]) For him, the only explanation lay in Scripture. Revelation as contained in "Sacred Scripture" was the only source of truth. When dealing with the big questions of life, death, morality, Dostoevsky quotes Scripture, not the thoughts of philosophers. There are over eighty scriptural references in The Legend of the Grand Inquisitor. In the mature novels there is a well-defined epistemological structure built on the proposition that by itself humanity cannot know about what is of real importance —humanity will not find its destiny through science and reason. Only the path to God through revelation is the way to humanity's destiny. Yes, Dostoevsky shows respect to science and reason and believed that they can teach us important facts about existence; however, science and reason rely upon human faculties and therefore cannot teach us anything that in the final analysis is of any real importance. The meaning of existence is to be found in "Sacred Scripture." Characters that represent reason and science—Raskolnikov (*Crime and Punishment*) and Ivan Karamazov (*The Brothers Karamazov*)—do not hold ultimate truth. The truth from above is found in Sonya (*Crime and Punishment*) and Father Zossima's (*The Brothers Karamazov*) Bible. But the path of Sonya and Zossima is characterized by negation: humility, restraint, denial, puzzlement. The path of Prince Myshkin (*The Idiot*) demonstrated that any human-generated attempt at "Christlikeness" would ultimately fail because we are human and not divine. Many of those who believe in science and reason (identified by Dostoevsky with Western liberal intellectuals—the "endarkeners") end up committing suicide. For example, Svidrigailov (*Crime and Punishment*), Smerdyakov (*The Brothers Karamazov*), and Stavrogin (*The Devils*). Suicide is also characteristic of those whom these nihilists destroy—for example, Matryosha (*The Devils*), the twelve-year-old girl who hangs herself after being raped by Stavrogin. What saves Raskolnikov (*Crime and Punishment*) from this path is Sonya, who— reading and preaching from the Bible—convinces him to repent publicly and to confess to the police and to be saved: resurrection is the underlying theme of Dostoevsky's mature work—Sonya's axiom is: confess publically and God will give you your life back. Indeed, the key passage that Sonya reads to Raskolnikov is the resurrection of Lazarus. If there is anything approaching a synthesis for this revelation/reason dialectic it

18   Trace, *Dostoevsky and the Brothers Karamazov*, 151; See also, Dostoevsky, *The Diary of a Writer*.

is resurrection: the grace (rebirth) and action (resurrection) from and of God. Then there are those characters that are undecided. Dmitri Karamazov (*The Brothers Karamazov*) who eventually will be saved from despair, not by reason, but through revelation; not by philosophy, but by faith. Ivan Karamazov, the archetypal frustrated pessimistic atheist, has adopted the "European ideas," that is, the Enlightenment dogma that revelation in the form of the Scripture is not a valid means of truth: human reason must ascend to take its place; apparent or so-called enlightenment takes over from faith. Ivan rejects revelation and thereby faith, only to be enslaved by reason. His discussion[19] with his brother, Alyosha, illustrates that even if God was proved to him he would reject God's creation, his rationality rejects a supernatural/inspirational basis for Scripture. Despite the fact that he confesses that he believes in God, this "god" is very much the result of natural theology, and a "god" that is the object of his arrogant intellectual refutation—without revelation he continues to be trapped by his demon.

iii. Dialectical Theological Anthropology

The characters in Dostoevsky's novels are there to draw an analogy. That is, a comparison, in many ways a portrait, of humanity. This analysis is in the relation between God and humanity. Without God these people are fallen, broken, sinful—they cannot get it right. With God they still fail, and *fall*. Without God, humanity is nothing; with God humanity *might* be of value. As we have seen previously, this is grounded on a devastatingly pessimistic theological anthropology. Dostoevsky uses this dialectic throughout his mature novels, but through it all he expresses a vast compassion for people in their *fallen* condition, except when they entertain or act upon atheistic principles (not, that is, the atheism of someone who is struggling to believe, but sincerely cannot and still loves through self-sacrifice). In *The Brothers Karamazov* he presented the understanding that there is some good in humanity—the *imago Dei* is not totally obscured or lost, but not enough good is left to enable people to get along without God. Without God there is no limit to the depths of depravity, sin, debauchery, and cruelty that humanity can sink to; worse, as people perpetrate these acts they convince themselves that

19   Dostoevsky, *The Brothers Karamazov*, Bk. 5 Pro and Contra, ch. 3 The Brothers get Acquainted, and, ch. 4 Rebellion.

what they are doing is right. For Dostoevsky, the serpent is still very much present in the world; a dark force, animated and conscious, that beguiled and seduced, flattered and corrupted, that whispered thoughts into the minds of men and women; a dark strength that deluded, willfully; personified evil which seduced men and women to corrupt children; an evil that convinced responsible adults of the vanity of their thoughts. Often, the person's involvement in these actions cannot be reconciled with the beliefs—religious or otherwise—that he or she has held. With the perception of an external morality an unresolvable tension emerges: enjoyment is countered by judgment. This tension may lead to suicide. All sins can be forgiven; this is the dialectical paradox. But suicide is perhaps (as we noted earlier) the worst manifestation of the sin against the Holy Spirit that Jesus warned about. Suicide rejects God's forgiving judgment; the person simply passes judgment on him- or herself with all the consequences of that action. Therefore, Dostoevsky's writings are about the dark side of humanity, the dark side of desire, but above all about the corruption of love. Each human is constantly in a state of paradoxical, dialectical, disjuncture; this antinomy is only resolved eschatologically: in death to reign in hell, or to submit in heaven.

This is the fundamental dialectical conclusion of the theological anthropology in Dostoevsky's mature work. For Dostoevsky, there is so much evil in humanity that only God can keep people from totally destroying themselves. By contrast, he saw the intellectuals in Western Europe as having concluded that humanity was innately good. He received this idea essentially from Jean-Jacques Rousseau (1712–78) and Friedrich von Schiller (1759–1805), via the influence of Belinsky in his youthful days as a "European liberal," an influence that concluded humanity could get on without religion and God (but when asked where this goodness came from, they were undecided—Dostoevsky deals with the origin of goodness in his *magnum opus*: *The Brothers Karamazov*).

Ivan Karamazov is the epitome of Dostoevsky's theological anthropology. Several writers have noted a progression in the form and type of atheism in Ivan's beliefs, culminating in the dialogue between the devil and Ivan, which occurs after Smerdykov's confession of murder (the murder of their father inspired by Ivan's assertion that without God anything is possible), where Ivan is close to losing his mind he is so trapped by his demons. However, Ivan can still understand the dialectic between the true otherworldly God and the projected gods of human desire. Ivan is aware of the dialectic between religious projectionism and the wholly otherness of God, the real and true God, the God who is epistemologically unknowable in human terms. The dialectic of faith-unfaith, belief-unbelief, means that potentially he is closer to salvation than many religious people, if only his corrupt will were not so strong as to weigh him down. Compared with his believing brother, the monastic novice Alyosha, we have an almost dualistic dialectic—either/or. This is the result, dialectically, of Ivan's rebellion against God: fragmentation, disjuncture, and alienation. This dualistic element is often expressed in a dialectic between darkness and light: this unearthly battle between light and dark rages in the dialogue with the devil in Ivan's hallucination.[20] This is not the dualism of many ancient Middle Eastern religions: dark evil is created good by God—Lucifer the brightest of angels—but through free will *falls* and becomes the prince of evil. This is not a balanced duality; this is simply rebellion; a rebellion that humanity is now a part of.

iv. Dialectical Paradox
Regarding the Weak and Vulnerable

Blessed are the weak and vulnerable (the Beatitudes, Matt 5:3–10); the weaker you are, paradoxically the stronger you are: for Dostoevsky, Sonya (*Crime and Punishment*), Father Zossima (*The Brothers Karamazov*), and Prince Myshkin (*The Idiot*) hold to and represent the truth. The Westerners with their dogma of reason and enlightenment do not. But the path of those who believe in revelation is characterized by negation—humility, restraint, denial, puzzlement. The attempt at Christlikeness ultimately fails because we are human and not divine, yet we are called to Christlikeness. This is rooted in Russian Orthodox theology—that the *iurodivaia* (holy fool) knows nothing and can achieve nothing by the standards of this world, but paradoxically such a person radiates God's love and holiness. The Story of Maria or Myshkin's flawed efforts at saving Nastasya Filippovna (both in *The Idiot*); Zossima's refusal to shoot when he had the advantage in a duel, then his retreat to a monastery (*The Brothers Karamazov*); the witness of Sonya and her little step-sister living in abject poverty (*Crime and Punishment*) as compared to the sophisticated, worldly wise who appear to have everything in this life, but have nothing

20   Dostoevsky, *The Brothers Karamazov*, Bk. 11, ch. 9 The Devil—Ivan Fyodorovich's Nightmare.

in the next—these are all examples of a dialectical paradox: the foolish, broken, marginalized, those without power or status, are wise; the wise and rich and powerful are foolish. Dostoevsky often created a paradox between the fallen, the broken and sick, the suffering, the least of all in society, set off over and against the rich and powerful and intellectual. Here Dostoevsky is at his most prophetic and polemical, yet this is in many ways an exposition of the Beatitudes (Matt 5:3–10).

v. Dialectic Between
Bourgeois Religion and Piercing Atheism

A powerful dialectic occurs in *Crime and Punishment* and *The Idiot*. It is a dialectic between the godlessness of religion (church attendance by the St. Petersburg cultured classes) and a religion of godlessness (atheists, nihilists). For example, in *Crime and Punishment*, Pulkhéria Alexandrovna (Raskolnikov's mother) balks at Sonya who is forced to prostitute herself so as to feed her young brothers and sisters, yet is happy for her daughter, Dunya, to marry the middle-aged Lúzhin where there is no love, but simply lust, vanity, and status-seeking on the part of Lúzhin—and money for Pulkhéria Alexandrovna, who is poor after her husband's premature death. At least Sonya is honest about her plight as a prostitute—forced into the role through abject poverty and destitution. Pulkhéria is in effect prostituting her daughter, Dunya, so as to maintain her lifestyle. The implication is that Pulkhéria with her religious respectability is worse because Sonya is at least honest before God about her situation and has genuine faith, hates her life and longs for a miracle.

Madame Yepanchina (in *The Idiot*) represents the hypocrisy of institutionalized religion. Here Dostoevsky sets up a dialectic between the proud piety of the general's wife, Lizaveta Prokofievna, and the unconscious relatively innocent holiness of the actions of Prince Myshkin. For example, when a group of nihilist, proto-socialist, atheists descend on the Yepanchin's country villa, where Myshkin is recovering from an epileptic seizure, Lizaveta Prokofievna is disgraced by them—but also by Myshkin's refusal to reject them, expel them; worse, he gives in to the demands for money from one of them who claims he is vaguely related to Myshkin. Myshkin successfully disproves the claim of kinship but still gives him some money. The entire scene is reminiscent of the story in Luke's Gospel of the Pharisee who invited Jesus to eat with him in his house. While Jesus is eating with the Pharisee—a meal not given out of generosity but in order to find out what this man Jesus was about—a woman who is reputed to be a prostitute enters: "she stood behind him at his feet, weeping, and began to bathe his feet with her tears and to dry them with her hair. Then she continued kissing his feet and anointing them" (Luke 7:36–50). The Pharisee is outraged—but Jesus answers with a parable that exposes the self-righteousness of the Pharisee and how great repentance and humility will receive great forgiveness. Jesus does not rebuke her and send her away—he forgives her sins, which has the Pharisee's guests falling around in shock at the audacity of this man Jesus.[21] The self-righteous indignation of the Pharisees is analogous with Madame Yepanchina's vocal criticism of both the nihilists who have visited and Myshkin for not rejecting them.[22] There is, therefore, a dialectical tension between the nihilists and Madame Yepanchina; both have elements of truth, but are a long way from God—this dialectical tension can only be resolved in God. Myshkin tries, but fails because he is human and not divine, he may be *Christ-like* but he is not *the Christ*.

For Dostoevsky, proud, pious religiosity is not the way to be saved by God. As Thurneysen notes, Dostoevsky's triumph is to call into question everything of human achievement so that the only answer left is God.[23] Dostoevsky saw God and faith as the solution—applying a healthy skepticism in the form of a yes-no dialectic to the church. He suspected the power and authority of the church, but saw the value of the church, that is, its temporal necessity. Thurneysen comments,

> Without knowing Kierkegaard or Overbeck, he bore in himself the deepest mistrust toward a Christendom that had become church, and he loved in his Russian church just that which is not church in it—the reminders, still preserved pure, as he believed, of the early history of Christendom, free from compromise.[24]

---

21   In Dostoevsky's Russian New Testament verse 47 is mark with a pencil in the margin and the last sentence is marked "N.B." (shown here in bold): "Therefore, I tell you, her sins, which were many, have been forgiven; hence she has shown great love. **But the one to whom little is forgiven, loves little**." (NRSV)

22   Dostoevsky, *The Idiot*, Pt. 2, chs. 7–9.

23   For example, in Thurneysen, *Dostojewski* (1921): "nothing but a single great question, the question of the origin of his life, the question of God," 37; ET: "God is God. That is the one, central recognition of truth for Dostoevsky," 42–43.

24   Thurneysen, *Dostojewski* (1921), 6/ET: 10.

Thurneysen's realized that Dostoevsky held a mistrust toward a Christendom that had become church, and focused on what he perceived was still preserved of the early history of Christianity, free from compromise, in the Russian church of the late nineteenth century. Is this accurate? Considering what we have seen already of Dostoevsky spiritual rebirth through the New Testament read in a Siberian prison camp, the answer is a cautious yes. Not only is Dostoevsky primarily influenced by the theocentricity of the New Testament, but the background of the Russian Orthodox Church remains from his childhood: the heritage of Russian Orthodoxy theology generally, Eastern soteriology specifically, and Eastern Platonism, because this was the Christianity in which Dostoevsky was raised and nurtured. Although it is the theocentricity brought about by the New Testament—his sole reading matter in the Siberian prison camp—that brings him back to faith, the cultural upbringing from his childhood is still there. Church and religion were regarded ambivalently to a degree by Dostoevsky, but God was everything: the God revealed specifically by the Christ of John's Gospel.

Why did Dostoevsky show so much respect for the nihilists, the atheists, a love and respect that was not echoed in the criticisms of Madam Yepanchina? As was so often the case, Dostoevsky spoke through his characters. This dialectically paradoxical respect for atheists is echoed by the Orthodox starets, Father Zossima (*The Brothers Karamazov*):

> Hate not those who reject you, who insult you, who abuse and slander you. Hate not the atheists, the teachers of evil, the materialists—and I mean not only the good ones—for there are many good ones among them, especially in our day, hate not even the wicked ones. Remember them in your prayers thus: Save, O Lord, all those who have none to pray for them, save too all those who will not pray. And add: it is not in pride that I make this prayer, O Lord, for I am lower than all men . . . .[25]

---

25   Dostoevsky, *The Brothers Karamazov*, Part 2, Book IV, Lacerations, chapter 1 Father Ferapont (Constance Garnett translation).

vi. Dialectic Between Religion and Faith

~ Dialectic between Religion and Faith: European Nihilism

Dostoevsky developed a great respect for religion in the form of the Russian Orthodox Church when it was true to the gospel and reflected the spiritual traditions of the hermits and startsy.[26] If the Christian religion had become corrupted, as he believed it had in the Europe of his day, then it was worse than bad: liberal Protestants in Germany, Roman Catholic "infallibility," and the annexing of religion as the preserve of the well-off in England. Further, because of what he saw across Europe, he was convinced that Protestantism was moving into atheism because of its fragmentation, whilst Roman Catholicism was moving into socialism (a form of proto-Marxism).[27] Furthermore, he saw religion often as an obstacle between God and God's creation, particularly when it was humanist religion, self-generated and self-referential, and self-reverential. Faith was the opposite of religion in this dialectic. But, for Dostoevsky, herein lies the dialectical tension—we must not sit back and accept the church and the world as it is, we must rant against the situation as it is, but also value this tension. Wealth—financial, or in terms of status and power—denies this tension, smothers it! This tension is dialectical and it points to the eschaton. It is this eschatological tension that gives life meaning; therefore, any attempt to solve the problem of the church will fail. He believed that Rome had negated this dialectical tension by claiming the mantle of authority and power from the Roman Empire, and by declaring infallibility. In other words, it had sold out to the world, to mammon: to the devil.

26   Starets: an elder in a Russian Orthodox monastery, venerated as an adviser to "the way," teacher, spiritual father, charismatic leader, characterized by wisdom achieved from ascetic experience, ascetic struggle, self-denial, wisdom conferred by the Holy Spirit, generated preveniently.

27   In June 1862 Dostoevsky visited Western Europe to consult specialists about his epilepsy and to see the result of the Western ideology he believed was corrupting Russia. He visited Berlin, Paris, London, Florence, Milan, and Vienna. He published his observations in "Winter Notes on Summer Impressions," published in *Vremya* (*Time*, the periodical he edited) February-March 1863. These observations were later reordered and published in book form: Dostoevsky, *Winter Notes on Summer Impressions* (trans. Kyril Fitzlyon).

~ Dialectic between Religion and Faith: Dostoevsky, "The Idea,"
The Tower of Babel, The Crystal Palace, and The Ant Heap

"The Idea" for Dostoevsky is the path of unrighteousness, this is one
of four propositional metaphors that he uses to frame the theological
ethics underpinning his work. "The Idea" is initially found in *Notes
from Underground* (1864); then it forms the central plan in *Crime and
Punishment* (1866); then it is brought to its fullest expression in *The
Brothers Karamazov* (1877/8–80). To summarize: "The Idea" is a sequence
of decisions and actions. The initial decision is to disbelieve in God or to
reject God for one's own agenda, therefore the individual must decide to
redefine human morality and ethics according to his or her own principles
(the individual will reject morality, while simultaneously becoming a
very moralizing and judgmental person); this amounts to a storming of
heaven through the attempt to redefine human morality/ethics. This leads
to the realization that without God there are no limits or constraints on
human behavior and even if confronted by God's reality the logical course
of action is suicide: to return the ticket of life to God. (We will examine
"The Idea" in more depth later.)

In the same manner that "The Idea" occupies Dostoevsky's thinking
throughout his post-Siberian work, two other all-pervading propositional
metaphors are "the Tower of Babel" and "the Crystal Palace." These two
are used in the same way and complement "The Idea." Kroecker and Ward
see the use of them starting with Dostoevsky's *Notes from Underground*
(1864):

> According to the underground-man, modern progressivism places
> great emphasis on the notion that world history is ultimately
> rational. . . . [This] is apparent in the very phrase philosophy of
> history, which was invented by Voltaire . . . . For the underground
> man, reason is merely the tip of the iceberg, amounting to
> "perhaps one-twentieth" of what constitutes human being. Under
> his scrutiny, the modern idea of progress is revealed not as the
> expression of dispassionate reason but as the symptom of fervent
> hope—hope for the "Crystal Palace" of the future.[28]

"The Tower of Babel" and "the Crystal Palace" are supplemented by
a fourth, "the Ant-Heap." These three are used to represent related

---

28   Kroeker and Ward, *Remembering the End*, 67. Kroeker and Ward are referring
to Dostoevsky, *Notes from Underground*, chs. 8 and 10.

phenomena: human progress as symbolized by the economic and social ideals of the utopian socialists in France, the religio-capitalist system in England, and the nineteenth-century liberal neo-Protestant humanist-Idealist agenda in Germany. Chapple notes, "the underground man muses about the perversity of humanity's history and the hopelessness of efforts to plan rationally humanity's utopia on earth. . . . [H]e asserts The Crystal Palace will be built as a symbol of the success of human reason."[29] For Dostoevsky, the Tower of Babel is the symbol of humanity's attempt to go it alone without God. Ellis Sandoz, on the political apocalypse that Dostoevsky predicted, wrote:

> [This] is represented by three symbols: (1) The Tower of Babel— the ideal society of the revolutionary wishing to insure without God the happiness of mankind: the symbol of idolatry; (2) The Crystal Palace—society illumined from within by the power of human reason but opaque to the light of faith which is rejected, together with tradition, as irrational mystery: rationalism, symbol of the pride of mind; (3) the Ant Heap—the future ecumenical society of man devoid of humanity and reduced to the level of an insect in the name of humanitarianism: the symbol of the end of secular history.[30]

In *Crime and Punishment* Dostoevsky uses these three metaphors— "the Tower of Babel," "the Crystal Palace," and "the Ant-Heap"—and goes one step further by inventing a fashionable restaurant/cafe, frequented by liberal humanists and proto-socialists, named The Crystal Palace, which is mentioned in the movements of Razumikhin and Raskolnikov.[31] Babel, as a motif, is often complemented by the use of the term Babylon as a metaphor of wickedness and confusion—Semyon Yegorovich Karamazinov and Pyotr Stepanovich Verkhovensky (*The Demons*) agree that Western Europe is Babylon and will fall.[32] This image of The Crystal Palace comes from Dostoevsky's European tour (Summer 1862). He believed Europe had been corrupted by this Tower of Babel/ Crystal Palace. Therefore, we can find the genesis of all three metaphors in Dostoevsky's scathing critique of London. On return from his travels

29   Chapple, *A Dostoevsky Dictionary*, 138, 164, 251 and 302–3.

30   Sandoz, *Political Apocalypse*, 137.

31   Dostoevsky, *Crime and Punishment*, Pt. 2 chs. 4, 6 and 7, 106–17, 154–74 and 175–93.

32   Dostoevsky, *Demons*, Pt. 2, ch. 6, Pyotr Bustles About, 343–87.

he wrote of overwhelming deprivation and poverty in the East End of London. [33] He noted the noise and pollution and the filthy state of the Thames, as compared to the progress and engineering achievements represented by The Crystal Palace and the Great Exhibition held in it:

> Now London is in this respect something entirely different, . . . the typically Western principle of individual isolation[;] . . . even the very leaders of progress lack faith, and bow down in worship of Baal.
>
> The immense city, forever bustling by night and by day, . . . the daring of enterprise, the apparent disorder, . . . the polluted Thames, the coal-saturated air, the magnificent squares and parks, the town's terrifying districts such as Whitechapel with its half-naked, savage and hungry population, the City with its millions and its world-wide trade, The Crystal Palace, the Great Exhibition. . . . [Y]ou realize the grandeur of the design; you feel that something has been achieved here, here is victory and triumph. And you feel nervous. It is a Biblical sight, something to do with Babylon or Babel, some prophecy out of the Apocalypse being fulfilled before your very eyes. You feel that a rich and ancient tradition of denial and protest is needed in order not to yield, not to succumb . . . not to idolize Baal, that is, not to take the actual for the ideal. [34]

Dostoevsky writes at length about the poverty and depravity of the working class, and how Catholic priests try to care and convert them,

> But an Anglican minister would never visit a poor man. The poor are not even allowed inside a church because they have not the money to pay for a seat. . . . Anglican ministers and bishops are proud and rich, live in wealthy parishes and dioceses and wax fat. . . . It is a religion of the rich, and undisguised at that. They travel all over the earth, penetrate into darkest Africa to convert one savage, and forget the million savages in London. . . . [I]n fact all the Golden Calves in that country are extremely religious. . . . Baal reigns and does not even demand obedience, because he is certain of it. Baal does not close his eyes . . . . [35]

Thus we have the origin of the image/metaphor of "the Crystal Palace"/"the Tower of Babel" as representing humanity trying to go it

33 Dostoevsky, *Winter Notes on Summer Impressions*, ch. 5, "Baal," 42–43.
34 Ibid., 43–44.
35 Ibid., 51–52.

alone without God, fed by corrupt religion, with the mass of humanity as "the Ant-Heap."

Further, because of what he saw, he was convinced that Liberal neo-Protestantism in Germany was moving into atheism because of its fragmentation, whilst he declared socialism the illegitimate offspring of Roman Catholicism, and was convinced that socialist atheism would lead to inhumanity and materialism.[36] Much of this works through into *Crime and Punishment* (1866)—with Raskolnikov representing "the Tower of Babel" in his arrogant assertion of his own will. Babel functions in Raskolnikov as a measure of the modern hope that human history is progressing toward its fulfillment in a new kind of social order. This new order was indelibly associated with the French revolutionary principle of *liberté, égalité, fraternité*:[37] Hence Raskolnikov's Napoleonic delusion— *eritis sicut Deus*, building his Babel tower. Where is this leading? At the end of the book,[38] in real time within the narrative, Dostoevsky gives Raskolnikov a dream; this is the same dream that Dostoevsky had experienced while in prison in Siberia: a vision of humanity having lost the ability to agree on what is good and what is evil and therefore the sight of teeming millions killing each other in meaningless spite (a highly prophetic vision given the ideologically driven mass carnage of the twentieth century).[39]

Therefore, the combined metaphor of "the Tower Babel"/"the Crystal Palace"/"the Ant-Heap" represented for Dostoevsky the dis-ease of humanity: primarily, proto-socialist liberal humanist atheism, secondarily, the authority of the Roman Catholic Church, coupled with the religious-capitalist pride and elitism of Victorian England, complemented by the drive towards atheism in some quarters of Liberal neo-Protestantism in Germany. This is taken to its logical conclusion in the Grand Inquisitor who explicitly invokes/voices "the Tower of Babel,"[40] as does Stepan Trofimovich Verkhovensky (*The Demons*). [41] Babel represents not just

36   See, Dirscherl, S.J., *Dostoevsky and the Catholic Church*, 95.

37   Kroeker and Ward, *Remembering the End*, 67.

38   Dostoevsky, *Crime and Punishment*, "Epilogue," 533–52.

39   Kroeker and Ward, *Remembering the End*, 75, quoting from the Epilogue to *Crime and Punishment*.

40   Dostoevsky, *The Brothers Karamazov*, Pt. 1 Bk. 1 ch. 5, Elders, 25–33, and Pt. 2 Bk. 5 ch. 5, Grand Inquisitor, 246–64.

41   Dostoevsky, *Demons*, Pt. 1, ch. 1, 7–11.

corrupt Roman authority but is a prophetic forewarning of Marxism in Russia. Therefore Dostoevsky used the metaphor of The Tower of Babel explicitly in The Grand Inquisitor to describe *eritis sicut Deus* (which in turn epitomized "the Idea"):[42] totalitarianism, whether Roman Catholic or political (socialist or free market), was a Tower of Babel, which could be communal (Rome, or French socialism) or individualistic (the schismatic Raskolnikov).

vii. Dialectic Between Goodness and Comfort

Dostoevsky understood the existential decision that people were forced to take between a spiritual advantage and an earthly advantage. This tension was because people were primarily spiritual creatures. For many of his characters their actions are sheer foolishness—resulting in mockery, scorn, derision. The decisive purpose of life is goodness not comfort. The purpose of life is goodness—but this makes no sense unless God exists. But then, the existence of God is not enough. What underpins all of Dostoevsky's dialectics is, as Arthur Trace terms it, God-and-immortality: "the purpose of life as goodness makes no sense unless God-and-immortality exist, and that comfort should be the end of life if God-and-immortality do not exist."[43]

Raskolnikov's decision even after Svidrigailov's suicide still to go ahead and confess his crime (the murder of the elderly pawnbroker and her sister) and his rejection of the hope of being a Napoleon figure (a proto-Nietzschean superman) is an example of living for eternal goodness, not worldly comfort. Likewise, Ivan Karamazov's decision even after the suicide of Smerdyakov to testify in court to what the latter, his half-brother, has done in murdering their father, even though it implicates him. Despite all the atheistic ramblings we have heard from Ivan, he decides to live for goodness, the Good, not worldly comfort. His other brother Dmitri is another example—Mitya is innocent of the murder (though knows not that Smerdyakov his illegitimate half-brother, is the murderer), he has lived the life of a debauched libertine and though he knows he is innocent of his father's murder he will accept conviction, accept the suffering, be transported to Siberia. Another example is Zossima's actions in the duel and afterwards living for the Good and not self-interest, not only in his

---

42   Kroeker and Ward, *Remembering the End*, 63, 67, 75, 102, 185, and 227 n.1.

43   Trace, *Dostoevsky and the Brothers Karamazov*, 97

own life but also in the pressure he puts on Mikhail to go and confess to his crime.

viii. Dialectical Eschatology

In the work of Dostoevsky, dialectic is engrained into life. This example of Dostoevsky's dialectic is also characterized by *diastasis*—separateness, fragmentation, and as such the antinomies are irreconcilable. In Dostoevsky, these factors are always opposing each other and never resolved (complementary dialectics). The resolution of these open-ended antinomies was in God—more pertinently in the eschaton. Dostoevsky's work therefore reflects an eschatological tension—these dialectical paradoxes and antinomies are held in the dialectical tension between this life and the life to come. This raises the question, "how does Dostoevsky's negation relate to the dynamic tension inherent in Russian Orthodox theology between the apophatic and the cataphatic?" Apophatic theology can be seen here as an assertion of the inadequacy of human understanding in matters divine and therefore a corrective within theology (a necessary corrective to the affirmative, the reliance upon human language, human constructs for God, or "gods"). In the Eastern Church apophatic theology is regarded as fundamental, as an affirmation that God cannot be an object of knowledge at all (for example, the teachings of St. Gregory Palamas that God's essence is unknowable, while he makes himself known to us through his energies; also the writings of Vladimir Lossky). Apophatic knowledge is here to be understood not as post-modernist deconstruction, which in the end can say nothing except to appear to deny everything; apophatic theology here is a way of knowing that employs negative statements. To say what God is not, to state in humility that we simply cannot know all that there is to God, is not to deny God's existence. To state that God is *no thing* (i.e., no particular thing) is not the same as saying God is *nothing*. Gregory of Nyssa writes that God is named by those who call upon him, but this does not tell us what God's nature is.[44] There is therefore a dynamic tension between the apophatic and the cataphatic in Orthodox theology, which is also in the theology that underpins the writings of Dostoevsky.

---

44   Gregory of Nyssa, *Select Writings and Letters*, in *The Nicene and Post-Nicene Fathers*, Vol. 5, 2nd series, 1892 (trans. William Moor and Henry Wilson), 265.

This dynamic tension is seen dialectically as thesis and antithesis, and may pose a paradoxical contradiction, but any synthesis could only occur with the eschaton. This raises another question: what is the importance of existentialism in Dostoevsky's writings? An existential gospel represents a salutary corrective against utopian optimism based on science and belief in the inevitable technological advance of nations and of human progress. Such utopianism was redolent of nineteenth-century German Liberal Protestantism. In Dostoevsky's work, we find brutal, raw humanity stripped of pretense (religious or scientific)—fallen humanity totally dependent upon the grace and forgiveness of God; echoes again of Paul's theology of inner conflict in Romans: "I do not understand my own actions. For I do not do what I want, but I do the very thing I hate. . . . I can will what is right, but I cannot do it. For I do not do the good I want" (Rom 7:15 and 18b–19a). Eduard Thurneysen likened this eschatological tension to the idea of parallel lines never meeting in this reality, but with the potential to meet in eternity; he also used the analogy of the vanishing point always being outside the picture in an Expressionist painting—the vanishing point was therefore analogous with a dialectical synthesis.

> Rather, let us remember that the correctness of the most commonly and generally accepted drawing depends on that relationship of all lines to a single point of view that lies outside the picture, on that relationship that is called perspective. Not some fantastic addition or grotesque exaggeration, but rather just such a strict and exact relationship of all lines to a vanishing point in the beyond is what we mean by that course toward the beyond and toward infinity which we have recognized as characteristic of Dostoevsky's men and women[;] . . . the whole picture of life which is given by this psychology points on out beyond itself to this vanishing point.[45]

This dialectic is therefore fundamentally different from Hegel's concept of dialectic as it denies a synthesis in this reality, though both are characterized by movement. It is similar to the concept of a dynamic tension in Orthodox theology. Thurneysen derived this idea of the vanishing point, of parallel lines, from Ivan Karamazov. In his early discussion with his brother, Alyosha, in the room above the pub, the conversation that leads into Ivan reciting his narrative poem of The Legend of the Grand Inquisitor, he outlines his creed, stating how he believes that

45   Thurneysen, *Dostojewski* (1921), 35–36/ET: 40.

all these human dialectical contradictions, antinomies, paradoxes will be resolved in eternity:

> You must note this: if God exists and if He really did create the world, then . . . He created it according to the geometry of Euclid and the human mind with the conception of only three dimensions in space. Yet there have been and still are geometricians and philosophers . . . who doubt whether the whole universe, or to speak more widely, the whole of being, was only created in Euclid's geometry; they even dare to dream that two parallel lines, which according to Euclid can never meet on earth, may meet somewhere in infinity.
>
> . . . [In] the final result I don't accept this world of God's, and, although I know it exists, I don't accept it at all. It's not that I don't accept God, you must understand, it's the world created by Him I don't and cannot accept. Let me make it plain. I believe like a child that suffering will be healed and made up for, that all the humiliating absurdity of human contradictions will vanish like a pitiful mirage, like the despicable fabrication of the impotent and infinitely small Euclidian mind of man, that in the world's finale, at the moment of eternal harmony, something so precious will come to pass that it will suffice for all hearts, for the comforting of all resentments, for the atonement of all the crimes of humanity, of all the blood they've shed; that it will make it not only possible to forgive but to justify all that has happened with men—but though all that may come to pass, I don't accept it. I won't accept it. Even if parallel lines do meet and I see it myself, I shall see it and say that they've met, but still I won't accept it. That's what's at the root of me, Alyosha; that's my creed. I am in earnest in what I say.[46]

Ivan is, for Dostoevsky, the epitome of the Westerners—with their philosophy rooted in the Enlightenment. Like the Western "enlighteners," Ivan has lost his faith. His statement that he cannot accept God's world, especially in the context of an eschatological resolution, revolves around the fact that he cannot accept the supernatural (or more pertinently the super-rational) as this violates his faculty of reason. The greatest affront to him is therefore the supernatural revelatory basis of "Sacred Scripture." "Sacred Scripture" was to be seen as eschatological, and it is the possibility of a resolution of the antinomies and dialectically paradoxical contradiction of human existence in eternity that most affronts Ivan. He

46   Dostoevsky, *The Brothers Karamazov* Bk. 5, Pro and Contra, ch. 3 The Brothers Get to Know Each Other (Constance Garnett translation).

cannot cope with this eschatological tension. Thurneysen referring to this eschatological tension commented on the character of Prince Myshkin (*The Idiot*), the holy fool, God's fool (*iurodivaia*):

> He never disturbs the boundaries of the last things, and never shortens the eternal distances. But he guards them. He is always seeking with all the power of his soul that ultimate point where everything has its end and its beginning in God, that ultimate point which is comparable only with birth and death.
>
> . . . [T]here is the root of the "supreme rationality of this idiot," as his enemy and friend Rogozhin says . . . .
>
> It is always as if he were trying to discover in all men and all things the traces of the original creation and the secret tendency toward resurrection that is within them.[47]

4. DIALECTICAL ONTOLOGY

Dialectic in Dostoevsky's work is related to the nature of truth and existence: life is ontologically on a knife-edge, moving teleologically towards an unseen conclusion in the eschaton. Every single human being that lives is either moving towards God during their life or away from God, often towards or away at different times in a life: death confirming their position/relation to God. Truth, in Dostoevsky's novels, lies in the extremes, not in a compromise. As such Dostoevsky's dialectic is opposed to Hegelian dialectics. Truth lies at the ends of a dialectical extreme, not in a compromise, not in the middle. Resolution is deeply desirable, but cannot be achieved in this life

---

47   Thurneysen, *Dostojewski* (1921), 29–30/ET: 33

6

Dostoevsky: Religion and Atheism

1. RELIGIOUS AMBIVALENCE

Eduard Thurneysen notes, "Yet the most fearsome attack which Dostoevsky led with the assembled power of his knowledge and all the passion of his heart was directed against religion and the church. This attack runs through all his works, but reaches its high point in The Grand Inquisitor, and in Ivan Karamazov's nightmare of the devil."[1] As we have seen already, belief in a "god" is not enough; humanity is obsessed with and possessed by "idols" and "goddesses." Dostoevsky drives a hard, clear dialectic between the truly real otherworldly God and the "gods" of human invention and projection. (This issues, to a degree, in his opposition to Feuerbach's projectionist theories.) This belief of Dostoevsky's is grounded, ontologically, in the otherness of God. As we have noted, Arthur Trace sees this in Dostoevsky's thinking not as "god" but "God-and-immortality."[2] God-and-immortality implies that God is real, different, distinct, *and*, in addition, that each and every human being has an immortal soul and that there is eschatological judgment and the human is responsible before God. But what of religion? Where is religion in this theological understanding? What role does it play?

Religion was regarded in a somewhat ambivalent way by Dostoevsky, yet the more he read the Bible and stayed in Russian Orthodox monasteries, the more he realized that society needed religion to solve the

---

1   Thurneysen, *Dostojewski* (1921), 45/ET: 50.

2   Trace, *Dostoevsky and the Brothers Karamazov*, 97

problems of the human condition. But he was well aware of the dangers of corrupted religion, especially political and sociological belief systems that mimicked religion—for example, socialism. *Religion* and *faith* were often seen dialectically by Dostoevsky. And he was well aware, as we have seen, of the appropriation of religion to bolster self-righteousness in the cultured and educated classes as compared to the simple faith of the ordinary Russian people—the peasants. Religion when it became corrupt was evil to him. For example, the Parable of the Pharisee and the Tax Collector[3]—the proud Pharisee who is only too aware of the public's gaze as he prays loudly and confidently and informs all of the size of his charitable donations and his fasting; by comparison, the tax collector bows his head and stands afar off, barely entering the Jerusalem Temple, pleading to God for mercy as he is a sinner. This parable resonated with Dostoevsky's criticism of those who trusted in themselves that they were righteous and regarded others who did not practice public religion with contempt. This is comparable with the antinomy between the characters of Marmeladov and Lúzhin in *Crime and Punishment*: Marmeladov's drunken confession of unworthiness in his adaptation of the Parable of the Sheep and the Goats to the pub landlord as compared to Lúzhin's self-reliance and respectability as a society lawyer who believes in the innate goodness of mankind whilst denying the dark side of his own personality. Again, this antinomy could only be resolved in the eschaton—only God in Christ knew the secrets of all hearts.

2. DOSTOEVSKY'S DIALECTICAL CRITICISM OF RELIGION

Dostoevsky is an early proponent of the school of suspicion[4] that criticizes and questions religion. However, unlike many liberal humanists and atheistic academics in the twentieth century, he is critical of religion *theistically*, that is, from the perspective of God, and *evangelically* from the perspective of the gospel: God for Dostoevsky transcends religion. Nietzsche and Freud, father figures in many ways of the school of suspicion, are to be considered atheist; however, Dostoevsky is a believer, a Christian. The European Enlightenment produced a number of critics who throughout the ensuing nineteenth century produced significant

3   Luke 18:9–14
4   See, Ward, "Dostoevsky and the Hermeneutics of Suspicion," 270–83.

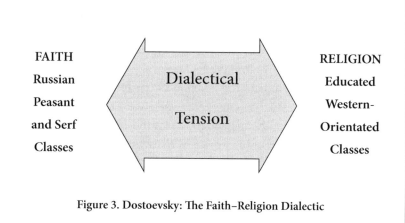

Figure 3. Dostoevsky: The Faith–Religion Dialectic

Diagram showing the tension which was never resolved in his work between on the one hand the ordinary Russian peasants, most of whom were rural and uneducated, and, on the other, the urban, Western-orientated, educated and cultivated, classes of, principally, St. Petersburg.

theories of religion, from the purely psychological explanations of Freud to the anthropological work of Frazer,[5] and from the Christological skepticism of Strauss to the atheist projections of Feuerbach. The unifying factor was reductive: religion and "gods" were seen as products of cultural evolution, or of survival drives in individuals, or the communal in the form of a society protecting itself. From a theological perspective, the work of Ludwig Andreas Feuerbach (1804–72) is of significance to our investigations. The young Dostoevsky, in his theologically formative years, read him and took his ideas on board. Feuerbach, who was initially a Hegelian, moved on to formulate his own projectionist theories. He claimed that his movement from Hegelianism to these theories was the logical development of Kant and Schleiermacher (who unlike Feuerbach were theists). Feuerbach argued that if Kant and Schleiermacher were correct, then all of our supposed knowledge of God was merely an enlargement of ideas about our experiences and ourselves. He built on a post-Kantian belief that we could not know the world in itself and that our minds contribute to a conception of what is. He accepted the Kantian

---

5   Frazer, *The Golden Bough*—an anthropological study of religious culture across the world.

belief that we impose categories in our minds on phenomenal objects; furthermore, he concluded that humans cannot possess knowledge about noumenal reality, though he took this one step further and doubted the existence of noumenal reality, especially the supernatural. Feuerbach's writings were to have a profound effect on Marx and Engels; his theories were used to help formulate the concept of existential materialism (the importance of this will become clear when we examine Dostoevsky's critique of socialism in The Legend of the Grand Inquisitor). Feuerbach's thinking is encapsulated in his work *The Essence of Christianity* (1841) in which he wrote, "God is himself the realized wish of the heart, the wish exalted to the certainty of its fulfillment[;] . . . the secret of theology is nothing else than anthropology—the knowledge of God is nothing else than the knowledge of man."[6] Human-god-speak and religious experience, to Feuerbach, is therefore nothing more than the externalization of human experience, abstracted desire.

Published in 1841, Feuerbach's *Essence of Christianity* was taken up by modern thinkers all over Europe and in St. Petersburg—which was the most Europeanized (Frankophile) of Russian cities. The burgeoning middle class and the cultured intellectuals in St. Petersburg were either in one of two camps—the Westerners or the Slavophiles. The latter were more traditional, conservative, and religious, and were nationalistic with regards to *mother Rus* (Russia); the former took on board the affectation of speaking French and sought to identify with everything associated with Western European culture—novelists and poets, sociologists and political thinkers, philosophers, artists, and scientists. Religion in Russia in the mid-nineteenth century was in many ways subservient to political authority—which merely added fuel to the arguments of the Westerners.

Into this world came Dostoevsky to attend the St. Petersburg academy and to graduate as an army engineer. However, he drank in the European influence and as we have seen fell under the influence of Belinsky. Dostoevsky, as Boyce Gibson puts it, "[though] uncertain in foreign languages, he had mastered the essentials of the Hegelian left, especially Feuerbach. *The Essence of Christianity* is always a work to be reckoned with in the study of Dostoevsky, and whether he read it or not is beside the point, he was profoundly influenced. . . . [H]e took over Feuerbach in the warmer Russian style which Belinsky had provided for

6   Feuerbach, *Essence of Christianity*, 121, 207

him."[7] For the impressionable young Dostoevsky any statement about God was to be seen as a statement about humanity—this meant atheism. Belinsky took an affirmation of human solidarity from Feuerbach and wedded it to the group's socialist leanings. In 1845, Dostoevsky ceased attending Holy Communion, though he became something of a "Christian atheist"—"Dostoevsky remained devoted to the figure of Christ. That was not wholly inconsistent with his new convictions. . . . [S]o long as Christ can be delivered of his shroud of deity he can be revered as the best man ever. . . . [Dostoevsky held his] atheism concealed as sociological description, and Christ raised to the height of human excellence."[8] This was the belief system of Dostoevsky when he rallied the Petrashevsky circle around him, was arrested, and with the others sentenced to death by execution for political sedition in 1849. He was a thoroughgoing socialist, religious projectionist, veiled self-confessed atheist, convinced of the ultimate value of Western culture. And he held to the writings of, first, Belinsky, and then the Europeans he valued most: Auguste Comte (1798–1857), the initiator of sociology and scientific ethics (representing French-utopianism), the poet/dramatist and philosopher Friedrich von Schiller (1759–1805), and the theologian Ludwig Feuerbach (these latter two representing the German-philosophical-Idealist tradition). (Although Dostoevsky did not read Hegel himself, he knew Hegelian philosophy well through Belinsky.) The belief in religious projections would stay with him, but he would add to it the transcendent God, the one true God beyond religion. Dostoevsky was not a systematic theologian so he did not set out this belief in the manner in which professional theologians did. God was wholly other, but reveals himself in Jesus Christ—this revelation was not, however, dependent on anything human. Religion at its best was to be seen as a response to God's self-revelation, but religion was still to be considered human. This was very much a view that Dostoevsky would have concurred with in his middle (1860s) and mature (1870s) period of writing after his return from Siberia, though he did not articulate it as such. Undergirding valid religion, indeed the focus and heart of religion for Dostoevsky is the Christ: Dostoevsky saw this as the "Russian Christ," whom he saw in the ordinary Russian people, their lives, their sufferings, and their joys.

---

7   Gibson, *The Religion of Dostoevsky*, 10; also Dostoevsky, *The Diary of a Writer.*

8   Ibid, 12–13; also Dostoevsky, *The Diary of a Writer.*

Dostoevsky attempts to articulate something like this in his mature writings. In looking at some of these, we will understand his criticism of religion—that is, a criticism of religion *when it worked against the gospel.* This is a critique of religion and the church seen as human culture, piety seen as social respectability. To this end we will briefly look at three of his works: *Notes From Underground, The Idiot,* and *The Dream of a Ridiculous Man* in relation to key elements of Dostoevsky's critique of religion. The novel *Notes From Underground* will be looked at in relationship to Nietzsche and the "Idea" underpinning Dostoevsky's theological ethics; *The Idiot* in the context of Dostoevsky's portrayal of holiness and sanctification and how these characteristics relate to religion; *The Dream of a Ridiculous Man* in relationship to the Christian doctrine of the *fall* and original sin.

i. Notes From Underground and Nietzsche—the "Idea"

Notes from Underground (literally *podpolya*—"beneath the floor") was published in 1864, five years after Dostoevsky's return from Siberia. On the surface it appears totally unchristian—save that what Dostoevsky was presenting was the logical outcome of rejecting the gospel: humanity without God. Dostoevsky's theological ethics are about the human rejection of God and the psychological state humanity falls into. The work is about a retired civil servant living alone in a bleak, grey, nihilistic world. This is an early example of the dictum presented by Ivan Karamazov that without God there is no morality, no humanity—anything goes, there are no constraints on human behavior. *Notes from Underground* is a portrait of the weakness and fragmentation, psychologically, of the human soul. The "underground man" (the narrator) purposely lives in squalid conditions, loveless and with a corrupt and self-serving will that is all that is left of the human psyche: that is, the ego. This is the logical conclusion of liberal atheism and humanism. Any love for humanity is a fraud without God. To Dostoevsky European idealism was just such a fraud—just "intellectual prattle."[9] The reason for all the dusty nihilism of the underground man is to show the necessity for Christ and for faith, and the struggle in an individual's soul between good and evil, between love and ego. Religion is permissible in developing this inner struggle and in developing faith in the Christ—but Dostoevsky saw little of this

9   Gibson *The Religion of Dostoevsky,* 84.

amongst the respectable Christian classes in St. Petersburg and Moscow. Indeed many of these people, like the character of Madame Yepanchina, would have gone out of their way to avoid thinking about these issues and considered themselves innately good (contrary to Mark 10:18[10]); by contrast, this work builds on what he experienced of prison life in Siberia (the prison experiences were initially the subject of *Notebooks from the House of the Dead*, published in 1862).

What is important for our study about *Notes from Underground* are two points: first, the work contains the psychological basis of Dostoevsky's entire study of postlapsarian humanity (a condition that for Dostoevsky still applied to his contemporaries—Christian or otherwise); second, the work, along with much of the rest of Dostoevsky's corpus (with the exception of *The Brothers Karamazov*), had a profound influence on the German philosopher Friedrich Nietzsche, who unlike many German Idealists and European humanitarians saw that if people were to abandon Christianity then the Christian basis for human behavior went as well. All that was left was what we have seen of Dostoevsky's underground man: the corrupt will, fragmenting into alienated insanity.

This understanding led Nietzsche to propound his theory of will-to-power. In *Twilight of the Idols*, Nietzsche acknowledges the profound debt he owed to Dostoevsky.

> The testimony of Dostoevsky is relevant to this problem—Dostoevsky, the only psychologist, incidentally, from whom I had something to learn; he ranks among the most beautiful strokes of fortune in my life, even more than my discovery of Stendhal. This profound human being, who was ten times right in his low estimate of the superficial Germans, lived for a long time among the convicts in Siberia—hardened criminals for whom there was no way back to society—and found them very different from what he himself had expected: they were carved out of just about the best, hardest, and most valuable wood that grows anywhere on Russian soil.[11]

The difference from our perspective is that Nietzsche saw this reality and followed the path of atheism, which logically led to moral nihilism. Dostoevsky's message was that this is the limit of human freedom without

---

10   Mark 10:18—"Jesus said to him, 'Why do you call me good? No one is good but God alone'" (Luke 18:19).

11   Nietzsche, *Die Götzen-Dämmerung*, 99.

"The Idea"

The Path of Unrighteousness
The Theological Ethics Underpinning Dostoevsky's Work

"The Idea" is initially found in *Notes from Underground* (1864);
then it forms the central plan in *Crime and Punishment* (1866);
it is brought to its fullest expression in *The Brothers Karamazov* (1877/8–80)

Actions/decisions:

to disbelieve . . .
in God, or to reject God for one's own agenda

to be . . .
therefore, as God (*eritis sicut Deus*)

to decide
. . . to redefine human morality and ethics according to one's own principles
(i.e., Raskolnikov's Napoleonic agenda in *Crime and Punishment*)

to storm heaven
. . . in attempting to redefine human morality/ethics (i.e., the "Tower of Babel")

to realise
. . . that without God there are as a result no limits
or constraints on human behaviour

to rebel
. . . even in the face of theism,
to "Return the Ticket of Life to God" (insanity/suicide)
i.e., Ivan Karamazov and Smerdyakov in *The Brothers Karamazov*,
Stavrogin in *The Demons*, Svidrigaylov in *Crime and Punishment*,

. . . because of the gravity, the weight and the delusions, of sin

Figure 4 Dostoevsky: "The Idea" 1.
Dostoevsky's "The Idea," the path of unrighteousness, and the theological ethics
that underpin "The Idea" as found in the in major works.

"The Idea"
The Path of Unrighteousness
The Theological Ethics Underpinning Dostoevsky's Work

From the novels of Dostoevsky "The Idea" is initially found in
Notes from Underground; then it forms the central plan in *Crime and Punishment*
to be further expounded in *The Demons*; then it is brought to its fullest expression
in *The Brothers Karamazov*.

This is "The Idea" that if Christianity is abandoned then so too is Christian
morality; the underground man is an example of the depths of nihilism and
alienation in the human psyche without God, as is Raskolnikov.

"The Idea" is taken to its logical conclusion in *The Brothers Karamazov*
in the statement of Ivan Karamazov that without God there are no constraints on
human behaviour, human will. This is the theological ethic for Dostoevsky of the
anti-Christ represented by the titanic intellectual sins of the man-god
(the antithesis of the God-man, Jesus Christ).

For an explication of "The Idea" by Dostoevsky, see, for instance:

Crime and Punishment, Pt. 3, Ch. 6, especially, 274
Raskolnikov expounding Napoleon's freedom to enact his will.

The Brothers Karamazov, Pt. 1, Bk. 2, Ch. 6, specifically 69
Dimitri and Fr. Paissy on Ivan's theory that everything is permitted.

The Brothers Karamazov, Pt. 1, Bk. 3, Ch. 8, specifically 133–4
Ivan's theories and his "no-god."

The Brothers Karamazov, Pt. 2, Bk. 5, Ch. 6, specifically 272
Smerdyakov's appropriation of Ivan's expounding of "The Idea."

The Brothers Karamazov, Pt. 4, Bk. 11, Ch. 8, specifically 625
Smerdyakov quoting Ivan's "everything is permitted" back to him.

**"You used to be brave once, sir, you used to say 'Everything
is permitted,' sir, and now you've got so frightened!"
Smerdyakov murmured to Ivan . . .**

Figure 5. Dostoevsky: "The Idea" 2.
Dostoevsky's "The Idea," the path of unrighteousness, and the theological ethics
that underpin "The Idea" as found in the in major works.

God—all that is left is the necessity for Christ and the slender hope of faith. Unfortunately the Czar's official censor expunged the passage that made this explicit. Dostoevsky writing to his brother made his frustration felt:

> It would have been better not to print the last chapter but one at all (it is the most important, where the essential idea is expressed), than to print it as it is, that is, with cobbled-up sentences and full of contradictions[:] . . . those brutes of censors—where I made a mock of everything and sometimes blasphemed for form's sake, that is passed, but where I deduced from all this the necessity of faith in Christ—that is suppressed![12]

He never restored the passages that had been removed and there is no record of it in the archive of his work. However, he went on to present the idea more explicitly in *Crime and Punishment* two years later. To achieve the understanding of the absolute necessity of Christ and the inability of the human psyche to solve the problem of life on its own Dostoevsky had to cut through human culture and religion.

ii. The Idiot and Holiness: Iurodivaia/Smireniye

We have examined Dostoevsky's *The Idiot* already and have seen how there is a dialectical tension between the innate holiness of Prince Myshkin and the pious religiosity of the respectable Christian classes in St. Petersburg. Of crucial importance to Russian Orthodox theology is the idea of a *holy fool*, the *fool for God*—someone poor and foolish by the standards of this world, but not the next, not compared to eternity and the redeemed. This is central to Dostoevsky's construction of *The Idiot*. There are a number of points that relate to the criticism of religion that we can consider here.

First, *The Idiot* is about *Christlikeness*, not the name of *Christian*. Christlikeness is about the adjective, not the noun: in German, *Christlich* (adv.), rather than *Christin* (noun); unfortunately in English the word *Christian* is used for both the adjective and the noun. Claiming the name of Christian is seen as a religious act; being *Christ-like* is not necessarily a religious act—the distinction is clarified, qualified, by holiness/ sanctification. Holiness is something that is measured from outside of a person (self-effacing humility is an essential characteristic); therefore

---

12   Dostoevsky to his brother, April 5, 1864 (March 26, 1864 old calendar), in Coulson, *Dostoevsky, a Self-Portrait*, 124.

holiness/sanctification is eschatological because the measure in the final analysis is Christ. Therefore, this move into holiness/sanctification is generated by the Holy Spirit and is the rekindling of the *imago Christi*, and as such is a gradual process.

Second, a dialectic between religion and holiness/sanctification: On the one hand, Madame Yepanchina, the paradigm of the cultured (though aristocratic) religious classes, attends church and passes judgment on those she considers unchristian (whilst proclaiming to her friends and relatives that we are all Christian). On the other hand, by contrast, Myshkin is not consciously religious. He attends church occasionally, but not to ingratiate himself with God, but rather, for example, to extend his sympathy to those grieving at the funeral of General Ivolgin. Myshkin is an example that religiousness diminishes as holiness/sanctification increases. Myshkin is not a conscious practitioner of religion, not a regular churchgoer, but he exudes the love of God. In the study notebooks for *The Idiot* Dostoevsky wrote in capital letters *"MYSHKIN IS THE CHRIST"*;[13] in addition, he is to be considered "the perfect human being,"[14] and as such he is predestined to fail.

Third, those attracted to Myshkin are irritated at his unworldliness (e.g., Aglaya, to whom he is engaged for a while). By contrast, Rogozhin, the drunken wealthy rogue, and Nastasya, who was abused systematically by her childhood protector and is now a mature woman and sexual predator, both recognize his holiness and implicitly accept him and try to do him no harm.

Fourth, Dostoevsky uses important Russian words to convey Myshkin's holiness: *iurodivaia* (*holy fool* or *God's fool*, which has a strong tradition in Russian Orthodox theology), but there is also *smireniye* and *sostradanie*. *Smireniye* involves the curbing of the passions; it is characterized by humility and spiritual peace and is considered the opposite of pride, self-assertion, and spiritual revolt. There is a degree of *submergence* in *smireniye* in the sense of knuckling under and allowing events and people to press, even oppress, and accepting the pressure and suffering that results. In the case of Myshkin, this *humility/smireniye* is characterized by restraint, self-denial. The character of Myshkin exemplifies *smireniye*—a *smireniye* verging on pressing, oppression. Why

13   Dostoevsky, *Notebooks for The Idiot*, 198 and 201.
14   Ibid., 14, 198.

this *smireniye?*—because of love. Dostoevsky's work is about the message of love conveyed through people—*sostradanie* (sympathy verging on the empathetic). In the notebooks for *The Idiot*, he wrote, "Compassion is the most important and perhaps the only law for human life[:] . . . compassion, that is the whole [the essence] of Christianity."[15] Dostoevsky's portrayal of Myshkin has been seen as the failure of Christianity by critics—both Soviet and Western literary critics.[16] Ironically this criticism is a compliment—it acknowledges the limits of religion. Holiness/sanctification—the *imago Christi*, as distinct from religion—is important; what is more, holiness for Dostoevsky is not of this world. Therefore, the world will judge holiness to be a failure, and also religion as failure if it reflects this holiness (the holiness of the *iurodivaia* characterized by *smireniye*); when religion reflects worldly standards it is considered a success. Myshkin's failure is a negation—a gospel paradox—and stands to condemn the worldliness of religion.

Fifth, suffering is a hallmark of the *iurodivaia* and in the example of Myshkin it is his epilepsy that sets him apart. Myshkin's naivety and innocence is in part caused by his epilepsy, which marks him as different so that he does not play the games that other men and women play—pseudo-Machiavellian politics and sexually charged relationships. The more stressed Myshkin becomes at the gossiping and destructive behavior among the people he associates with the more his seizures increase, to the extent that when he sees that Rogozhin has murdered Nastasya (Mary Magdalene?), whom he would have done anything to save, the epilepsy overwhelms him (*status epilepticus*) and he returns to the asylum. It is important to remember that for Dostoevsky epilepsy is not automatically a mark of holiness. The other epileptic character in his mature work is Smerdyakov (*The Brothers Karamazov*), but he is presented as evil, deranged, and twists everything he hears to promote his own agenda; he even fakes an epileptic seizure to give himself an alibi for the evening of the murder. Only when he is confronted by the nihilistic thinking that characterized his deliberate murder of his father does he then commit suicide, ostensibly to prevent Ivan Karamazov (his half-brother) reporting his, Smerdyakov's, guilt at the trial of Dimitri (their half-brother by yet another woman) for their father's murder.

15   Ibid., 192, and 395.
16   Gibson, *The Religion of Dostoevsky*, 114.

iii. The Idiot and Holiness: The Dead Christ

The relationship between holiness/sanctification and religion is illustrated well in Part Two, chapter 4 of *The Idiot*. On entering Rogozhin's house, Myshkin is almost paralyzed by the sight of a copy of Holbein's painting, *The Dead Christ* (which we encountered earlier—Anna Dostoevsky's reminiscence when her husband saw the painting in the museum in Basel).[17] Holbein used as a model, a corpse, which had suffered greatly in death. What Dostoevsky projects into Myshkin's reaction was his own experience upon seeing this painting when he was on his European tour in 1867. Anna's journal entry, describing the deep impact on her husband at witnessing the painting in Basel Museum is very similar to Myshkin's reaction to the painting in Part 4, chapter 2: "That picture! That picture!" cried Myshkin, struck by a sudden idea. "Why, a man's faith might be ruined by looking at that picture!" Anna Grigoryevna's diary entry for August 12, 1867 reads: "it struck him with terrific force, and he said to me then, 'A painting like that can make you lose faith.'"[18] Why? Why did Dostoevsky say this—and repeat it through the mouth of Myshkin? The answer may be that the painting represents the point where religion must cross over completely to faith. The painting presses on the viewer, leaving the viewer in no doubt as to the brutality and depths of depravity that the human is capable of—from the Christian perspective, this is what has been done to God, when God sought our salvation. This is at the heart of an existential gospel. Further, in the narrative context, Myshkin is in some way experiencing a premonition of his own suffering and destruction at the hands of those he is trying to save.

17   Hans Holbein the Younger (b. 1497, Augsburg. Germany, d. 1543, London), *The Body of the Dead Christ in the Tomb* 1521, Oil on wood, 30.5 x 200 cm, Kunstmuseum, Öffentliche Kunstsammlung, Basle. It appears that Holbein intended to stress the miracle of resurrection and its imminence, since the minutely observed level of decay in the body's wounds suggests that Christ's body is seen three days after death, therefore close to the point of resurrection. A tradition around the production of the painting claims that a drowned body was fished out of the Rhine, which then served the painter as a model for the figure of Christ. Even if it is only a legend, it is a testimony to the terrifying realism of Holbein's depiction of a corpse brutalised by extreme torture and death, and in a state of rigor mortis and decay.

For details and images search *Wikipedia* using "The Body of the Dead Christ in the Tomb" (specifically: https://en.wikipedia.org/wiki/The_Body_of_the_Dead_Christ_in_the_Tomb). See also, *The Web Gallery of Art,* www.wga.hu (specifically, http://www.wga.hu/frames-e.html?/html/h/holbein/hans_y/1525/03deadch.html).

18   Anna Dostoevsky, *Dostoevsky Reminiscences*, ET by Beatrice Stillman (1975), 393.

3. THE RELIGION-FAITH DIALECTIC

i. Rogozhin's Atheism?

Rogozhin, after Myshkin's encounter with the Holbein painting, asks him if he is religious: does he believe in God?[19] Myshkin does not answer the question in a straightforward manner; indeed, it is similar to the encounters in the Gospels between Jesus and individuals. Myshkin's answer is parabolic (that is, it is reminiscent of the way Jesus answered questions somewhat obliquely with a story, a parable):

> "Lef Nicolaievitch," said Rogozhin, after a pause, during which the two walked along a little further, "I have long wished to ask you, do you believe in God? . . . I meant to ask you before—many people are unbelievers nowadays, especially Russians, I have been told. You ought to know—you've lived abroad."[20]

Myshkin then comments about the picture and how it could upset a person's faith—thereby setting the content of his answer: faith above religion. Myshkin continued, "'As to faith,' he said, smiling, and evidently unwilling to leave Rogozhin in this state—'as to faith, I had four curious conversations in two days, a week or so ago.'"[21]

Myshkin, voicing Dostoevsky's own beliefs and concerns, then recounts his four stories—parabolic comments on religion and faith. The first is about an encounter on a train where he fell into conversation with a stranger who was bright, clever, kind, and considerate, but claimed to be an atheist—"He doesn't believe in God, and he talked a good deal about it, but all the while it appeared to me that he was speaking outside the subject."[22] There was a clear dichotomy between what the man was and his belief system. Myshkin then contrasts this with the story of two people who were great friends. One of them spots that the other has a silver watch and chain. Neither was really poverty stricken, they were respectably poor but comfortable—

> [One of them] was by no means a thief . . . but this watch so fascinated him that he could not restrain himself. He took a knife,

---

19   Dostoevsky, *The Idiot*, 218.

20   Ibid.

21   Ibid., 219.

22   Ibid.

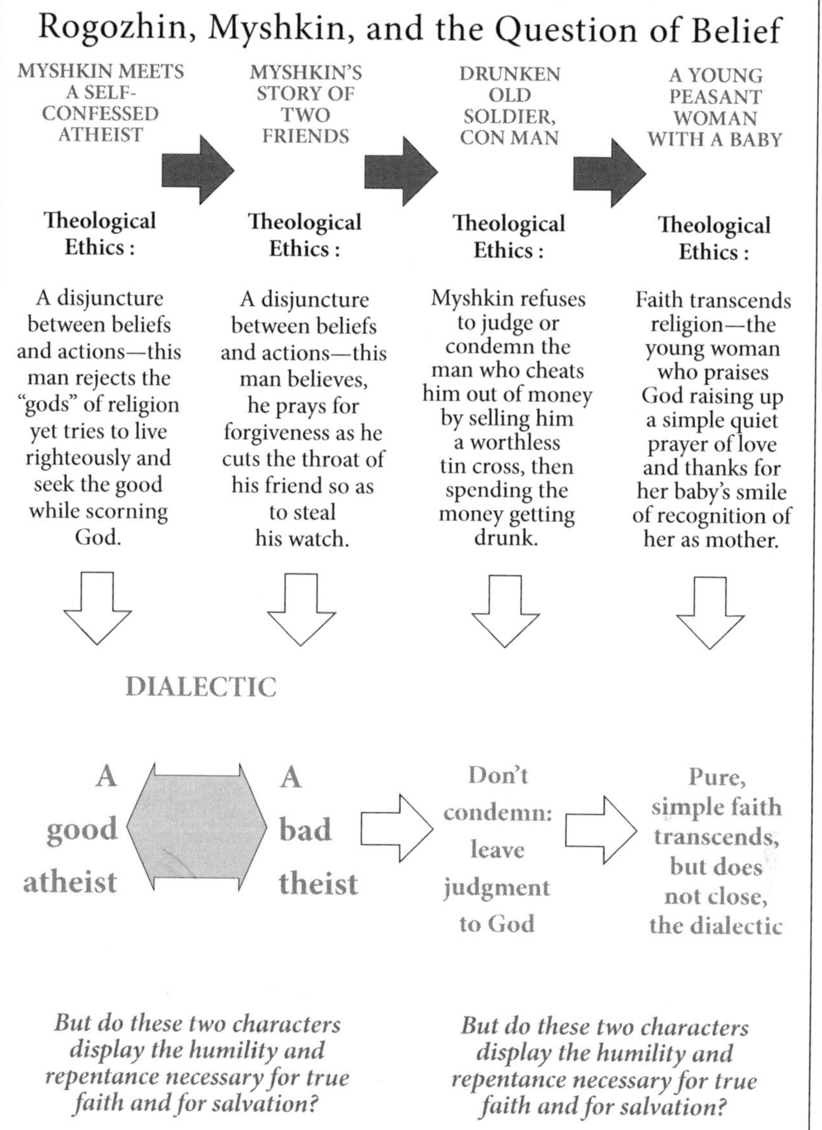

Rogozhin, Myshkin, and the Question of Belief

MYSHKIN MEETS A SELF-CONFESSED ATHEIST	MYSHKIN'S STORY OF TWO FRIENDS	DRUNKEN OLD SOLDIER, CON MAN	A YOUNG PEASANT WOMAN WITH A BABY
Theological Ethics :	**Theological Ethics :**	**Theological Ethics :**	**Theological Ethics :**
A disjuncture between beliefs and actions—this man rejects the "gods" of religion yet tries to live righteously and seek the good while scorning God.	A disjuncture between beliefs and actions—this man believes, he prays for forgiveness as he cuts the throat of his friend so as to steal his watch.	Myshkin refuses to judge or condemn the man who cheats him out of money by selling him a worthless tin cross, then spending the money getting drunk.	Faith transcends religion—the young woman who praises God raising up a simple quiet prayer of love and thanks for her baby's smile of recognition of her as mother.

DIALECTIC

A good atheist	A bad theist	Don't condemn: leave judgment to God	Pure, simple faith transcends, but does not close, the dialectic

But do these two characters display the humility and repentance necessary for true faith and for salvation?

But do these two characters display the humility and repentance necessary for true faith and for salvation?

Figure 6. Prince Myshkin's Answer to Rogozhin
Diagram showing the progression of Myshkin's parabolic answer to Rogozhin's question: "Do you believe in God?" Human religion is seen as dialectical, judgment is with God—simple faith transcends the question and the dialectic by appealing to God in simple prayer and love. This is a well-constructed progression in theological ethics (i.e., beliefs and actions) by Dostoevsky.

and when his friend turned his back, he came up softly behind, raised his eyes to heaven, crossed himself, and saying earnestly— "God forgive me, for Christ's sake!" He cut his friend's throat like a sheep, and took the watch.[23]

Rogozhin's responded:

"Oh, I like that! That beats anything!" he [Rogozhin] cried convulsively, panting for breath. "One is an absolute unbeliever; the other is such a thorough-going believer that he murders his friend to the tune of a prayer! Oh, prince, prince, that's too good for anything! You can't have invented it. It's the best thing I've heard!"[24]

Hence we have the relative value of religious belief. Simply declaring belief in God is not enough; likewise denial of God's existence is not irrefutably damming (particularly as it raises the question of which particular "god" a person does or does not believe in)—holiness/ sanctification is what is important. The remaining two parables/stories qualify this. The third is about an old drunken soldier who cons Myshkin into buying what he claims is a solid silver cross on a chain, but it is really only made of cheap tin. Myshkin buys it, laments that the old soldier has probably gone off to drink the proceeds of the sale, but comments, "I thought, 'I will wait awhile before I condemn this Judas. Only God knows what may be hidden in the hearts of drunkards.'"[25] The fourth and final parable/story defines Myshkin's answer:

I came across a poor woman, carrying a child—a baby of some six weeks old. The mother was quite a girl herself. The baby was smiling up at her, for the first time in its life, just at that moment; and while I watched the woman she suddenly crossed herself, oh, so devoutly! "What is it, my good woman," I asked her . . . (I was never but asking questions then!) "Exactly as is a mother's joy when her baby smiles for the first time into her eyes, so is God's joy when one of His children turns and prays to Him for the first time, with all his heart!" This is what that poor woman said to me, almost word for word; and such a deep, refined, truly religious thought it was—a thought in which the whole essence of Christianity was expressed in one flash—that is, the recognition of

23   Ibid.
24   Ibid.
25   Ibid., 220.

God as our Father, and of God's joy in people as His own children, which is the chief idea of Christ."[26]

So joy and love are the touchstone of true religion. In recounting the stories Myshkin has told Rogozhin of his implicit belief in God, more pertinently what God values and wants from *his* creation, *his* children: love and joy, characteristics of holiness/sanctification.

Rogozhin's response to these stories is to insist that the two of them exchange crosses (an ancient Russian Orthodox tradition which binds the two as spiritual brothers). Rogozhin insists that he exchanges his expensive cross for the cheap tin cross that Myshkin bought from the old soldier.

ii. The Story of Marie

The other side of this, the negative side of religion, has already been established early in *The Idiot* in the story of Marie.[27] Myshkin recounts this when the Yepanchin girls ask the Prince, on their first meeting, if he has ever been in love (this is shortly after his return to Russia from being treated for his epilepsy in Switzerland). His answer is "no," but with a qualified "yes." Though a "yes" not in the manner in which they mean (*eros*). His love was more to do with *agapē* or *philia* (altruistic love or friendship). In answering yes he then recounts the story of Marie and how he loved her. Marie is presented as an example of *iurodivaia* characterized by *smireniye*—her life and death at the hands of the mean-spirited, evil-minded villagers sets the scene for the whole novel and particularly what happens to Nastasya. Dostoevsky in the notebooks for *The Idiot* comments that Marie was crucial for understanding the story—that like Mitya in *The Brothers Karamazov*, it is not primarily licentiousness in itself that destroys people, but bad ideas. And here we have bad religion: Marie is a poor girl of about seventeen who works slavishly and obediently for her cantankerous mother in a small Swiss mountain village; Myshkin comes to know her whilst walking the mountains and then living for a while in the village after being treated for his epilepsy at a Swiss clinic. One day a traveler seduces her, takes her away, and then dumps her. She returns to the village in bare feet, penniless, and to the disgrace of her mother and the villagers who taunt her for losing her virtue; they then encourage the

26   Ibid., 220–21.
27   Ibid. Pt. 1, ch. 6.

children to pelt her with mud as she hobbles about in her rags—"Sometimes on Sundays, if they [the men of the village] were drunk enough, they used to throw her a penny or two, into the mud, and Marie would silently pick up the money. She had begun to spit blood at that time." Then the local minister[28] decided to start preaching against her whilst conducting her mother's funeral: "The parson, a young fellow ambitious of becoming a great preacher, began his sermon and pointed to Marie. 'There,' he said, 'there is the cause of the death of this venerable woman'—(which was a lie, because she had been ill for at least two years)—'there she stands before you, and dares not lift her eyes from the ground, because she knows that the finger of God is upon her.'" The children of the village turn against her at the behest of their parents and the village schoolteacher. But Myshkin teaches them not to—to look kindly on her (the children are as subject to the *fall* as the adults, but are presented as more open to change, more capable of kindness than adults). By the time Marie dies of consumption, the children and Myshkin love her deeply, do everything to try to help her, but the men and women of the village, and the minister, still condemn her as a fallen woman and self-righteously go to church— and they are deeply concerned about the influence of Myshkin on their children! They are blind to the sanctity of the *iurodivaia*. At no point does Marie answer them back or challenge their prejudiced beliefs, such is her restraint, her submerged humility (*smireniye*). In the story of Marie, Dostoevsky is dialectically setting-off holiness/sanctification against formal self-righteous religion. The villagers could have helped Marie, when it was clear that she has repented of the foolishness of her actions. Marie's behavior was not how she should have behaved before God, but neither was the prejudiced, vindictive attitude of the villagers. No one is righteous before God: to humbly refuse to partake in these human power games on the world's terms is the only way forward; this is the way of the holy fool, characterized by humility and self-denial.

---

28   The minister is either Lutheran or Reformed (most probably the latter) and would have been the result of what Dostoevsky witnessed of judgmental Pietistic preaching in Switzerland and Germany from his winter tour of 1862—see, Dostoevsky, *Winter Notes on Summer Impressions*, published in *Vremya*, Feb–Mar 1863, also, Dostoevsky, *Diary of a Writer*.

4. SONYA AND RASKOLNIKOV:
A DIALECTIC OF SIN AND GRACE

i. To Believe . . . or Not To Believe, That is the Question

We have established that a central idea in the theology underpinning the novels of Dostoevsky is this *diastasis* between world and God. The characters in his novels do not sit cozily in religious piety, mistaking (as Dostoevsky saw it) their own self-love for an experience of God, but are broken and fallen sinners, wretched in the irrational nihilism of their depravity. Change happens: after an existential decision to turn, to alter the way of thinking that has brought them to the state they find themselves in, they live different, "resurrected" lives, but they are still human, still mortal, still fallen, though reformed. The world is still the world and God is still God—transcendent and other. This change, this decision, must be seen as generated by the Holy Spirit—previeniently.

The central character in *Crime and Punishment* is a young student, an intellectual, originally from the country, who having dropped out of university is living in a squalid garret in the poorest district of St. Petersburg: Rodion Romanovich Raskolnikov. We noted earlier his obsession with the idea of the superman, the superiority of the rebellious intellectual: he believes that there are some human beings who have the right to transcend existing law and custom so as to establish new laws and customs, Napoleon being his favorite example—in the story he has even published an article in a law journal proposing his theory:

> I maintain in my article that all . . . , well, legislators and leaders of men, such as Lycurgus, Solon, Mahomet, Napoleon, and so on, were all without exception criminals, from the very fact that, making a new law, they transgressed the ancient one, handed down from their ancestors and held sacred by the people, and they did not stop short at bloodshed either, if that bloodshed—often of innocent persons fighting bravely in defense of ancient law—were of use to their cause. It's remarkable, in fact, that the majority, indeed, of these benefactors and leaders of humanity were guilty of terrible carnage. In short, I maintain that all great men or even men a little out of the common, that is to say capable of giving some new word, must from their very nature be criminals—more or less, of course. [29]

29   Dostoevsky, *Crime and Punishment*, Bk 3, ch. 5.

Therefore, because Raskolnikov considers himself to be extraordinary, he conceives the design of murdering Alyona Ivanova not primarily to steal from her, but to rid the world of what he regards as a louse! But it all goes wrong—having smashed an axe into the elderly pawnbroker's head he is caught trying to mop-up the blood around her corpse by the early return of Lizaveta, her younger sister. He is forced to kill the sister in the same way to cover his crime.

We established earlier how the righteousness of God presses in on him. His conscience will not allow him to settle, it convicts him of the depravity and awfulness of his crime. He is plagued by hallucination and guilt-ridden nightmares for weeks after the murders. Salvation comes in the form of Sofya Semyonovna Marmeladova (Sonya): a prostitute. Sonya is responsible for bringing in an income to feed and clothe her consumptive stepmother and her stepbrothers and stepsister. Her father having lost his job with the civil service through drinking, she becomes the sole breadwinner—no other paid employment is open to her. It is the pressure and witness of Sonya, the seventeen-year-old prostitute, on one occasion through her reading the story of the raising of Lazarus to him from St. John's Gospel, that contributes to a cataclysmic change in Raskolnikov's thinking. He admits his guilt publicly, confesses to the authorities, and takes his punishment: exile to a Siberian prison camp. Sonya follows and waits for him to serve his sentence: this, as we have established, is for Dostoevsky, resurrection as it is woven into the heart of existence.

ii. Trespass and Reparation

Crime and Punishment is about sin and guilt, about human fallenness, about the nihilism resulting from bad decisions. The Russian title of the book is *Prestuplenie i nakazanie*. *Prestuplenie* means literally, a *stepping over*, a *transgression*, therefore it relates to the English verb to *transgress*—or, more pertinently, *to trespass*. *Nakazanie* relates to the English noun *reparation* (or verb, if there is one—*to reparate*).[30] The work is therefore about humanity when it oversteps the limits imposed not just by convention and human law, but rationality and, ultimately, God's

---

30   The verb *nakazat*, from which is derived the noun *nakazanie*, can under certain circumstances be used for, *to order*, or *to instruct*, as well as relating to *punishment* and *reparation*: does not Sonya effectively instruct Raskolnikov?

law. The phrase *Prestuplenie i nakazanie* has been taken over by many world languages to mean *crime and punishment*—Dostoevsky has to a large extent given this phrase to the world! We must remember that in the original Russian the wording had these strong connotations of sin and transgression; trespass and atonement; guilt, expiation, and reparation— with obvious theological associations. It is also important to remember that the name Dostoevsky gave to this anti-hero was significant: *raskolnik* means literally a schismatic in Russian (from *raskol*—schism, primarily, then dissent, the related verb being *raskolot*—to split). Why is Raskolnikov a schismatic—because he separates humanity from God, his actions split, rend, humanity from God. Dostoevsky knew that to his Russian readers a schismatic was one representing a small group who had broken away from the Russian Orthodox Church—for example, the *Raskolniki* or Old Believers, who were members of a sect that broke away in the seventeenth-century. But what Dostoevsky was saying was that this man, this murderer and intellectual, is prepared to "sacrifice fellow human beings on the altar of theoretical premises and his own satanic pretensions to moral freedom";[31] furthermore, that this is "startlingly modern and by now distressingly familiar" [32] and is in many ways representative of the history of Western civilization in the twentieth century, and as such represents the schism brought about by the fall of humanity away from God through original sin.

iii. Atheism

Is Raskolnikov an atheist? Dostoevsky presents characters that are full of contradictions with regard to beliefs and ethics. The questions arise, in which "god" does someone not believe? or which "god" does another profess? For Dostoevsky atheists *might* (note the subjunctive) have a better grasp of the one true God as revealed, than polite respectable Christians; likewise both question whether pious Christian religion really did proclaim the gospel of God's forgiveness through Christ's redemption. These are polemical points. The terms atheist and atheism are likewise contentious. It is important to remember that this cautious

31   Leatherbarrow, "Introduction," in Dostoevsky, *Crime and Punishment*, xxvi. Much of this analysis of the title of *Crime and Punishment* is derived from Leatherbarrow's work.

32   Ibid.

respect for atheism served in distancing him from his theological and ecclesial heritage.

If Myshkin's parabolic answer to Rogozhin's question, "Do you believe in God or not?"[33] established a dialectical paradox with regard to theism/atheism, this is taken further with the story of Marie,[34] which, as we established earlier, pushes this dialectic between, on the one hand, simple partisan declarations of religious belief and, on the other, faith. Marie was the victim of religious prejudice and self-righteous moralizing by the local minister and his congregation because she loses her virtue and dies as an outcast, an untouchable. Marie was forced into the role of the village idiot, yet she exudes love, holiness, and forgiveness to all—reminiscent of a martyr or saint from the early church; this completes this paradox of human-centered religion established by Myshkin's parabolic answer to Rogozhin.

Is Raskolnikov an atheist? It is difficult to say—his belief system can be interpreted as such, but more pertinently it is characterized by rebellion. The more he rebels, the more he denies the love of God by his actions, the more he then dissolves into the nightmarish *surd*-like[35] nihilism of sin, the irrationality that flows from his belief system. For example, Raskolnikov affirms the existence of God in answer to Porfiry's questions (the investigating officer), yet earlier he derides Sonya's faith, the existence of her God, and the way this God has left her and her family in poverty and illness. Ivan Karamazov (*The Brothers Karamazov*) by contrast goes through what can be identified as various phases and types of so-called atheism, his theologoumena being characterized by rebellion against God more than logical atheism (the divine object of his fury being at times realistic, at others non-realistic). However, for Dostoevsky there is some value in atheism—it *might* not always lead to destruction and fragmentation; but conversely, self-confessed, so-called atheists, are to be seen as skating on thin ice and in many instances their beliefs will lead to their self-willed death and destruction in a self-generated hell: for many, the gates of hell are locked from the inside (by the condemned)

---

33   Dostoevsky, *The Idiot*, 218.

34   Ibid, Pt. 1 ch. 6, 67–76.

35   *Surd*-like: *surdus*, "deaf, dumb" is the Latin translation of the Greek *alogos* primarily without speech or word, however, also without reason, irrational. Theologically this is Raskolnikov's irrational nihilistic contradiction of the Word of God in Christ through his behaviour and beliefs.

while the gates of heaven stand wide open and welcoming. But a period of atheisn may lead to a clarification, a clearing out of false religious ideas leaving the individual open to God's grace. As we noted, the first story Myshkin recounts in his answer to Rogozhin was of a man who professed atheism but was honest and righteous in his heart and yearned for what the Christian should. There are elements here of The Parable of the Two Sons (Matt 21:28–32)—one son says to his father he will not work in the vineyard, but does; the second son says he will, but does not. The parable is about obedience to the will of God—the first son does the will of the Father (N.B. Matt 7:21). This is the paradox of atheism and rebellion.

5. THE DREAM OF A RIDICULOUS MAN: RELIGION AS THE RESULT OF THE FALL

Eduard Thurneysen commented that "In *The Dream of a Ridiculous Man*, a late, deeply meaningful short story that says in a few pages all that Dostoevsky had to say, it is told how humanity turns away from God, from the true, living God, and thereby make the earth into hell."[36]

Dostoevsky is concerned throughout the 1870s with the question of *Christlikeness* (the *imago Christi*) in relation to religious belief. This culminated to a degree in *The Dream of a Ridiculous Man*, a short story published in 1878.[37] In *The Dream* Dostoevsky focuses on the relationship between religious belief and theological anthropology; that is, religious belief and the invention of human gods seen in relation to the theological anthropology that he outlined in his other works. Written in the form of a story or parable, and recounted as narrative by the "ridiculous man," the work deals with the state of humanity prelapsarian/postlapsarian, the nature of original sin as a decision (and therefore existential), and it raises issues to do with the "invention" of religion by fallen humanity. The "ridiculous man" is very similar to the "underground man"—he is withdrawn, isolated, in a shroud of self-imposed loneliness. This results in alienation, spiritual desolation, moral indifference, and nihilistic beliefs. The "ridiculous man" is above all modern and individualistic.

36   Thurneysen, *Dostojewski*, 74/ET: 80.

37   Dated 1877, it appeared in *The Diary of a Writer* the following year. Quotation here are from a translation by Alan Myers in Dostoevsky, *A Gentle Creature and Other Stories*, 107–28. References hereafter are from the Constance Garnett translation at http://www.kiosek.com/dostoevsky/library/ridiculousman.txt.

This individuality is important to Dostoevsky's critique—the counter is the communal characterized by compassion and a sense of responsibility for other human beings, but above all by *sobornost'*.

i. The Fall

The first part of the story details the state of alienation in the "ridiculous man." He is given no name therefore he is representative of the many but isolated modern individuals (Adam—fragmented?). Above all nothing matters to him; he is indifferent to all other people and even to meaning. Living in his "Voltaire-style" apartment he contemplates suicide, the denial of his own existence, as the only act worth doing. One evening, having contemplated the revolver and the potential for months, he decides to go through with the act of shooting himself. However, he is confronted by a small pauper girl whilst on his way home late at night. He ignores her pleas even when she tries to stop him, crying simply, "Mummy, Mummy!" He is indifferent to her plight. He is proud to have sent her away. When he returns home he sits at the table contemplating the revolver trying to get the image of the little girl out of his mind. He falls asleep. He dreams. In his dream he does shoot himself, and—possessed by the same sense of nihilism—continues existing through his funeral and burial. From the grave he prays from the heart:

> Whoever you may be, if you exist, and if anything more rational than what is happening here is possible, suffer it to be here now. But if you are revenging yourself upon me for my senseless suicide by the hideousness and absurdity of this subsequent existence, then let me tell you that no torture could ever equal the contempt which I shall go on dumbly feeling, though my martyrdom may last a million years![38]

The prayer is answered and he is exhumed by a creature that transports him through the infinity of space till he then recognizes a star as the sun he knew from earth and then finds himself back on earth in the Aegean amongst people who are not subject to original sin. These prelapsarian people are genuinely innocent. Dostoevsky goes into some depth in describing them, their virtue, kindness, but above all their freedom from

---

38   Dostoevsky, *The Dream of a Ridiculous Man* (trans. Constance Garnett), Section 3, Para. 5 (the work is a little over 8,000 words in length—21 pages in print).

deceit, jealousy, lying, subterfuge, cruelty, barbarity, murder. . . . They are as happy and frolicsome as children. However, although he says they are like children, Dostoevsky is not implying that contemporary children are prelapsarian. It is important to remember that Dostoevsky is not Pelagian, even though he has great admiration for the state of the child— Rogozhin's indictment of children as brutal savages (*The Idiot*) or the pack of boys who systematically bully[39] (*The Brothers Karamazov)* are but two examples. Although these passages in *The Brothers Karamazov* seem to be a side issue compared to the main thrust of the story, they are crucial to understanding the nature of original sin—adults are merely grown up children; children are to all sense and purpose immature adults. Children are as subject to the *fall* as adults, but as Father Zossima states, they are also like little angels. There is therefore the *potential* for them to be both angels and demons. Ivan Karamazov in his rebellious preamble to the Legend of the Grand Inquisitor cites children as his defense against an incompetent and unjust god, claiming that children are totally innocent and therefore unworthy of any suffering—Ivan is therefore the Pelagian heretic. However, the "ridiculous man" does witness prelapsarian humanity as truly innocent:

> They loved and begot children, but I never noticed in them the impulse of that cruel sensuality which overcomes almost every man on this earth, all and each, and is the source of almost every sin of mankind on earth. They rejoiced at the arrival of children as new beings to share their happiness. There was no quarrelling, no jealousy among them, and they did not even know what the words meant. Their children were the children of all, for they all made up one family.[40]

These people are not religious as such, but from the portraits Dostoevsky paints of them they radiate holiness without affectation and an unconscious oneness with God. In this prelapsarian world, God appears to suffuse the world and these people. There is no sin in this world prior to the arrival of the "ridiculous man" with all his West-inspired Petersburg sophistication—this world is created, the "ridiculous man" arrives, the people fall (though from the way the parable is presented, it

---

39   See: Dostoevsky, *The Brothers Karamazov*, Pt. II, Bk. 4 Strains, ch. 3 He gets involved with Schoolboys; also, Pt. IV, Bk. 10 Boys, ch. 1—7; and Epilogue ch. 3 Ilyushechka's Funeral.

40   Dostoevsky, *The Dream*, §. 4, para 2

took very little to tip them over, just the simple decision to lie). In their prelapsarian state, the holiness of these people is the result of innocence, not the attainment of saintliness. Illness was scarce; death regarded as natural "as though falling asleep, giving blessings and smiles to those who surrounded. . . . I never saw grief or tears on those occasions, but only love . . . made perfect and contemplative." They implicitly believed in immortality and were "convinced of it without reasoning. They had no temples, but they had a real living and uninterrupted sense of oneness with the whole of the universe . . . ."[41] But this was not to last; "Now I will tell the truth. The fact is that I corrupted them all!"[42]

His dream appears to last for millennia—and little by little, gradually over immense periods of time, these people were corrupted. The "ridiculous man" is placed in the role of the serpent:

> I only know that I was the cause of their sin and downfall. . . . [L]ike a germ of the plague infecting whole kingdoms, so I contaminated all this earth, so happy and sinless before my coming. They learnt to lie, grew fond of lying, and discovered the charm of falsehood. Oh, at first perhaps it began innocently, with a jest, coquetry, with amorous play . . . that germ of falsity made its way into their hearts and pleased them.[43]

This one man, the "ridiculous man," taught one individual to take the decision to lie. It may have seemed just a small step, a little thing but this decision bred other lies and so on—the germ of sin was sown. What followed? "Sensuality was begotten," then jealousy, then cruelty, soon the first murder—blood was shed. They began to separate into groupings, classes, and eventually racial groups. They formed into unions; reproaches and upbraidings followed. They came to know shame, which led them to invent virtue. Honor sprang up, and flag waving nationalism. "They began torturing animals, and the animals withdrew from them into the forests and became hostile to them. They began to struggle for separation, for isolation, for individuality, for mine and thine. They began to talk in different languages." They knew sorrow and loved it, even thirsted for it— eventually believing that truth could only be attained through suffering. "Then science appeared. As they became wicked they began talking of

41   Ibid.
42   Ibid.
43   Ibid., §. 5, para 1.

brotherhood and humanitarianism, and understood those ideas. As they became criminal, they invented justice and drew up whole legal codes in order to observe it, and to ensure their being kept, set up a guillotine."[44]

As time passed they forgot what they had been in their innocence. They refused to believe that they had ever been happy and innocent. They called it a dream; they lost all faith and invented the notion of legends to account for these memories. They longed to be happy and innocent once more so they crafted an idol of it, statues proliferated; they set up temples and worshipped this idea—which they acknowledged as no more than their own projected desire. They reverenced and worshiped these idols even though they fully believed that what they represented was unattainable and could not be realized; yet they bowed down to it and adored it and their leaders encouraged the people to do so. Thus they invented religion, including theories of religion to explain that it was really all nothing—however, this was a secret kept for the priestly caste, the ruling class. The "ridiculous man," realizing what he had caused, was beside himself with grief and guilt:

> I wept over them, pitying them. I stretched out my hands to them in despair, blaming, cursing and despising myself. I told them that all this was my doing, mine alone; that it was I had brought them corruption, contamination and falsity . . . .
> Then such grief took possession of my soul that my heart was wrung, and I felt as though I were dying; and then . . . then I awoke.[45]

Because of what he had seen in this dream/vision he does not commit suicide but does seek out the pauper girl and helps her. He does change—

> I will not and cannot believe that evil is the normal condition of mankind. And it is just this faith of mine that they laugh at. But how can I help believing it? I have seen the truth. It is not as though I had invented it with my mind, I have seen it, seen it, and the living image of it has filled my soul for ever. I have seen it in such full perfection that I cannot believe that it is impossible for people to have it.
> The chief thing is to love others like yourself, that's the chief thing, and that's everything; nothing else is wanted, you will find out at once how to arrange it all. And yet it's an old truth which

44   Ibid.

45   Ibid., §. 5, para 3.

has been told and retold a billion times—but it has not formed part of our lives! The consciousness of life is higher than life, the knowledge of the laws of happiness is higher than happiness, that is what one must contend against. And I shall. If only everyone wants it, it can be arranged at once.

And I tracked down that little girl . . . and I shall go on and on![46]

ii. Godless Religion

The story is about the importance of *sobornost* over individuality; it is about the importance of faith and the recognition of God-and-immortality. But what of religion? This work is in many ways Dostoevsky's answer to Feuerbach: what blinds Feuerbach to God is sin. If he were not blinded by sin then he would see through the cacophony of human religion and understand that *God is*. What we have here in this short story is the closest that Dostoevsky gets to a theological statement on religion—albeit presented in the style of a parable (though unusually for a parable, the narrator is the lead character). In religious terms Dostoevsky considers the state of humanity: that is, the role for humanity of religion as belief system as well as the formality of worship, gatherings, and so on. So, when these people in *The Dream* invent religion what happens? The first casualty was truth—sin was sown like a germ, they learnt to lie. They split up and formed groups around the individual belief systems of dominant members (therefore the fragmentation of beliefs into religion)—they formed into unions (socialism?), they came to know shame, and shame brought them to virtue. Respect was the next casualty—they began torturing animals, they polluted the earth; they struggled for separation, for isolation, they spoke in different languages. They developed a form of religious belief in sorrow and thirsted for suffering, and said that truth (axiomatic beliefs) could only be attained through suffering. Science appeared; they became wicked, they began talking of brotherhood and humanitarianism (socialism, liberalism). Ethics followed: they became criminal, they invented justice and drew up legal codes and set up a guillotine (the French Revolution). They scorned innocence; they lost all faith in their past happiness. Faith was derided, but legends and mythology encouraged. They made idols and set up temples (religion)

46   Ibid., §. 5, para 3 & 6.

and worshipped their own ideas, their own projected desire (Feuerbach); they bowed down and adored with tears!

> They said: "We may be deceitful, wicked and unjust, we know it and weep over it, we grieve over it; we torment and punish ourselves more perhaps than that merciful Judge Who will judge us and whose Name we know not. But we have science, and by the means of it we shall find the truth and we shall arrive at it consciously. Knowledge is higher than feeling; the consciousness of life is higher than life. Science will give us wisdom, wisdom will reveal the laws, and the knowledge of the laws of happiness is higher than happiness."[47]

Love was subjugated into sensuality, lust, and self-love; individual rights were championed. Slavery followed; the weak eagerly submitted to the strong, on condition that the latter aided them to subdue the still weaker.[48]

Religion did challenge people in their state of sinfulness; but it also patronized and complimented them. Whatever belief system these people came up with (overtly religious, political, sociological) it did nothing to change the underlying ontological nature of their original sin or the existential effect in the present of their corrupt nature. Religious consciousness arose outside of the officially sanctioned elite: saints came to these people, weeping, and talked to them of their pride, of their shame. The prophets were laughed at or stoned: "holy blood was shed on the threshold of the temples" (religious sacrifice and martyrdom). Socialism developed: intellectuals began to formulate doctrines so that everybody might live together in something like a harmonious society. Wars were fought over this idea. But they still firmly believed that science and rationalism (the age of reason and the Enlightenment), and the instinct of self-preservation (free-market economic theories of the nineteenth century) would force all people at last to unite into a harmonious and rational society:

> Then there arose people who began to think how to bring all the people together again, so that everybody, while still loving himself best of all, might not interfere with others, and all might live together in something like a harmonious society. Regular wars sprang up over this idea. All the combatants at the same

47   Ibid. §. 5, para 2.
48   Ibid. §. 5, para 3.

time firmly believed that science, wisdom and the instinct of self-preservation would force men at last to unite into a harmonious and rational society; and so, meanwhile, to hasten matters, "the wise" endeavored to exterminate as rapidly as possible all who were "not wise" and did not understand their idea, that the latter might not hinder its triumph.[49]

In presenting the elite, the "revolutionary guard"/"the Inquisitor," exterminating those they did not consider wise because they had not understood their beliefs, Dostoevsky was writing at his most prophetic. Although in one way he is referring back to the French Revolution (in particular, the appropriation by the revolutionaries of Rousseau's theories of social contract) the description here is uncannily like the belief system, the religion, of Soviet Marxism: the collectivizations, the Stalinist purges of anyone who did not conform to the changing party line and so on. In addition, his comments are applicable to many twentieth-century dictatorial systems, from National Socialism in Germany with their religion of "Blood and Soil" to Third-World dictators towards the end of the century. Finally, in Dostoevsky's parable there arose religions with a cult of non-existence and self-destruction for the sake of the everlasting peace of annihilation: suicide. The wise, the humanitarians (the ruling elite) were happy for there to be religion—though they knew there was nothing in it—as it kept the people happy.

iii. Feuerbach and Dostoevsky

After study with the philosopher Hegel, Ludwig Feuerbach (1804–72) underwent something of a philosophical conversion, represented by his first major work, *The Essence of Christianity*.[50] This work explicated his anti-Hegelian stance, by ironically drawing on Schleiermacher's focus on religious experience. But where Feuerbach differed from both Kant and Schleiermacher (who were theists) was that he did not hold to belief in God—Feuerbach argued that if they were correct then God (indeed all "gods") was merely an enlargement of our ideas, experiences, and aspirations. He wrote, "God is the realized wish of the heart, the wish exalted to the certainty of its fulfillment."[51] Furthermore, the secret, so

49   Ibid.
50   Feuerbach, *The Essence of Christianity* (1841).
51   Ibid., 1973 edition, 121.

to speak, of theology is that it is nothing more than anthropology.[52] Both Feuerbach and Schleiermacher had focused, or grounded, Christianity on human religious experience. Alister McGrath commented:

> This approach has enormous attractions. However, as Ludwig Feuerbach demonstrated, it is also enormously problematical . . . .
> The leading idea of the work is deceptively simple: Human beings have created the gods, who embody their own idealized conception of their aspirations, needs, and fears. Human "feeling" has nothing to do with God; it is of purely human origin, misunderstood by an overactive human imagination.[53]

McGrath notes that this proposition is a severe critique of human-centered religion—and Christianity is not excluded. But, "[i]t may be noted that Feuerbach's critique of religion loses much of its force when dealing with non-theistic religions, or theologies (such as that of Karl Barth) which claim to deal with a divine encounter with humanity from outside."[54]

Dostoevsky as a naïve Europeanized liberal student at the University of St. Petersburg read Feuerbach and drank in his theory about religion. And like many inspired by Feuerbach's writings, he, along with the rest of Petrashevsky circle, invented a morality and ethic centered on their own values and ego.[55] He dismissed religious belief on the grounds of Feuerbach's theology, but substituted a system of ethics based on supposed universal brother/sisterhood(!) with everyone being innately nice to each other—a sort of pseudo-Christian ethic, or more pertinently, a parasitic-atheistic creed derived from the Christian gospel. The theologian Robert Jenson has commented:

> But just if Feuerbach is right, if there is in fact no antecedent one God, there also can be no one antecedent community of humankind. Feuerbach dreamed of a universal humanity and so of a shared eternal vision of human value, but therein he remained

52   Ibid., 207.

53   McGrath *Christian Theology*, 230.

54   Ibid., 231. See also, Gerrish, "Feuerbach's Religious Illusion," 362–65, and 367.

55   For example, the British novelist George Eliot, who translated Feuerbach's *Essence of Christianity* into English, along with *The Life of Jesus* by David Friedrich Strauss. See, Hill "Translating Feuerbach, Constructing Morality: The Theological and Literary Significance of Translation for George Eliot," 635–53; also, Creeger (edited and compiled), *George Eliot: A Collection of Critical Essays,* in particular: Paris, "George Eliot's Religion of Humanity," 1–23, and U. C. Knoepflmacher, "George Eliot, Feuerbach, and the Question of Criticism," 74–93.

parasitic on the faith he debunked. Thus Western unbelief has since had to abandon that dream and now knows only classes and genders and races and cultures. Insofar as religion interprets itself by the resultant neo-Feuerbachian theory, religion is revealed as a struggle for metaphysical power, for each such group necessarily projects its ideal or compensatory vision of itself to be the final good. It is just so that Scripture sees the gods of the peoples as idols and "nothings." Exactly as neo-Feuerbachian theory says, what each of the gods does is validate and enforce the particular human situation, with its structure of values, from which she/he/ it is projected—in all the alienation and tyranny of every such situation.[56]

An observation similar to Jenson's (though Jenson is writing more than a century after Dostoevsky's death) led Dostoevsky to realize that without God, if there was no God, then there were no limits to human morality, human depravity: a proposition that frames his final work, *The Brothers Karamazov*. Without God all human ethics become a pretense; all human ethics become a demand by the most powerful group to set out how others should behave. Feuerbach, as well as others at this time, asserted that he could perceive a common harmonious human ethic, and that given time this could be applied to all humanity (whether they wanted to go along with it or not!).[57] Dostoevsky along with Kierkegaard[58] are the two nineteenth-century Christian prophets who challenge this notion of universal harmony through a tyrannous imposition.

What is important for us is this idea that religion is often invented by people to mask the existential crisis of their lives. But this religion may not be acceptable in God's sight. Though people may start off by inventing gods and idols to complement them, they eventually come to realize that these gods/idols do not exist: teleologically this is "godless" religion. But they fail to perceive the possibility of God beyond this incestuous world of human-centered religion. Feuerbach promoted a criticism of religion; so did Dostoevsky. But in Dostoevsky's case this is a criticism in the service of the gospel. If he were not blinded by sin then he would see through the cacophony of human religion and understand that *God is*. From the time of his rediscovery of Christian faith in the

56   Jenson, *Systematic Theology. Volume 1. The Triune God*, 53.

57   Smart, *Nineteenth Century Religious Thought in the West*, see, Vol. 1 *Ludwig Feuerbach and Karl Marx*.

58   Arbaugh, "Kierkegaard and Feuerbach," 7–10.

prison camp at Omsk, Siberia, Dostoevsky struggled with how to refute Feuerbach; such was the influence this German theologian had had on him in his student days.[59] Robert Jenson's remarks quoted above echo what Dostoevsky has the ruling elite believing and saying in *The Dream*, that is, that Western humanity knows only classes and genders and races and cultures, that the common values of liberal humanism can only be, at best, imposed.[60] Is this what Dostoevsky is presenting where the elite seek to impose harmony and common values? Dostoevsky was prophetic of the dealthy nihilism of Communism, Stalinism, National Socialism, legions of twentieth-century religio-political thought systems.

This short story is the closest that Dostoevsky gets to a theological statement on religion—albeit presented in the style of a parable.

iv. An Indictment

Primarily, the statement is a savage indictment of humanity, more pertinently humanity without God, humanity that has turned its back on God and deludes itself with all sorts of beliefs systems—religious, political, individualistic, socialist, nihilist. This is a *postlapsarian* humanity, which will try everything except turning to God. This is an existential crisis. What is left after this critique of human religion, of human belief systems, is faith. Faith is, for Dostoevsky, in the one true God and the revelation of Jesus Christ. There are actually two stories here in *The Dream of the Ridiculous Man*. There is the parable of the human race as another race on another earth-like planet who (unlike the human race on earth) have no name for God, that is, no revelation as in the Old Testament—"that merciful Judge Who will judge us and whose Name we know not."[61] Furthermore they have no real revelation of the *nature* of that God/Judge as in Jesus Christ (they only have natural theology and religious cults) and therefore there is for them no atonement—these people are truly lost. Then there is also the story of the "ridiculous man." Is Dostoevsky saying that this man must go through the period of doubt, alienation, finally to come back to the truth and be saved? There is evidence for dialectic

---

59   A point made by Gibson, *The Religion of Dostoevsky*, 10–11 and 161f.

60   Regarding the assertion, "there also can be no one antecedent community of humankind," Jensen refers to Pannenberg *Systematische Theologie Bd. 1*, 151–66.

61   Dostoevsky, *The Dream*, §. 5, para 2

here: the "ridiculous man" (as representative of the human race, not the people in his vision), moves from innocence through sin and death to saintliness. If this is so, there is dialectic, but not dualism: the world of the people in his vision is not inherently evil, it is good (there is no hint of Manichaeism here).

Amongst the people the "ridiculous man" corrupts in his dream there is no Christ, no savior; they are—in their fallen and corrupt state—forsaken. What is essential to Dostoevsky, therefore, is the figure of Christ, and it can be argued that Christ was implicitly present in this community that the "ridiculous man" visits in his dream prior to their *fall*. Boyce Gibson comments: "for Dostoevsky, God was in Christ to such a degree that he had difficulty in envisaging the divine transcendence. Merging God in the community of Christ-seekers was a temptation to him at all times."[62]

Further, Boyce Gibson and others have suggested that it is as if Dostoevsky was trying to set out "the Christian truth anonymously: to confront us with the content . . . ."[63] But the people in his dream are left suspended with no forgiveness: what is missing, what they cry out for (though they do not realize it) is the grace and forgiveness of a criminal class bestowed from the God of love—tangibly revealed in Christ. In many ways *The Dream* is a lead up to Father Zossima in *The Brothers Karamazov*, who sees the gospel in the dictum "each is responsible for all." In the words of the "ridiculous man," the chief thing is Christlikeness: to love others like yourself. After his conversion the "ridiculous man" called upon this eternal truth with tears and not words.[64]

The *fall*, for Dostoevsky, is transmitted among these people, proto-humans, though nurture, education, and conditioning. If someone arose who tried to challenge the state of humanity, that person was corrupted and absorbed. It is as if the germ was there in them from the start, all it took was one tiny incident to trigger the *fall*. Transmission therefore appears for Dostoevsky to be sociological, social interaction that exploits an inherited flaw. Were they born with this flaw or does it appear in them after the fall, to be transmitted? Is Dostoevsky right to consider there to be a flaw in creation? So although there is no explanation of transmission,

62   Gibson, *The Religion of Dostoevsky*, 168.
63   Ibid., 166.
64   Dostoevsky, *The Dream*, §. 5, para 4/5

there *appears* to be an hereditary element in Dostoevsky's story, which both affirms and appears to contradict Russian Orthodox teaching on the *fall*.

7

Sin and Grace: A Dialectic of Salvation

1. DIALECTICAL DELUSIONS

Dostoevsky's understanding of the human condition before God is presented analogically through character portraits: Dostoevsky's men and women. Key characters from the novels illustrate the theological anthropology we have established. In all this sordidness and depravity, the movement is towards resurrection and the key is grace. Coming to a full and true understanding of the depravity of humanity is only tolerable and acceptable in the light of sanctification and resurrection. Negation and denial are important, but must be in the context of affirmation. Therefore it is not the radical nature of the negations we find in Dostoevsky's novels that are important, but the superior affirmations that issue from the negations. To stay with the negations is simply to wallow in the sordidness of human depravity. Grace moves the individual toward resurrection. Without the promise of resurrection attested to at the end of *Crime and Punishment*, humanity is truly lost and condemned. As Thurneysen notes of Dostoevsky's own personal journey, "[His] Hosanna has passed through the great purging fire of doubt."[1]

Despite his Napoleonic delusion, Raskolnikov has to recognize this *diastasis*, this unresolved antinomy between God and humanity. His salvation is dependent on this realization, preveniently generated by the Holy Spirit, but closure can only come from God's side. It is the utter necessity of resurrection as the solution to the human problem. But this

---

1   Thurneysen, *Dostojewski*, 10/ET: 14.

may not always be the case, as *The Brothers Karamazov* illustrates. The Karamazovs illustrate a truism: the meaning of life is buried so deep that the wise and clever, the proud and powerful, cannot find it; furthermore, the one who does understand the meaning of this life as a denial before God will be seen as a fool, as weak, as sickly. Therefore life crowds out this truth for the popular, the leaders, the self-righteous to the extent that for Dostoevsky those who do perceive this truth are the harlots and the murderers, the insane, the desperate: this is a dialectical paradox. The popular, the leaders, the self-righteous—the politicians, philosophers, and intellectuals—have locked themselves into an hermetic hell of their own making. But the harlots and the murderers, the insane and the desperate *may* perceive it and move towards salvation, or conversely they may not and may be condemned before God. Grace is everything.

Therefore, the answer and solution posed by the question of humanity is in God. But this is not the self-generated, Feuerbachian, pagan "gods" and "goddesses" of humanity. Because of the mystery at the heart of suffering it is Christ who points the way, and is the way—certainly for Dostoevsky—and therefore the answer is Trinitarian, though not being a systematic theologian Dostoevsky does not state this explicitly. This is the action and event of the triune God: the unfathomable distance and mystery of the Father, the compassion and mysterious sacrifice of the Son, and the enigmatic wrenching and remodeling of the human by the Holy Spirit. Once humanity understands how sick it is, captured and imprisoned as all are in the tempest of their passions, in the confusion of their thoughts, if they can recognize how they can be moved by something unspeakably great, distant, and yet near, something beyond and yet here, then they can begin to perceive the answer to the problem of life in this triune God. God's messengers and martyrs, his prisoners, his heralds, point the way: the holy monks and priests, but equally ordinary humans who have turned to God—for example, Sonya.

There is therefore a dialectic between sin and grace. A key to Dostoevsky's understanding of sin and grace is in the long encounter between Raskolnikov and Sonya, where he forces her to read the story of the resurrection of Lazarus from St. John's Gospel to him.[2] He taunts her that she has also destroyed a life. He may have murdered, but she has destroyed her own life through the depravity of her prostitution. Yet he

2   Dostoevsky, *Crime and Punishment*, pt. 4, ch. 4, 314–31.

can perceive the effect of grace in her: her sanity and sanctity. This leads him to bow down and kiss her feet.[3] This is a graceful act, acknowledging on a subliminal level her holiness and her God. However, sensing that she perceives the change in him and in an attempt to reassert his rebellion, he states, "I was not bowing to you but to all human suffering."[4] He enquires of her faith; then he teases her laughingly, gloatingly, that "maybe there isn't any God,"[5] and that her stepsister, the innocent and charismatically holy Polenka (Pólya), will end up following her into prostitution when Sonya inevitably falls sick. Sonya likewise admits in abject humility that she is a fallen creature, that she is "dishonorable, a great, great sinner."[6] When he finally forces her to read the raising of Lazarus she stumbles over the words, her voice falters and she trembles with fear:

> Raskolnikov partly understood why Sonya was hesitant to read to him, and the more he understood it, the more rudely and irritably he insisted on her reading. He understood only too well how hard it was for her now to betray and expose all that was hers. He understood that these feelings might indeed constitute her secret, as it were, real and long-standing, going back perhaps to her adolescence, when she was still in the family, with her unfortunate father and her grief-maddened stepmother, among the hungry children, the ugly shouts and reproaches. But at the same time he now knew, and knew for certain, that even though she was anguished and terribly afraid of something as she was starting out to read, she also had a tormenting desire to read, in spite of all her anguish and apprehension, and precisely for him, so that he would hear it, and precisely now—whatever might come of it afterwards! . . . He read it in her eyes, understood it from her rapturous excitement. . . . She mastered herself, suppressed the spasm in her throat that had made her voice break at the beginning of the verse, and continued her reading . . . .[7]

It is as though Sonya—the great sinner—is holding her very soul in her hands, exposing it in her frailty before Raskolnikov, fearful that he may mock and destroy her faith, the slender thread that holds her from falling into a depraved nihilistic nothingness. Sonya's existential crisis in

3   Ibid., Pt. 4, ch. 4, 321.

4   Ibid., Pt. 4, Bk. 4, 325.

5   Ibid.

6   Ibid.

7   Ibid., Pt. 4, Bk. 4, 326.

facing Raskolnikov is not nervous emotionalism, it is not to be seen as pietistic religion, it is about facing the truth of one's sinful nature whilst exercising the divine imperative to witness to the truth of the gospel. This is not to be considered subjective because this existential experience is defined by and in relation to the pneumatological action of the love of the God who is love, a love that measures and judges all.

The antinomy between sin and grace is resolved ultimately in the eschaton, however, the path towards the eschaton is defined by repentance. Sonya knows she is wrong in her behavior, yet despite this she can bear witness to God's truth to Raskolnikov. She knows her situation, it is informed by orthodox Christian morality, and she waits for the time when she can change.

2. FORGIVEN–UNFORGIVEN

Eduard Thurneysen notes, "The absolutely final word of his novels is 'resurrection.' Over the dark abysses of the humanity which he depicts there glows from the beyond the light of a great forgiveness."[8] Forgiveness is God's response to the huge rebellion of humanity, the *fall* into the original sin.

i. Ivan Karamazov and Rebellion

Ivan Karamazov represents Dostoevsky's most fearsome attack, which is leveled at the assembled power of the church and religion as the ultimate example of the lie *eritis sicut Deus* (you shall be as God). Ivan Karamazov is the chief protagonist and spokesman for a frustrated pessimistic atheism in *The Brothers Karamazov*, of a gigantic intellectual rebellion against God: a Babel-like tower of rebellion against God that is pseudo-religious escapism. In some cases this atheistic rebellion may lead to repentance, and for the atheistic, a clearing-out of false religious ideas, to be replaced, subsequently, by a true understanding of God and immortality; but equally, it may not, as Dostoevsky demonstrates in Ivan Karamazov, the lost soul, dissolving into insanity—having placed itself beyond redemption.

Dostoevsky asserts that humanity cannot cope with its creatureliness, with the negativity of the relationship with this critically realistic God; humanity cannot cope with standing under God's judgment. The human

8   Thurneysen, *Dostojewski*, 39/ET: 44.

solution is to be rid of God through secular, politicized, humanistic atheism, or to control God by creating religion, an idol. Dostoevsky is asserting, to a degree, that the ultimate and most dangerous of revolts is the illusion of religion and the claim to be obedient to a "god," "goddess," or "idol." The presentation and explication of this insurrection is seen at its fullest in story of The Grand Inquisitor.

ii. The Ultimate Rebellion

The story of The Grand Inquisitor is the protest and rebellion of Ivan Karamazov. Dostoevsky uses the visual analogy of lines of perspective meeting outside of the picture plane in a painting, comparing this to two parallel lines never meeting according to Euclidean geometry, arguing that in eternity they will meet in the same way that all the irreconcilable antinomies of suffering and evil on earth in this life will be resolved in eternity. Therefore, this angry rebellion, this atheism (pseudo-atheism—for in the end Ivan argues that even if God is proved to him he will still rebel), can often lead over into true faith, faith beyond religion, as it begins to for Raskolnikov: "The great, passionate negations of the false gods make room once again for the knowledge of the true God."[9] But if not, if atheism does not lead to perception of the one true God and therefore repentance, then suicide becomes the ultimate act of rebellion. Dostoevsky pours these negations into Ivan's theological ramblings, his rebellion, his story of The Grand Inquisitor and the long dialogue with the devil. Are Dostoevsky's rebels sick with God in whom they claim not to believe? Sick because of the judgment and righteousness of God that presses on them, yet they will die without there being the supreme inconceivable possibility of being healed by God, and of rising again, resurrected, being born again? That is, unless they turn in repentance and submit to God, unless they lay down the crowns of their rebellion.[10] For Dostoevsky, the real evil working against God was to be seen in the cultural and political atheism embodied in the West (that is, the civilized nations of Western Europe): Ivan is therefore, to a degree, a Western construction. Thurneysen raises the question of whether Dostoevsky presents the Russian Orthodox Church as the alternative to this Western atheism, having already demolished the Roman Catholic Church through

---

9   Thurneysen, *Dostojewski*, 45/ET: 51.
10   Rev 4:10.

The Grand Inquisitor, even though Dostoevsky's critique of religion in the service of the gospel applies as much to the Russian Orthodox Church as to other churches and denominations.

3. DOSTOEVSKY—*THE BROTHERS KARAMAZOV*

The Brothers Karamazov (serialized, initially between 1878–80) is about a father, Fyodor Karamazov, and his four sons—Ivan, Dmitri, and Alyosha, and the illegitimate Smerdyakov. Ivan, in his mid-twenties, is highly intelligent, and has already published. Dmitri is sensual, a womanizer, and is all too fond of drink. Alyosha, the youngest, is in the novitiate at the local Russian Orthodox monastery. Fyodor's two wives died, as did the servant woman Lizaveta that bore Smerdyakov—this fourth son working for his father as manservant. Both Fyodor and Dmitri are trying to seduce a young woman—Grushenka. Against this is Father Zossima, a starets at Alyosha's monastery, along with Rakitin, a seminarian and religious atheist. Half way through the story Fyodor is brutally murdered—suspicion and arrest fall on Dmitri because of the rivalry for Grushenka, and because of stolen money. Dmitri is convicted of the murder even though Smerdyakov has confessed secretly to Ivan of his guilt. Woven into this story are Ivan's theological speculations. There are several scenes at the monastery contrasting the holiness of Father Zossima with the worldly ambitions of Rakitin; the faith of the Russian peasants is extolled; and the all-too-fleshly worldly desires and obsessions of Fyodor and his son Dmitri and the scheming of Grushenka are laid bare. Then we have the character of Ivan Karamazov, who is not prone to the sins of the flesh, so to speak, but to the titanic intellectual sins of the mind: *eritis sicut Deus*. When Ivan meets up with Alyosha, having returned home after many years away in Moscow and St. Petersburg we have three long chapters where they become reacquainted.[11] In this, Ivan off-loads all his atheistic philosophy onto Alyosha, the seventeen-year-old novice, in the chapter entitled Rebellion, then recounts the prose poem he has created, entitled The Grand Inquisitor. Later, as Ivan's mind becomes more and more unhinged due to his belief system, especially his denial of everything except his own ego, Dostoevsky presents a nightmare hallucinatory conversation Ivan has with the devil. By the time of Dmitri's

11   Dostoevsky, *The Brothers Karamazov*, Pt. II, Bk. V ch. 3 The Brothers Make Friends, 228–35, ch. 4 Rebellion, 236–45; ch. 5 The Grand Inquisitor, 246–64.

trial and wrongful conviction for the murder of their father Fyodor, Ivan appears to have succumbed to a mental breakdown and his testimony before the court that Smerdyakov confessed to the murder of Fyodor before he committed suicide is ruled inadmissible. The story ends with Alyosha leaving the monastery (having been advised by Father Zossima that he should serve Christ in the world); Dmitri being transported to Siberia, Grushenka announcing she will follow and wait for him. Into *The Brothers Karamazov* Dostoevsky poured all his skill and talent as a writer illustrating the fallenness of humanity: broken, depraved, egocentric. But this is balanced by the proposition from Christian soteriology: repent and be forgiven; face sin in all its depth, and accept God's forgiveness. Ivan does not—and loses his mind; Dmitri does and lives. Alyosha, still only a naïve seventeen-year-old, has to face coming to terms with the world, whilst retaining his faith. Sin therefore is gargantuan and manifold, deceptive and possessing, deceitful, alluring, deluding—but forgiveness and grace are always available. Sin and grace are forensic: repentance being the only path to life. This was Dostoevsky's doctrine, as such, of Christian soteriology in *The Brothers Karamazov*.

In the chapter entitled Rebellion, Ivan focuses on the antinomy between an omnipotent and merciful God and the cruel, bleak reality of relatively innocent suffering (relative that is to the fall); this can also be seen as a *diastasis* between divine mercy and affliction. Dostoevsky's dialectics are rooted in theodicy: *Si Deus justus—unde malum?*: if God is righteous, good, and omnipotent, then why is there evil and the suffering that flows from it? Ivan speculates that if the suffering and death of an innocent child could solve this paradox and close the antinomy, then it would never be acceptable. Ivan refuses to accept that the sufferings here on earth can be assuaged, dismissed—as the persecuted and persecutor are reconciled by God. At this juncture in the story Ivan is not a logical atheist, he does not examine everything in terms of a denial of the existence of God and a denial of any meaning in life. It is his perception of suffering in the world that causes him to refuse to acknowledge God or God's creation (Ivan is not seeking simply, philosophically, to prove the non-existence of God). For Dostoevsky, the problem of humanity is the man-god, characterized by a rebellion against human limitations; the infinite pretensions of the human self are summarized by the determination of men and women to be God: *eritis sicut Deus*. Salvation lies not in the man-god but in the God-man: Jesus Christ.

At the center of this is the story of the Grand Inquisitor. Set in sixteenth-century Seville, The Grand Inquisitor, having supervised an *auto da fé* of over one hundred heretics, is then confronted with Jesus Christ having returned to earth (the second coming?), only to be arrested by the Inquisition. His crime?—To have healed a little girl. Confronted by the inquisitor in his cell, Christ is silent. After a long monologue (in the course of which the inquisitor reveals himself to be a religious atheist) looking at the temptations of Jesus in the wilderness, the nature of the devil that tempted him, the role of miracle, mystery, and authority, further the authority of the church (Peter's rock), the inquisitor's objection is that Christ should not have returned, that all power and authority had been handed over, and could not be drawn back, that Christ had no right to interfere with the church. Furthermore, Rome had taken the power to forgive people their sins, make them happy. By contrast Jesus's expectations of humanity are too great, too unattainable: the burden of freedom is too much for them. Christ does not speak a word in his defense, merely sits and listens; however, at the end he rises and places a kiss of peace gently on the inquisitor's bloodless lips as if to say, "I forgive you." The inquisitor, instead of holding Christ to be burnt at the stake the next morning, opens the door and orders him to go, and not to return.

Dostoevsky is not so naïve as to aim the criticism that is the Legend of the Grand Inquisitor only at Rome.[12] His polemic is also aimed at the liberal humanists that had influenced him in his youth—the proto-socialist sympathizers with the French revolution who led to his conviction for sedition and imprisonment/exile in Siberia, following a mock execution. Dostoevsky is criticizing any dictatorial authority claiming to act as God (again, *eritis sicut Deus*). The Grand Inquisitor refers to the anthill for humanity and the Tower of Babel for the role of the church, though Dostoevsky also used these metaphors for a denunciation of atheistic socialism.[13] He is writing a few years after the First Vatican Council, which had declared infallibility for the papacy; therefore, in the context of Roman oppression and attacks on the Russian Orthodox Church over the previous eight hundred years, it is easy to see why Dostoevsky takes this stand.[14] The Grand Inquisitor is characterized by dialectic between the

---

12   Summarized in Dirscherl S.J., *Dostoevsky and the Catholic Church*, 79f.

13   Dostoevsky, *The Diary of a Writer*.

14   Dirscherl S.J., *Dostoevsky and the Catholic Church*.

freedom of Christ and religious oppression. Dostoevsky is also tackling the subject of atheism—again in the form of a dialectic between theism and atheism. For Dostoevsky atheism may be of value—for instance, the clearing away of all human preconceptions. Dostoevsky knew only too well that self-confessed atheists might often have a better grasp of the truth of God than pietistic Christians immersed in religious culture, though their lifestyle and beliefs scorned such theism. Thurneysen notes that Ivan's atheism is dialectical and develops in three stages: first, Ivan's passionate protest against the reconciliation of the riddles and torments of life within the divine order of the world that is asserted by the gospel (that the immeasurable suffering of a child is tolerable when measured against the joy of the life to come); second, Eduard Thurneysen notes[15] how Ivan then moves from what he calls "dialectical-animated atheism" to a "rigid-satanic atheism" (he systematically attacks and denounces anything to do with the church and/or religion); third, in consequence, Ivan moves from "rigid-satanic atheism" to "demonic-satanic atheism" (the stage at which he begins to lose his mind): the Grand Inquisitor is in the role of the devil, Ivan Karamazov appears to be the Grand Inquisitor—he projects his rebellion into his creation of the Grand Inquisitor—therefore Ivan Karamazov is becoming the devil.

Ivan's theological counterpart is Smerdyakov. It is through Smerdyakov that Dostoevsky voices the central ethic that if there is no God then there are no limits on human behavior, human depravity. Michael V. Jones comments that there are

> four, or possibly five, stages in Ivan's thought[;] . . . they span the period between his eighteenth and twenty-fourth year: they are the legend of the philosopher who refused to believe in paradise, the story of the grand inquisitor, the article on the ecclesiastical courts, the conversation with Alyosha on rebellion and the theory of geological upheaval set forth by Ivan's hallucinatory devil. Each of them represents a stage in Ivan's wrestling with questions of theodicy, God and the world-order. And they feed back into the plot through the axiom which so impresses Smerdyakov, that if there is no God there is no morality.[16]

15   Thurneysen, *Dostojewski*, 45f. English translation, (1964), Ch. IV Ivan Karamazov, the Grand Inquisitor and the Devil,' 49–52, specifically, 51.

16   Michael V. Jones "Introduction," in Dostoevsky, *The Brothers Karamazov*, ix–xxv.

Dostoevsky foresaw and prophesied through Ivan the chaos and nihilism of twentieth-century history: the Soviet-Marxist-Stalinist catastrophe; National Socialism, the holocaust of the Jews, and so forth. The German philosopher and novelist Hermann Hesse, studying Dostoevsky commented:

> Humanity is now on the point of realizing this. Already half Europe, at all events half of Eastern Europe, is on the road to Chaos. In a state of drunken illusion she is reeling into the abyss and, as she reels, she sings a drunken hymn such as Karamazov sang. The insulted citizen laughs that song to scorn, the saint and seer hear it with tears.[17]

17   Hesse "Die Brüder Karamasow oder Der Untergang Europas," *Blick ins Chaos*, 1920. ET: Hesse "The Brothers Karamazov or the Downfall of Europe," *The Dial magazine*, 607–18. Hesse was writing three years after the Russian revolution, and a matter of months after the end of the First World War.

Conclusion

1. DOSTOEVSKY'S THEOLOGICAL VISION

What are the theological beliefs that underpin Dostoevsky's writings? Dostoevsky's novels are predicated on two theological propositions: anthropological and ethical. First, there is insufficient good left in humanity for people to get along without God, to be saved without God; despite human arrogance we cannot save ourselves from the condition we have willed ourselves into. Second, without God there are no constraints or restraints on human behavior; human ethics are therefore foundationless, relative, transitory. In response, humanity will invent all manner of gods and goddesses, religions, myths, and cults for comfort in this *fallen* depravity, and all manner of self-centered and reverential laws with which to protect their *fallenness*: from a human perspective concepts of criminality are relative, transitory, ephemeral, but also tyrannous and often punitive, retributive, and politicized. Those in power and authority will always convince themselves of the rightness of their enacted criminal law, particularly when it contradicts God's law. Before God, *actual* criminality is demonically driven, as we saw in Rodion Raskolnikov, also Smerdyakov and Ivan Karamazov, *et al.* Such propositions are doctrinal. Such concepts are theological and ethical.

But what of religion? Is all religion, for Dostoevsky, a human invention that fails to penetrate the philosophically generated glass ceiling between humanity and God? The patristic and Russian Orthodox traditions valued the relationship between the two realms, the two realities: heaven and earth. The sharp Cartesian dualism between matter and mind, physical and spiritual, earth and heaven, that has bedeviled the West since the seventeenth century, and that served as the condition of reductivist materialism (which, finding no role for the spiritual, simply eliminated it and was left with nothing but matter) has no place here. In the older, more sacramental worldview represented by the Russian Orthodoxy of Dostoevsky, there was no hard barrier between the material and the spiritual, but something analogous to a permeable membrane. Indeed, the material and the spiritual were flip sides of each other: the spiritual was in the material; the material was in the spiritual. Neither aspect of creation made sense apart from the other: this is incarnational.

This is an understanding of reality that contradicts much of the basis of modern philosophy, particularly the philosophical and intellectual endeavors of the academy since the Reformation. A Kantian closed universe is where there is no perceived or acknowledged commerce between the two realms leading to doubts as to the existence of heaven and eternity, and then hardening into skepticism, a skepticism that is formulated into scientific and doctrinal certainty.

The problem for the academy lies with the hermetic concept of reason adhered to in the West since the Enlightenment, enforced, by the philosopher Immanuel Kant's glass ceiling, philosophically installed between humanity and God, whereby a philosophical barrage cuts humanity off from God (because the philosophers argued that there was no commerce, no connection between us and God, if there was a God). In effect, the people who subscribe to this isolationism are, from Dostoevsky's perspective, merely creating a mental model that appears to seal them off from God's Holy Spirit, as the characters in his novels create a grey, nihilistic world in their own image.

This raises questions about the veracity of our religious ideas, about the models we have constructed in our minds about God, salvation, and humanity: is not the generic mono-god(dess) of human invention legion and possessing in its Feuerbachian illusion? Are not these mental models of a god(dess) entirely human-generated, a fantasy and illusion? Or is the pertinent question the degree to which these mental models cohere, coincide, and concur with the reality of God, and the triune reality of Christ's salvation. And, crucially, if these mental models that control our beliefs and actions differ too greatly from God-given reality, then these very religious models may prevent us from knowing God and accepting the salvation proffered for us on the cross. Therefore, in addition to Kant's glass ceiling, there may indeed be mental—psychological—barriers that we have created: Feuerbachian projections may not coincide and correspond with God's revelation. Such projections—often emotional—may not be from without; they may be no more than the heartfelt desires, the deepest longings, of the complex and manifold psyche of each individual, only seemingly projected outside the self, reinforcing Kant's glass ceiling. Such was Ivan Karamazov's self-generated hell.

Is humanity, for Dostoevsky, blind to God because in its veiled desperation it invents all manner of gods, goddesses, and demonic divines? Religion is of value if it serves the gospel, but it can all too easily turn into human-centered culture and become Feuerbachian—the equivalent of holding up a mirror to itself: the humanly conferred and generated glass ceiling merely reflects the human desire for salvation back onto the human individual: therefore human-projected desires, aspirations, and fears, codified into religious comfort. Faith and holiness/sanctification in a communal context are in many ways more important than religion. Therefore, Dostoevsky does force a dialectic out of the issue of religion and faith.

For Dostoevsky, religion—indeed, Christian religion—may serve the gospel, it may genuinely bring people to God in Christ, but it can also be dangerous in the authority and power structure of organizations. For Dostoevsky this was seen in the Roman Catholic Church (and also in bad priests within the Orthodox tradition, for example in the character of Rakitin), but also the proto-Marxist revolutionary, and in the humanist religion of socialism. Pushed to its limit, religion as socially acceptable and respectable piety was a denial of an existential gospel; human-centered religion masked the alienation and suffering that was inherent in the gospel.

Revelation and reason are implicitly complementary for Dostoevsky. Reason is, by its very nature, analytical, therefore it is separatist, fragmentary, and individualistic. Reason cannot solve the problem of humanity, indeed for Dostoevsky there are times when it only makes things worse. Only divine revelation as attested to in "Sacred Scripture" will suffice. Dostoevsky's epistemology is grounded in reason and revelation: reason is essential to perceiving and understanding God's revelation, but is not in itself the answer; revelation is all. Jesus, the Christ, is God's highest revelation and, as we saw, Dostoevsky was so possessed by the vision of Christ that he at times found it difficult to conceive of the triune nature of God.

The human, for Dostoevsky, cannot cope without God. The radical contradictions of human existence become more pronounced as the depths of the human psyche and the corrupt nature of the will are encountered: selfishness breeds delusions, which in turn hide this fragmented psyche. Such are—for Dostoevsky—the manifold delusions of atheism. A delusion may exhaust itself, may burn itself out (Raskolnikov) or it may condemn the individual human before God (Ivan Karamazov). Therefore, the problem of humanity is the man-god, characterized by a rebellion against the limitations of humanity; the infinite pretensions of the human self are summarized by the determination of men and women to be God. Escape, for Dostoevsky, a lesson he had to learn painfully following the mock-execution and exile in Siberia, escape from the human condition—that is, salvation—lies not in the man-god, but in the God-man: Jesus Christ. This is dependent upon the recognition that *God is God* and humanity is only mere humanity: without God humans have no future or meaning.

Therefore, Dostoevsky pursued a devastating critique of Western civilization and of the power and authority of the church: Western civilization was seen by Dostoevsky as the attempt to build a tower of Babel up to heaven, the "endarkeners" were attempting to colonize heaven itself through science, culture, human achievement, socialism and capitalism. This delusion, he prophesied, would end in confusion and destruction: in the twentieth century it did, and continues to wreak havoc in the twenty-first century. Socialism (characterized by slavish obedience) was the "ant-heap" and as such was a denial of a God-given human freedom, and in many ways, a denial of charity, where charity demonstrates the fundamental need for dependence upon God (as demonstrated in the Parable of the Sheep and the Goats: if a socialist government was truly successful there would be no place for individual's charity).

The church in general (though Dostoevsky seems to have a particular bias against the Roman Catholic Church) was seen as the human attempt to silence the cry for God in ordinary mortals, to still the passionate hunger for God, substituting slavish obedience to human gods (explicated in The Legend of the Grand Inquisitor). The Roman Catholic Church, aligned for Dostoevsky with socialism, was also the "ant-heap." God was not in the possession of human beings, least of all princes and prelates; God was other, transcendent, beyond: only through revelation can we know anything of God, and—given that we live after the Christ event—Sacred Scripture was, for Dostoevsky, the fount of that revelation.

A key leitmotif for Dostoevsky was resurrection: in discovering and accepting the limits of their humanity, Dostoevsky's characters realize their reliance upon God and the need for the absolute transcendence of human limitation by God through resurrection (a limitation characterized by death, death as the price of the *fall*, the original sin, the corrupted will). Without God-and-immortality (and in consequence resurrection) the characters in his mature writings are driven mad by their sublimated hunger for God, a hunger sublimated into personal egoism. Resurrection is eschatological and bodily. But resurrection, though bodily—consider Dostoevsky's emphasis on the importance of the story of Lazarus—is also seen in this life in the way that way that Dostoevsky's characters undergo a radical transformation of their life; this is not only in their beliefs, but also in the manner of their relationships with other people (for example, Raskolnikov—but he has to accept the reparation and purgation of imprisonment and exile).

2. MYSHKIN AND ALYOSHA— CHRISTLIKE ARCHETYPES

Christ is all; it is Christ we should be moving towards, Christlikeness is the hidden teleology in Dostoevsky's novels. Therefore, Myshkin and Alyosha are seen as Christlike archetypes. Why? Because in not being able to answer or refute his brother's rebellious atheistic theologoumena, Alyosha is not failing. Neither does Myshkin fail when he does not save the St. Petersburg middle classes, drunken rogues, prostitutes, the cultured bourgeoisie, even the aristocracy, from themselves. Likewise Job is righteous before God because of his honesty, but also through his acceptance of the mystery of God. Is it not the mystery of God—central to Russian Orthodox theology—that is the answer to the problems and questions that radical evil raise against the faith (as demonstrated by Dostoevsky in the theodicean questions raised by Ivan's atheistic attack on faith), as compared to the certainties offered by Job's so-called comforters?

No amount of systematization in theology and philosophy will close the antinomies between God and humanity, between suffering in this life and the resolution and reconciliation to come. We saw this was central to Dostoevsky's work, especially as theodicean objections are central to Ivan Karamazov's rebellion.

Myshkin and Alyosha are an example of the *answer* as *no-answer*. Alyosha bears witness to the futility of Ivan's assertions by merely standing for what he knows to be the way of truth: the naïve and halting way he mimics Christ at the end of Ivan's prose poem about the Grand Inquisitor by offering Ivan the same kiss of forgiveness. Alyosha and Myshkin, and important here, likewise Marie from *The Idiot*, and Lizaveta from *Crime and Punishment*). Such a one represents the holy fool, or God's fool (*iurodivyi*), found in the Russian Orthodox tradition, who exhibits foolishness in Christ; that is, one who transcends the cognitive limits of theological epistemology, and thereby witnesses to God's forgiveness through altruistic love.

Marie in particular is presented by Dostoevsky as an example of *iurodivyi* characterized by *smirenie* (a form of humility and meekness, often deeply submerged, marked by, above all else, restraint, holy restraint: that which Christ exhibited at the hands of his tormentors at his trial and execution). Marie dies as a consumptive outcast, rejected by the mean-spirited, self-righteous, pietistic moralizing of the village minister and his congregation. Dostoevsky in the notebooks for *The Idiot* comments that Marie was crucial for understanding the story,[1] that like Mitya in *The Brothers Karamazov*, it is not primarily licentiousness in itself that destroys people, but bad ideas. Furthermore, in relation to the character of Marie, Dostoevsky wrote how "*smirenie* is a great force,"[2] and how "*smirenie* is the most terrible force that can ever exist in the world!"[3] He also noted the importance of the apostle Paul's comments that we are to be fools for Christ (1 Cor 4:10), how our discipleship should be characterized by a foolishness in Christ, how this is *iurodstvo*, a holy foolishness for Christ's sake, a concept commonly found in Russian Orthodox hagiography.

And the dialectical antithesis of *iurodivyi* characterized by *smirenie* is the assertive human-centered religion of Raskolnikov, Ivan Karamazov, and others. At no point does Marie answer her persecutors back or challenge their prejudiced beliefs, such is her restraint, her submerged humility (*smirenie*). In the story of Marie, Dostoevsky is dialectically setting-off holiness/sanctification against formal self-righteous religion. The meaning of life is concealed so that the wise and the proud and powerful will never find it, and such a one is regarded as foolish and weak.[4] Hence *iurodivyi* characterized by *smirenie* are traditional marks of saintliness and Christlikeness in Russian Orthodox thinking.

1   Dostoevsky, *The Notebooks for The Idiot*, 97, 107, 172, 193, 203. See also Boyce Gibson, *The Religion of Dostoevsky*, 105, 114, 122 and 177.

2   Dostoevsky, *The Notebooks for The Idiot*, 172.

3   Ibid., 193.

4   Thurneysen, *Dostojewski*, 23/ET: 27.

In many ways this is a Christian tragedy; but we are wrong to interpret such Christlike worldly failure as wrong before God in Christ, for was not Christ himself forced outside of the formal respectable religion of his day and crucified outside the city walls? Boyce Gibson claims,

> The fact is, Myshkin is physically and psychologically unequal to the task; despite his odd remark to Ippolit, he is not sufficiently a materialist. It is not his "Christian heart" which is lacking; it is the equipment and the expertise which Christians in the various spheres are expected to draw upon. The "Christian tragedy" might have been avoided, but only on the following conditions:
> (a) If Myshkin had been physically more robust and normal, and less of a *yurodivy*, a God's fool.
> (b) If he had had the support of an integrated religious community. Myshkin is anthropologically Christian, but shows no sign anywhere of corporate affiliations . . . .
> The tragedy of *The Idiot* is the tragedy of a natural-born, but non-participating Christian. Human compassion needs roots to nourish it and affiliates to work with.[5]

Did Dostoevsky, considering his severe gospel-inspired criticism of religion, intend to place Myshkin simply as a Christian soul, a lost saint in this world? Martyrs die as witnesses to Christ and cannot be preserved by their religious—Christian—community. Being unprotected by a religious community may actually generate Christlikeness. Sonya and Marie are manifestly outside the support and protection of a religiously minded community. Indeed, Sonya and Lizaveta actually form an ecclesial community when they study the Bible, but both are outside the conventional community of pietistic well-to-do church-goers in St. Petersburg: "For where two or three gather in my name, there am I with them" (Matt 18:20); but Myshkin and Marie are bereft of even the support of one other. For Dostoevsky, perceiving such holy foolishness is not beyond the most demonic of fallen and willful people: Svidrigailov perceives it in Sonya and her little sister Polenka (though it does not stop him exercising his predilection for little girls, though he is not without graceful acts of charity). Raskolnikov, at the height of his paranoia, curses the presence of these holy fools for Christ, and when visiting Sonya and demanding she read the raising of Lazarus to him, and realizing how she

5   Boyce Gibson, *The Religion of Dostoevsky*, 121–22.

had spent her evenings in Bible-study with Lizaveta, complains that "One might well become a holy fool (*iurodivyi*) oneself here! It's catching!"[6]

But perhaps it is in the apparent curse of saintliness that such people will always be outside of the religious norms of a type of religion that draws its sustenance from this world, not from eternity. Hence the importance and value of negation, provided it points ultimately to positive assertions about God, assertions that could only be validated by God: God can only be known by and through God (the *Deus dixit*). Such negativity clears the way for a more positive affirmation. Such love is defined by negation, by altruistic self-denial. Such love is defined in 1 Corinthians 13: "love is not . . ."; Paul phrases in the negative, not in the positive. Such love is shown in the quiet way Alyosha and the starets Father Zossima refute Ivan's rebellious atheism merely by standing and not by indulging in a Socratic dialogue in an attempt to disprove the other (again, *iurodivyi*).

That the *answer* is *no answer* is exactly what happened when the Grand Inquisitor finishes haranguing Christ: the answer as such is the placing of a kiss of forgiveness on the Cardinal's bloodless lips. It is also *no answer* as an *answer* that Ivan Karamazov receives at the end of his long diatribe against a divine reconciliation of the antinomies of suffering in this life.

3. THE MARK OF ABEL

We can be alienated from Christ and treasured by the world; or we can be reconciled to the Christ and be alienated from the world. We cannot be reconciled to both: we cannot serve two masters (Matt 6:24; Luke 16:13). We are heirs of Cain or heirs of Abel (in effect we serve Cain or we serve Abel). There is a dialectic here between heaven and the world; the world is possessed by personified evil and if we serve the world in the form of the mark of Cain we align our ownership with such evil.

Because she is victimized and oppressed, Marie is discernable by the mark of Abel; she does not fight back so does not become emblazoned with the mark of Cain. This is a dialectic that is central to Dostoevsky's theological anthropology and to his realized eschatology. This same is true with Sonya: Sonya admits in abject humility that she is a fallen creature, that she is "dishonorable, a great, great sinner."[7] Sonya does not exude "prostitute pride," or organize a "prostitute pride rally" to march

6   Dostoevsky, *Crime and Punishment*, Pt. 4, ch. 4, pp. 324–25.

7   Ibid.

through the streets of St. Petersburg, she does not form an agitprop group to campaign for "prostitute rights," she does not demand a special form of marriage for prostitutes (perhaps one that does not require fidelity); she does not get a socialist government elected that passes legislation to have anyone who says anything offensive about prostitution charged with aggravated prostitute-phobia (or pornephobia) with a potential punishment of five years imprisonment. Sonya does not in her unrepentant state seek to become a member of a fraternal order, an ecclesial hierarchy of religious professional (i.e., bishops); she is not seeking power, authority, and status—in an ecclesial context—as a means of justifying her sin.

The example of Sonya is not a license for liberal Western morality; repentance is the key, and, if necessary, shame for one's behavior. If Sonya did become proactive and politicized, taking pride in her prostitution and demanding change in society's approach to prostitution, then she would have changed from the mark of Abel to the mark of Cain. Sonya is afflicted by the mark of Abel regardless of her sin. If she crossed the line into proactive demonstration and vengeance, however veiled or politically legitimized, she would be moving over to the mark of Cain. However oppressed the Russian peasants and working classes considered themselves to be, the Bolshevik Revolution, with all the suffering and bloodshed that emerged from it, denied the mark of Abel. If we follow through Dostoevsky's logic, then the Bolshevik Revolution was marked by the mark of Cain, by pagan rebellion.

The Swiss theologian Karl Barth outlined the eschatology of such a criticism of revolutionary demands in his second commentary on Romans, in the context of the 1917 Marxist revolution that, as he wrote, had just taken place in Russia. In relation to Dostoevsky's Grand Inquisitor he commented how revolutionaries—those seeking to redefine morality and ethics, politics, and the world order, indeed those seeking to redefine the very nature of the human—may often be mistaken for the Christ. However, such a person (and there are countless examples of them in Dostoevsky's novels as there are in the modern world) is not the Christ who stands before the Grand Inquisitor, but is, contrariwise, the Grand Inquisitor encountered by the Christ. Barth commented,

> The revolutionary must, however, own that in adopting his plan he allows himself to be overcome by evil. He forgets that he is not the One, that he is not the subject of the freedom, which he so earnestly desires, that, for all the strange brightness of his eyes,

> he is not the Christ who stands before the grand inquisitor, but is, contrariwise, the grand inquisitor encountered by the Christ. He too is claiming what no man can claim. He too is making of the right a thing. He too confronts other men with his supposed right. He too usurps a position which is not due to him, a legality which is fundamentally illegal, an authority which—as we have grimly experienced in Bolshevism, but also in the behavior of far more delicate-minded innovators!—soon displays its essential tyranny.[8]

Therefore, we may postulate that when members of one Christian denomination (in this particular instance, marked with the mark of Abel) stood before members of another Christian denomination (in this particular instance, marked with the mark of Cain) and were executed, they were at one with Christ. Likewise, when Protestants (in this particular instance, marked with the mark of Abel) stood before Queen Mary's religious forces (in this particular instance, marked with the mark of Cain) and were burned alive (or when Catholics were executed under Mary's younger sister, Queen Elizabeth), they were also at one with Christ—the perpetrators being of the devil, because they usurped the righteousness of God and lived according to the lie *eritis sicut Deus*? Are all such perpetrators—whether British slave traders, Nazi SS guards at the death camps, or today's abortionists—at one with Pilate in judging and condemning Jesus, or with Herod in the Massacre of the Innocents?[9] There is no space for compromise here: either we are the victims at one with Christ, or we are the perpetrators at one with Pilate and Herod. We are all either Cain or Abel: humanity, not God, defined this dualistic distinction. Humanity created the conditions of its own condemnation.

Like Cain's sin, human progress is intertwined with pseudo-religious self-justification. The story of Cain and Abel is about acceptable and unacceptable sacrifice, good and bad religion. Cain rejects God's wisdom and makes a sacrifice of his brother: this human solution to the question of right religion has echoed through human history. Cain and his spiritual progeny exhibit selfishness, jealousy, and aggression; they are divorced from the higher human nature characterized by altruistic love, they reject God's judgment on their innate religiosity, therefore they reject the wisdom of God. In so doing they first dehumanize the object of their religious hatred, often simply by classifying as inferior or

8   Barth *The Epistle to the Romans*, 505.
9   John 18:31 and Matt 2:16–18.

outside their company, then by gossiping and spreading malicious false slander and thereby destroying the person's character and reputation, costing them perhaps their job. By dehumanizing, by classifying some people as sub- or non-human, the Cainite elite merely dehumanize themselves. Therefore, we may ask, to what degree do the protagonists close themselves off to the redeeming influence of the Holy Spirit? This is why—to explore the theologic in Barth's axiom: the revolutionary is not the Christ, the Lamb, the victim, before the Grand Inquisitor, but was the oppressor, dehumanizing his or her victims. (Barth's revolutionary was explicitly based on the influence exerted on him by Dostoevsky's *Crime and Punishment*, specifically the character of Raskolnikov.) Being Pharisaic or puritanical merely generates self-righteousness and the impossibility of living up to the law (remember Marie's oppressors). This is the paradox in Dostoevsky's theological vision, and reconciliation can only come through the eschaton through the aegis of the Christ, in the Last Judgment.

4. GOOD AND EVIL: THE END TIMES

Although this book has been a relatively succinct journey, examining details in Dostoevsky's writings (dialectic, paradox, and negation) from which we may extrapolate his theological anthropology, what we have encountered is the ultimate fate of the human. The role the writer's epilepsy had in generating a dialectical understanding of reality is the key, in many ways, to his teleology and therefore his orthodox eschatology. Dostoevsky's novels are riven with God-given paradoxes, are deeply dialectical, and represent a criticism of religion in the service of the gospel.

This understanding, through the form and metaphor of literature, framed Dostoevsky's profound understanding of the human. For those who have eyes to read and ears to hear, his novels are heavily eschatological stories that parabolically chart the movement of the human into death. But herein lie two paths. First, the movement through paradox and Christlikeness into death leading to redemption: a salvation often characterized by the apophatic negation and self-denial of what we may term "the mark of Abel," leading ultimately to resurrection, and a blissful eternity with God. The second path is a death that is conversely the movement of those who refuse Christ's invitation to be redeemed, and thereby who continue to *fall* into a self-willed destruction and a self-generated hell. The choice of path issues from an individual human's decisions, a multitude of sometimes obscure and seemingly irrelevant decisions, but cumulatively they lead the human on one path . . . or the other. These decisions may be pneumatologically prompted suggestions, or demonically whispered flattery.

Critics working from within an essentially Enlightenment perspective or from what may be termed a modernist and/or liberal position will claim, with some justification, that there are no real angels and demons affecting the characters in Dostoevsky's novels, that Dostoevsky presents good and evil as psychological projections, relativistic modes of behavior. The opposite idea is the world of angels and demons is no mere psychological projection, but an accurate perception of the reality fallen humanity has willed itself into. Is Ivan's dream encounter with the devil simply a hallucination, or is it a genuine meeting between a human and a powerful spirit, a trans-corporeal being, who can influence the thoughts and actions of individuals? Was Dostoevsky being intentionally ambiguous by presenting this encounter as a dream? To try to claim one or the other—psychological projection, or real angels and demons—is to go beyond what Dostoevsky wrote. We can assert the truth of the biblical world—though critics would dismiss such a biblical mindset as belonging to primitive peoples who knew no better.

However, we might ask, where do ideas come from? Where does the existence of utterly depraved and evil thoughts and consequent actions come from? Dostoevsky does not have angels and demons appearing (like cherubs and imps in a Renaissance painting!) and enacting events of their own volition; no, Dostoevsky presents people who are being torn first one way then the other between evil and goodness. But if we do not accept the reality attested to in the Bible then where does the distinction come from: as was commonly stated in the 1970s, one man's terrorist is another's freedom fighter, one man's good is another man's evil. To many dictators evil is the ultimate good from their twisted perspective. But do good and evil exist in a way that transcends humanity?—good and evil as nouns, not as subjective verbs? Do ethics then come down to psychological relativism or do they reflect a God-given reality? Clearly Dostoevsky does believe that good and evil *are not* simply subjective and relative. However, believing that goodness is grounded in God and is not subjective does not require literal angels and demons as spirit persons to account for goodness and evil.

As an epileptic Dostoevsky's mind was driven into an understanding of the dichotomy between angels and demons (whether they were "literal beings" or psychological projections). Seemingly healthy people—who do not suffer from epilepsy—are often blind to this reality (whether the reality is literal or psychological, or some other explanation, the impact is still the same); they are also blind to the notion of demonic suggestion and interference (again whether literal or psychological). Eschatology is framed by angels and demons, whatever their ontological status, for they may generate in many ways the path the individual human travels: whether to heaven or to hell. This eschatology then becomes a theological axiom that underpins Dostoevsky's works: in his post-Siberian writings he was warning people of the two paths and the dangers of taking the wrong one. Startlingly original, stripped of all religious pretense (for Dostoevsky some prostitutes and criminals *might* just have a better understanding of salvation than many of the wealthy and cultured classes), Dostoevsky as a prophet warned not only of the eschatological reality that ruled individual lives, but also—prophetically—of the corporate politicized humanistic delusions of the twentieth century; he may have been a lone prophet crying out in the wilderness, but his theology resonates with that of the Russian Orthodox tradition and becomes more and more pertinent as the decades roll on and humanity becomes increasingly possessed by willful self-destruction.

Select Bibliography

NOVELS AND SHORT STORIES BY DOSTOEVSKY

English Editions

Dostoevsky, Fyodor Mikhailovich. *The Brothers Karamazov*. Translated by Constance Garnett, 1912. Open Access, Project Gutenberg: http://www.gutenberg.org/ebooks/28054.

———. *The Brothers Karamazov*. Translated by Richard Pevear and Larissa Volokhonsky. London: Everyman's Library, 1990.

———. *Crime and Punishment*. Translated by Constance Garnett, 1914. Open Access, Project Gutenberg: http://www.gutenberg.org/files/2554/2554-h/2554-h.htm.

———. *Crime and Punishment*. Translated by Richard Pevear and Larissa Volokhonsky. London: Everyman's Library, 1993.

———. *Demons (The Possessed)*. Translated by Constance Garnett, 1913. Open Access, Project Gutenberg: https://www.gutenberg.org/ebooks/8117.

———. *Demons*. Translated by Richard Pevear and Larissa Volokhonsky. London: Everyman's Library, 1994.

———. *The Diary of a Writer*. Translated by and annotated Boris Brasol. 2 vols. New York: Scribner's Sons, 1949.

———. *The Dream of a Ridiculous Man*. In *A Gentle Creature and Other Stories*, 107–28. Translated by Alan Myers. Oxford World's Classics. Oxford: Oxford University Press, 1995.

———. *Fyodor Mikhailovich Dostoevsky: Complete Letters*. Translated and edited by David A. Lowe. 5 Vols. New York: Ardis, 1989–91.

———. *Humiliated and Insulted*. Translated by Ignat Avsey. Richmond, UK: Alma Classics, 2012.

———. *The Gospel in Dostoevsky—Selections from His Works*. Edited by The Bruderhof Community, illustrations Fritz Eichenberg. Robertsbridge, UK: Plough, 1988.

———. *The Grand Inquisitor with Related Chapters from The Brothers Karamazov*. Translated and introduction by Charles B. Guignon. Chicago: University of Chicago Press, 1968.

———. *The Idiot*. Translated by Richard Pevear and Larissa Volokhonsky. London: Everyman's Library, 1993.

———. *The Notebooks for The Brothers Karamazov*. Translated by Edward Wasiolek. Chicago: University of Chicago Press, 1971.

———. *The Notebooks for Crime and Punishment*. Translated by Edward Wasiolek. Chicago: University of Chicago Press, 1967.

———. *The Notebooks for The Idiot*. Translated by Edward Wasiolek. Chicago: University of Chicago Press, 1967.

———. *The Notebooks for The Possessed*. Translated by Edward Wasiolek. Chicago: University of Chicago Press, 1968.

———. *Notes From Underground and The Gambler*. Translated by Jane Kentish. Oxford World's Classics. Oxford: Oxford University Press, 1999.

———. *Memoirs from the House of the Dead*. Translated by Jessie Coulson. Oxford World's Classics. Oxford: Oxford University Press, 2001.

———. *Winter Notes on Summer Impressions*. Translated by Kyril Fitzlyon. London: Quartet, 1985.

German Editions

Dostojewski, Fjodor Michailowitsch. *Der Idiot*. München/Zürich: Piper, 2002.

———. *Die Brüder Karamasoff*. Trans. E K Rahsin. München & Leipzig: R Piper und Co, 1908.

———. *Die Brüder Karamasow*. München: Deutscher Taschenbuch Verlag, 2002.

———. *Schuld und Sühne*. Berlin: Aufbau Taschenbuch Verlag, 1998.

ELECTRONIC RESOURCES

Online editions of Dostoevsky's novels (in Russian, German, and English) can be accessed at a number of websites:

Bibliography: https://en.wikipedia.org/wiki/Fyodor_Dostoyevsky_bibliography

Project Gutenberg: an online library of ebooks, open access, hi-quality and reputable translations: https://www.gutenberg.org/

The Christian Classics Ethereal Library: a website located at and run by Calvin College, 3201 Burton SE, Grand Rapids, Michigan, 49546: http://www.ccel.org/

> Братья Карамазовы (*Brat'ia Karamazovy* — *The Brothers Karamazov* translation Constance Garnett): http://www.ccel.org/d/dostoevsky/karamozov/htm/

> Преступление и наказание (*Prestuplenie i Nakazanie* — *Crime and Punishment* translation Constance Garnett): http://www.ccel.org/d/dostoevsky/crime/crime.htm

Christiaan Stange's Dostoevsky Research Station: run by an academic from Prague, The Czech Republic:

Notes from Underground (unacknowledged translation):
http://www.kiosek.com/dostoevsky/library/underground.txt

The Dream of a Ridiculous Man (translation Constance Garnett): http://www.kiosek.com/dostoevsky/library/ridiculousman.txt

The Literature Network: an American website selling audiobooks on CD and offering the text from 300 full books and over 1000 short stories and poems by over 90 authors on their website (plus a quotations database of over 8500 quotes)

The Idiot (unacknowledged translation):
http://www.online-literature.com/dostoevsky/idiot/

Dostoevsky's Image: a Russian website (2002, F.M.Dostoevsky Literary-Memorial Museum) devoted to photographs, graphics, paintings, et cetera of Dostoevsky: http://www.md.spb.ru/nd/e-people-1.html

OTHER BOOKS AND ARTICLES

Anonymous. "York Cycle, Play 48: The Mercers, The Last Judgment." In *English Mystery Plays*, edited by Peter Happé, 642. London: Penguin Classics, 1975.

———. *York Cycle of the Mystery Plays*, circa 14th C. Online text, medieval English, University of Michigan. http://quod.lib.umich.edu/cgi/t/text/text-idx?c=cme;idno=York.

Anselm of Canterbury. *Cur Deus Homo* (*Why the God Man*). In *Anselm of Canterbury— The Major Works*, edited by Brian Davies and G. R. Evans, 260–356. Oxford: Oxford University Press, 1998.

Arbaugh, George E. "Kierkegaard and Feuerbach." *Kierkegaardiana* 11 (1980) 7–10.

Athanasius, *The Incarnation of the Word. Being the Treatise of St Athanasius, De Incarnatione Verbi Dei*. Translated by Sr. Penelope CSMV. London: Bles, Centenary, 1944

Aulén, Gustav. *Christus Victor: An Historical Study of the Three Main Types of the Idea of the Atonement*. London: SPCK, 1931.

Barth, Karl. "Der Christ in der Gesellschaft." In Karl Barth, *Das Wort Gottes und die Theologie*, 33–69. München: Kaiser, 1924.

———. *The Epistle to the Romans*. 2nd ed. Translate by Sir Edwyn Hoskyns. Oxford: Oxford University Press, 1968.

Bauckham, Richard. "Theodicy from Ivan Karamazov to Moltmann." *Modern Theology* 4.1 (1987) 83–97.

Berry, Thomas. "Dostoevsky and Spiritualism." *Dostoevsky Studies* 2 (1981) 43–51.

Bettenson, Henry, trans. and ed. *The Early Christian Fathers: A Selection from the Writings of the Fathers from St Clement of Rome to St Athanasius*. Oxford: Oxford University Press, 1969.

Bloom, Harold. *Fyodor Dostoevsky*. New York: Infobase, 2004.

Bozanov, Vasily. *Dostoevsky and the Legend of the Grand Inquisitor*. Translated by Spencer E. Roberts. Ithaca, NY: Cornell University Press, 1972.

Breger, Louis. *Dostoevsky: The Author as Psychoanalyst*. New York: New York University Press, 1990.

Calvin, John. *Institutes of the Christian Religion*. Edited by John T. McNeill. Library of Christian Classics. Louisville, KY: Westminster John Knox, 2006.

Carr, Edward Hallett. *Dostoevsky*. London: Unwin, 1962.

Casiday, Augustine. *Tradition and Theology in St John Cassian*. Oxford: Oxford University Press, 2007.

Chapple, Richard. *A Dostoevsky Dictionary*. Ann Arbor, MI: Ardis, 1983.

Chisholm, F. Derek. "Dostoevsky as Political Prophet: Demons as Prophecy of Lenin, Stalin and the Foundations of Russian Communism." Online: www.fyodordostoevsky. com/essays/d-chisholm.html.

Coles, Alasdair. "Temporal lobe epilepsy and Dostoyevsky seizures: Neuropathology and Spirituality." Published online, Royal College of Psychology, 2013: https:// www.rcpsych.ac.uk/pdf/Alasdair%20Coles%20Temporal%20lobe%20epilepsy%20 and%20Dostoyevsky%20seizures.pdf

Comte, Isidore Auguste. *Cours de Philosophie Positive 1830–42*. Reprint. Paris: Éditions Hermann, 2012.

———. *The Positive Philosophy of Auguste Comte*. Translated, Harriet Martineau. Charleston, SC: BiblioBazaar, 2008.

Condradi, Peter J. *Fyodor Dostoevsky*. Macmillan Modern Novelists. Basingstoke, UK: Macmillan, 1988.

Coulson, Jessie. *Dostoevsky: A Self-Portrait*. Oxford: Oxford University Press, 1962.

Creeger, George R., ed. *George Eliot: A Collection of Critical Essays. Twentieth-century Views*. Englewood Cliffs, NJ: Prentice-Hall, 1970.

Crowder, Colin, "The Appropriation of Dostoevsky in the Early Twentieth Century: Cult, Counter-cult and Incarnation." In *European Literature and Theology in the Twentieth Century*, edited by D. Jasper, 15–33. New York: St Martin's, 1990.

Cunningham, David S. "The Brothers Karamazov as Trinitarian Theology." In *Dostoevsky and the Christian Tradition*, edited by George Pattison and Diane Oenning Thompson, 134–55. Cambridge: Cambridge University Press, 2001.

Davison, Ray. *Camus: The Challenge of Dostoevsky*. Exeter, UK: University of Exeter Press, 1997.

Delasanta, Rodney. "Putting Off the Old Man and Putting on the New: Ephesians 4:22–24 in Chaucer, Shakespeare, Swift, and Dostoevsky." *Christianity and Literature* 51.3 (2002) 339–62.

Dirscherl, Denis S.J. *Dostoevsky and the Catholic Church*. Chicago: Loyola University Press, 1986.

Dostoevsky, Anna Grigorievna. *Dostoevsky Reminiscences*. Translated by Beatrice Stillman. London: Wildwood House, 1975.

Edie, James M., James P. Scanlan, and Mary-Barbara Zeldin. *Russian Philosophy. Vol. I: The Slavophiles, The Westerners*. Chicago: Quadrangle, 1965.

———. *Russian Philosophy. Vol. II: The Nihilists, the Populists, Critics of Religion and Culture*. Chicago: Quadrangle, 1965.

———. *Russian Philosophy. Vol. III Pre-Revolutionary Philosophy and Theology, Philosophers in Exile, and Marxists and Communists*. Chicago: Quadrangle, 1965.

Esaulov, Ivan. "The Categories of Law and Grace in Dostoevsky's Poetics." In *Dostoevsky and the Christian Tradition*, edited by George Pattison and Diane Oenning Thompson, 116–33. Cambridge: Cambridge University Press, 2001.

Fanger, Donald. *Dostoevsky and Romantic Realism: A Study of Dostoevsky in Relation to Balzac, Dickens, and Gogol.* Cambridge: Harvard University Press, 1965.

Feuerbach, Ludwig. *The Essence of Christianity* [1841]. Gesammelte Werke, edited W. Schuffenhauer, vol. 5. Berlin: Akademie Verlag, 1973.

Florovsky, Georges. "The Quest for Religion in 19th Century Russian Literature: Three Masters: Gogol, Dostoevsky, Tolstoy." *Epiphany* 10 (1990) 43–58.

Frank, Joseph, and David I. Goldstein, ed. *Selected Letters of Fyodor Dostoevsky.* Translated by Andrew R. MacAndrew. Chapel Hill, NC: Rutgers University Press, 1987.

Frank, Joseph. "Introduction." In Fyodor Mikhailovich Dostoevsky, *Crime and Punishment,* translated by Richard Pevear and Larissa Volokhonsky, xi–xxxi. London: Everyman's Library, 1994.

———. "Introduction." In Fyodor Mikhailovich Dostoevsky, *Demons,* translated by Richard Pevear and Larissa Volokhonsky, xi–xxxi. London: Everyman's Library, 1994.

———. *Dostoevsky: The Mantle of the Prophet, 1871–1881.* Princeton, NJ: Princeton University Press, 2002.

———. *Dostoevsky: The Miraculous Years, 1865–1871.* Princeton, NJ: Princeton University Press, 1995.

———. *Dostoevsky: The Seeds of Revolt, 1821–1849.* Princeton, NJ: Princeton University Press, 1976.

———. *Dostoevsky: The Stir of Liberation, 1860–1865.* Princeton, NJ: Princeton University Press, 1986.

———. *Dostoevsky: A Writer in his Time.* Princeton, NJ: Princeton University Press, 2009.

———. *Dostoevsky: The Years of Ordeal, 1850–1859.* Princeton, NJ: Princeton University Press, 1983.

Frazer, Sir James George, *The Golden Bough: A Study in Magic and Religion.* 12 vols. London: Macmillan, 1911–15.

———. *The Golden Bough: A Study in Magic and Religion.* Abridged edition. Introduction by George W. Stocking Jn. 1922. Reprint. Harmondsworth, UK: Penguin, 1996.

Friedman, Maurice S. "Modern Job: On Melville, Dostoevsky, and Kafka." *Judaism* 12 (1963) 436–55.

Fuller, Michael. "The Brothers Karamazov as Christian Apologetic." *Theology* 98 (1995) 344–50.

Gerrish, Brian A. "Feuerbach's Religious Illusion." *Christian Century* 114, April 9, 1997, 362–65, and 367.

Gibson, Alexander Boyce, *The Religion of Dostoevsky.* London: SCM, 1973.

Gorodetzky, Nadejda. *Saint Tikhon of Zadonsk: Inspirer of Dostoevsky.* London: SPCK, 1951.

Gustafson, Scott W. "From Theodicy to Discipleship: Dostoevsky's Contribution to the Pastoral Task in The Brothers Karamazov." *Scottish Journal of Theology* 45.2 (1992) 209–22.

Hamilton, William, "Banished from the Land of Unity: A Study of Dostoevsky's Religious Vision through the Eyes of Ivan and Alyosha Karamazov." *Journal of Religion* 39 (1959) 245–62.

Hegedus, Lorant. "Jesus and Dostoevsky." *European Journal of Theology* 1.1 (1992) 49–62.

Hesse, Hermann. *Blick ins Chaos—Drei Aufsätze.* Bern: Verlag Seldwyla, 1920.

———. "Die Brüder Karamasow oder Der Untergang Europas." In *Blick ins Chaos—Drei Aufsätze,* 607–18. Bern: Verlag Seldwyla, 1920.

———. "Gedanken über Dostojewskis Idiot." In *Blick ins Chaos—Drei Aufsätze*, 199–204. Bern: Verlag Seldwyla, 1920.

Hill, Susan E. "Translating Feuerbach, Constructing Morality: The Theological and Literary Significance of Translation for George Eliot." *Journal of the American Academy of Religion* 65 (1997) 635–53.

Hollander, Robert. "The Apocalyptic Framework of Dostoevsky's The Idiot." *Mosaic* 6 (1974) 123–39.

Idinopulos, Thomas A. "Mystery of Suffering in the Art of Dostoevsky, Camus, Wiesel, and Grünewald." *Journal of the American Academy of Religion* 43 (1975) 51–61.

Jasper, David. "The Limits of Formalism and the Theology of Hope: Ricoeur, Moltmann and Dostoevsky." *Literature and Theology* 1.1 (1987) 1–10.

Jenson, Robert. *Systematic Theology. Volume 1: The Triune God*. Oxford: Oxford University Press, 1997.

Johae, Anthony, "Expressive Symbols in Dostoevsky's Crime and Punishment." *Scottish Slavonic Review* 20 (1993) 17–22.

———. "Towards an Iconography of Crime and Punishment." In *Dostoevsky and the Christian Tradition*, edited by George Pattison and Diane Oenning Thompson, 173–88. Cambridge: Cambridge University Press, 2001.

Jones, John. *Dostoevsky*. Oxford: Clarendon, 1983.

Jones, Malcolm V. "Introduction." In Fyodor Mikhailovich Dostoevsky, *The Brothers Karamazov*, translated by Richard Pevear and Larissa Volokhonsky, ix–xxv. London: Everyman's Library, 1990.

Kantor, Vladimir. "Pavel Smerdyakov and Ivan Karamazov: the Problem of Temptation." In *Dostoevsky and the Christian Tradition*, edited by George Pattison and Diane Oenning Thompson, 173–88. Cambridge: Cambridge University Press, 2001.

Kaufmann, Walter, ed. *Existentialism from Dostoevsky to Sartre*. New York: New American Library, 1975.

Kesich, Veselin. "The Grand Inquisitor." St Vladimir's Seminary Quarterly 2.3 (1954) 29–32.

Kierkegaard, Søren. *Philosophical Fragments, Johannes Climacus*. Edited and translated, Howard V. Hong and Edna H. Kong. New York: Princeton University Press, 1985.

King-Farlow, John, and Niall Shanks. "Theodicy: Two Moral Extremes." *Scottish Journal of Theology* 41.2 (1988) 153–76.

Kirillova, Irina. "Dostoevsky's Markings in the Gospel according to St. John." In *Dostoevsky and the Christian Tradition*, edited by George Pattison and Diane Oenning Thompson, 41–50. Cambridge: Cambridge University Press, 2001.

Kjetsaa, Geir. *Dostoevsky and His New Testament*. Oslo: Solum Forlag A.S., 1984.

———. *Fyodor Dostoyevsky: A Writer's Life*. New York: Fawcett Columbine, 1987.

Knoepflmacher, U. C. "George Eliot, Feuerbach, and the Question of Criticism." *George Eliot: A Collection of Critical Essays*, edited by George R. Creeger, 74–93. Englewood Cliffs, NJ: Prentice-Hall, 1970

Kraeger, Linda L., and Joe Barnhart. "The God-Nature Relationship in Dostoevsky's Personalism." *Scottish Journal of Religious Studies* 14.2 (1993) 71–88.

Kroeker, P. Travis, and Bruce K. Ward. *Remembering the End: Dostoevsky as a Prophet of Modernity*. Oxford: Westview Press Radical Traditions, 2001.

Lantz, Kenneth A. *The Dostoevsky Encyclopedia*. Westport, CT: Greenwood, 2004.

Lavrin, Janko. *Dostoevsky*. New York: Macmillan, 1947.

Leatherbarrow, William J. "Apocalyptic Imagery in Dostoevsky's The Idiot and The Devils." *Dostoevsky Studies* 3 (1982) 43–51.

———. *The Cambridge Companion to Dostoevsky*. Cambridge: Cambridge University Press, 2002.

———. *Fyodor Dostoevsky: A Reference Guide*. Boston: Hall, 1990.

———. "Introduction." In *Fyodor Mikhailovich Dostoevsky, Crime and Punishment*, translated by Richard Pevear and Larissa Volokhonsky, vii–xxii. London: Everyman's Library, 1993.

———. "Introduction." In *Fyodor Mikhailovich Dostoevsky, The Idiot*, translated by Richard Pevear and Larissa Volokhonsky, xi–xxvi. London: Everyman's Library, 1993.

Lewis, C. S. *The Problem of Pain*. London: Bles, 1940.

Lossky, Vladimir. *The Mystical Theology of the Eastern Church*. Cambridge: James Clarke, 1957.

McGrath, Alister. *Christian Theology*. Oxford: Blackwell, 1994.

Mochulsky, Konstantin. *Dostoevsky: His Life and Work*. Translated by Michael A. Minihan. Princeton, NJ: Princeton University Press, 1967.

Moltmann, Jürgen. "Dostoevsky and the Theology of Hope." In *Papin Festschrif: Essays in Honour of Joseph Papin Vol. 2*, edited by Joseph Armenti, 399–407. Villanova, PA: Villanova University Press, 1976.

Moreira-Almeida, Alexander. *Allan Kardec and the Development of a Research Program in Psychic Experiences*. Proceedings of the Parapsychological Association & Society for Psychical Research Convention. Winchester, UK, 2008.

Murav, Harriet. *Holy Foolishness: Dostoevsky's Novels and the Poetics of Cultural Critique*. Stanford, CA: Stanford University Press, 1992.

Murray, John Middleton. *Fyodor Dostoevsky: A Critical Study*. London: Secker, 1916.

Nestle-Aland. *Novum Testamentum Graece*. 1979. Reprint. Stuttgart: Deutsche Bibelgesellschaft, 1995.

Nietzsche, Friedrich. *Twilight of the Idols* (*Die Götzen-Dämmerung*). Translated by R. J. Hollingdale. Harmondsworth, UK: Penguin, 1985.

Nötzel, Karl. *Das Leben Dostojewskis*. Osnabrück: Biblio Verlag, 1925.

———. *Dostojewsky und wir: ein Deutungsversuch des voraussetzungslosen Menschens*. München: Musarion Verlag, 1920.

Onasch, Konrad. "Gleichzeitigkeit und Geschichte: Randbemerkungen zum Vergleich Dostojevskijs mit Kierkegaard." *Zeitschrift für Religions und Geistesgeschichte* 25.1 (1973) 46–57.

Padfield, Deborah. "Christianity: A Religion of Protest?" *Theology* 90 (1987) 186–93.

Panichas, George Andrew. *The Burden of Vision: Dostoevsky's Spiritual Art*. Chicago: Gateway Editions, 1985.

———. "Dostoevsky and Satanism." *Journal of Religion* 45.1 (1965) 12–29.

———. "F. M. Dostoevsky and D. H. Lawrence: Their Visions of Evil." In *The Reverent Discipline: Essays in Literary Criticism and Culture*, edited by George Andrew Panichas, 181–98. Knoxville, TN: University of Tennessee Press, 1974.

———. "Freedom's Dangerous Dialogue: Reading Dostoevsky and Kierkegaard Together." In *Dostoevsky and the Christian Tradition*, edited by George Pattison and Diane Oenning Thompson, 237–56. Cambridge: Cambridge University Press, 2001.

———. "Fyodor Dostoevsky and Roman Catholicism." *Greek Orthodox Theological Review* 4 (1958) 16–34.

―――. "In Sight of the Logos: Dostoevsky's Crime and Punishment as Spiritual Art." *St Vladimir's Theological Quarterly* 15.3 (1971) 130–50.

―――. "Pater Seraphicus: Dostoevsky's Metaphysics of a New Saintliness." In *The Reverent Discipline: Essays in Literary Criticism and Culture*, 212–23. Knoxville, TN: University of Tennessee Press, 1974.

Pannenberg, Wolfhart. *Systematische Theologie 1*. Göttingen: Vandenhoeck and Ruprecht, 1967.

Paris, B. J. "George Eliot's Religion of Humanity." In *George Eliot: A Collection of Critical Essays*, edited by George R. Creeger, 1–23. Englewood Cliffs, NJ: Prentice-Hall, 1970.

Parry, Ken, David J. Melling, Dimitri Brady, Sidney H. Griffith, and John F. Healey, eds. *The Blackwell Dictionary of Eastern Christianity*. Oxford: Blackwell, 1999.

Pattison, George, and Diane Oenning Thompson. *Dostoevsky and the Christian Tradition*. Cambridge: Cambridge University Press, 2001.

Peace, Richard. "Introduction." In Fyodor Mikhailovich Dostoevsky, *Crime and Punishment*, translated by Jessie Coulson, vii–xxiii. Oxford: Oxford University Press, 1995.

Pevear, Richard. "The Mystery of Man in Dostoevsky." *Sourozh* 66 (1996) 31–35.

Polka, Brayton. "Psychology and Theology in The Brothers Karamazov: Everything is Permitted and the Two Fictions of Contradiction and Paradox." *Literature and Theology* 5 (1991) 253–76.

Purinton, Carl Everett. "The Christ Image in the Novels of Dostoevsky." *Religion in Life* 16.1 (1946–47) 42–54.

Ramsey, Paul. "No Morality without Immortality: Dostoevsky and the Meaning of Atheism." *Journal of Religion* 36 (1956) 90–108.

Reik, Theodor. "The Study on Dostoyevsky." In *From Thirty Years with Freud*, 158–76. New York: Farrar and Rhinehart, 1940.

Rex, Helmut, "Dostoevsky: God-Man or Man-God." In *A Book of Helmut Rex*, edited by Albert C. Moore and Maurice E. Andrew, 198–220. Dunedin, NZ: University of Otago, 1980.

Roberts, Alexander, James Donaldson, Philip Schaff, and Henry Wace, eds. and trans. *The Early Church Fathers: Ante-Nicene Fathers: Translations of the Writings of the Fathers Down to A.D. 325; The Nicene and Post-Nicene Fathers of the Christian Church-First and Second Series*. 38 vols. Grand Rapids: Eerdmans, 1979.

Rochelle, Jay C. "The Gospel in Dostoevsky." *Currents in Theology and Mission* 17 (1990) 306–7.

Rosen, Nathan. "Freud on Dostoevsky's Epilepsy: A Revaluation." *Dostoevsky Studies* 9 (1988) 107–25.

Rosenshield, Gary. "Mystery and Commandment in The Brothers Karamazov: Leo Baeck and Fedor Dostoevsky." *Journal of the American Academy of Religion* 62 (1994) 483–508.

Rother, Siegfried. "Die Brüder Karamasow—Dostojewskijs Analyse menschlicher Existenz." *Internationale katholische Zeitschrift Communio* 18.6 (1989) 597–609.

Rousseau, Jean Jacques. *Rousseau: The Discourses and Other Early Political Writings: Vol. 1*. Edited by Victor Gourevich. Cambridge Texts in the History of Political Thought. Cambridge: Cambridge University Press, 1997.

Rozanov, Vasilii Vasilievich. *Dostoevsky and the Legend of the Grand Inquisitor*. Translated by Spencer E. Roberts. 1906. Reprint. London: Cornell University Press, 1972.

Russell, Henry M. W. "Beyond the Will: Humiliation as Christian Necessity in Crime and Punishment." In *Dostoevsky and the Christian Tradition*, edited by George Pattison and Diane Oenning Thompson, 226–36. Cambridge: Cambridge University Press, 2001.

Sandoz, Ellis. *Political Apocalypse: A Study of Dostoevsky's Grand Inquisitor.* Baton Rouge, LA: Louisiana State University Press, 1971.

Schroeder, C. Paul. "Suffering towards Personhood: John Zizioulas and Fyodor Dostoevsky in Conversation on Freedom and the Human Person." *St Vladimir's Theological Quarterly* 45.3 (2001) 243–64.

Sekirin, Peter, ed. *The Dostoevsky Archive: First-hand Accounts of the Novelist from Contemporaries' Memoirs and Rare Periodicals, Most Translated into English for the First Time, with a Detailed Lifetime Chronology and Annotated Bibliography.* Jefferson, NC: McFarland, 1997.

Sherry, Patrick. "Novels of Redemption." *Literature and Theology* 14.3 (2000) 249–60.

Simmons, Ernest Joseph. *Fyodor Dostoevsky: Columbia Essays on Modern Writers, no. 40.* New York: Columbia University Press, 1969.

———. *Introduction to Russian Realism: Pushkin, Gogol, Dostoevsky, Tolstoi, Chekhov, Sholokhov.* Bloomington, IN: Indiana University Press, 1965.

Smart, Ninian. *Nineteenth-Century Religious Thought in the West. Volume 1: Ludwig Feuerbach and Karl Marx.* New York: Cambridge University Press, 1985.

Snow, Charles Percy. *The Realists Portraits of Eight Novelists—Stendhal, Balzac, Dickens, Dostoevsky, Tolstoy, Galdós, Henry James, Proust.* London: Macmillan , 1978.

Spencer, Herbert. *Social Statics.* London: Chapman, 1851.

Steiner, George. *Tolstoy or Dostoevsky.* Harmondsworth, UK: Penguin, 1967.

Stirling, Jeannette. *Representing Epilepsy: Myth and Matter.* Liverpool, UK: Liverpool University Press, 2010.

Stoeber, Michael. "Dostoevsky's Devil: The Will to Power." *Journal of Religion* 74.1 (1994) 26–44.

Sykes, John. "Literature and Religion: Pascal, Gryphius, Lessing, Hölderlin, Novalis, Kierkegaard, Dostoevsky, Kafka." *Christian Century* 108 (1991) 945–46.

Terras, Victor. *A Karamazov Companion: Commentary on the Genesis, Language, and Style of Dostoevsky's Novel.* Madison, WI: University of Wisconsin Press, 1980.

Thompson, Dianne Oenning. "Problems of the Biblical Word in Dostoevsky's Poetics." In *Dostoevsky and the Christian Tradition*, edited by George Pattison and Diane Oenning Thompson, 69–102. Cambridge: Cambridge University Press, 2001.

Thurneysen, Eduard. *Dostoevsky—A Theological Study.* Translated by Keith R. Crim. London: Epworth, 1964.

———. *Dostojewski.* München: Kaiser, 1921.

Trace, Arthur. *Dostoevsky and the Brothers Karamazov.* Philadelphia: Xlibris, 2000.

Troyat, Henri. *Firebrand: The Life of Dostoevsky.* Translated by Norbert Güterman, woodcuts by S. Mrozewski. London: Heinemann, 1946.

Walsh, David. "Dostoevsky's Discovery of the Christian Foundation of Politics." *Religion and Literature* 19.2 (1987) 49–72.

Ward, Bruce K. "Christianity and the Modern Eclipse of Nature: Two Perspectives (Camus and Dostoevsky)." *Journal of the American Academy of Religion* 63 (1995) 823–43.

———. "Dostoevsky and the Hermeneutics of Suspicion." Literature and Theology 11.3 (1997) 270–83.

Webster, Alexander F. C. "The Exemplary Kenotic Holiness of Prince Myshkin in Dostoevsky's The Idiot." *St. Vladimir's Theological Quarterly* 28.3 (1984) 189–216.

Westphal, Merold. "The Phenomenology of Guilt and the Theology of Forgiveness." In *Crosscurrents in Phenomenology*, edited by Ronald Bruzina, 231–61. The Hague, Netherlands: Nijhoff, 1978.

Wienhorst, Sue E. "Vision and Structure in The Possessed." *Religion in Life* 45 (1976) 490–98.

Wikström, Owe. "Soul Recovery through Remystification: Dostoevsky as a Challenger of Modern Psychology." In *On Losing The Soul*, 119–36. Albany, NY: State University of New York Press, 1995.

Williams, Rowan, "The Archbishop on Dostoevsky's 'Devils'". Thursday 1st June 2006. An article for *The Reader Magazine*, Summer 2006, published on William's website. See: http://rowanwilliams.archbishopofcanterbury.org/articles.php/2003/the-archbishop-on-dostoevskys-devils.

Wink, Walter. *Engaging the Powers: Discernment and Resistance in a World of Domination*. Minneapolis, MN: Fortress Press, 1992

———. *Naming The Powers: The Language Of Power In The New Testament* (The Powers : Vol. 1). Minneapolis, MN: Fortress Press, 1959

———. *Unmasking the Powers: The Invisible Forces That Determine Human Existence* (Powers, Vol. 2). Minneapolis, MN: Fortress Press, 1986

Wolynski, Akim Lwowitsch. *Das Buch vom grossen Zorn*. Frankfurt: Literarische Anstalt Rütten and Loening, 1905.

———. *Das Reich der Karamosoff*. München: Piper, 1920.

Wood, Ralph C. "Dostoevsky on Evil as a Perversion of Personhood: A Reading of Ivan Karamazov and the Grand Inquisitor." *Perspectives in Religious Studies* 26.3 (1999) 331–48.

Zabolotsky, Nikolai A. "Fyodor Mikhailovich, Dostoevsky Today." *Scottish Journal of Theology* 37.1 (1984) 41–57.

Ziolkowski, Margaret. "Dostoevsky and the Kenotic Tradition." In *Dostoevsky and the Christian Tradition*, edited by George Pattison and Diane Oenning Thompson, 31–40. Cambridge: Cambridge University Press, 2001.

Index of Names

There are various ways of translating Russian names into the English language (and from Cyrillic into Latin script). Where relevant I have included the two most common translations, and allowed for the use of emphasizing acute accents when used in quoted translations.

Index of Subjects

supplementary 79

tangible 27–28, 30, 60
technological xiii, 105
teleology 31, 159, 165
tension 21, 65, 93, 96, 98, 103–5,
106–7, 111, 118
terrifying 57, 101, 121
terror 40
t/Theism 7, 116, 130, 153
t/Theist(s) 7, 111, 123, 138
theistic 8, 139
theocentric 85
theodicy 81, 151, 153
t/Theology xvi, 1, 2, 7–9, 16, 24, 35,
44–46, 48, 54, 56–57, 67, 73–74,
80, 82, 85–86, 89, 92, 94, 97, 104–5,
112, 118–19, 127, 139, 140–41, 159,
167, 171–75, 176–78
t/Theologian(s) xiii, 1, 8, 19,
36–37, 53, 56, 59, 84–85, 113,
139, 141, 146, 163
t/Theological(ly) xiii–xiv, 1–2, 4,
6–8, 16–17, 30, 32, 36, 42–43,
46, 48, 54, 56–57, 59–63, 65, 70,
79–81, 83, 85, 92–93, 99, 109,
111, 114, 116–17, 123, 129–31,
136, 139, 141, 145, 149–50, 153,
155, 160, 162, 165, 167, 173,
175, 177
theologies 71, 139
theological anthropology xiii–xiv, 2,
6, 17, 51, 56–57, 59–63, 65, 70, 80,
83, 92–93, 131, 145, 162, 165 See
anthropology
theories/theory 6, 16, 36–38,
60–61, 65, 68–69, 88, 109–12, 115,
117, 127, 135–37, 138–40, 153
time 8, 15–16, 19–21, 25–26, 29, 37,
46–47, 62, 64, 66, 73, 89, 102, 115,
124–26, 134–35, 137, 140, 147–48,
150 See *transdimensionality*
The Tower of Babel 99–103, 116, 152
tradition(al) 1, 3–4, 6–8, 24, 34,
45–46, 57, 59, 61, 74, 88, 100–101,
112–13, 119, 121, 125, 157, 160, 167

t/Transcendent 5–6, 27–28, 84–85, 89,
113, 127, 158
transcendence 4, 84–85, 142, 159
transcending 60
transdimensionality 46 See *time*
transform/transformation 40, 61,
69–70, 159
trespass 33, 128–29
transgress 69, 128
transgression 128–29
t/Trinity 4, 35, 49, 89–90
t/Trinitarian 49, 83, 89, 146, 172
t/Triune 2, 37, 47, 49, 90, 140,
146, 156, 157, 174
t/Truth xiii, xv, 3, 9, 19, 62, 64, 68–69,
75, 79, 81, 83, 88–92, 94–96, 107,
134–37, 141–42, 146, 148, 153, 159,
166
true xiv, 2–4, 19, 29, 34, 57, 87,
93–94, 98, 113, 123, 125, 129,
131, 141, 145, 148–49, 162
truly 11, 19, 31, 34, 66–67, 109,
125, 133, 141, 145, 158
truthful 10

unbridgeable 84, 89–90
understanding 1–4, 8–9, 16, 19,
22–23, 25, 28–30, 46, 49, 53, 56–57,
59, 61, 63–64, 66–67, 70–72, 80,
84–85, 92, 104, 109, 115, 118, 125,
133, 145–46, 148, 156–57, 160,
165–167 See *knowledge* and
epistemology
u/Universal/universalism 9, 36, 53,
139–40
unresolved 145
unrighteousness 99, 116–17
utopia/utopianism 40, 88, 100, 105,
113

West/Western xiii, 2, 6–8, 17, 29, 34,
36–38, 45, 57, 59–61, 71, 73, 80,
86, 90–91, 93, 98, 100, 101, 106,
111–13, 120, 129, 133, 140–41,
149–50, 155–56, 158, 163, 177
Westernize 62 See *East/Eastern*

Index of Dostoevsky's Works

The Idiot 2, 16–23, 29, 34–35, 41,
54–55, 63, 65–67, 71, 81, 91, 94–96,
107, 114, 118–22, 125, 130, 133,
160–61, 169, 170–71, 173–75, 177
Der Idiot 170
The Notebooks for The Idiot 160,
170

Notes from the House of the Dead 55,
63, 65
Notes from Underground 55, 63, 67,
99, 114–17, 170

Poor Folk 15, 63–64

The Double 15, 63–64

White Nights 15, 63–64
*Winter Notes on Summer
Impressions* 98, 101, 126, 170

Index of Secondary Source Authors

Sectional Contents

PART ONE
FYODOR MIKHAILOVICH DOSTOEVSKY,
WRITER AND PROPHET

DOSTOEVSKY: A THEOLOGICAL ENGAGEMENT